CONTEMPORARY
FIELD SOCIAL WORK

CONTEMPORARY FIELD SOCIAL WORK

Integrating Field and Classroom Experience

MARK DOEL
Sheffield Hallam University

STEVEN M. SHARDLOW
University of Salford

PAUL G. JOHNSON
University of Southern Maine

Los Angeles | London | New Delhi
Singapore | Washington DC

For information:

SAGE Publications, Inc.
2455 Teller Road
Thousand Oaks, California 91320
E-mail: order@sagepub.com

SAGE Publications Ltd.
1 Oliver's Yard
55 City Road
London EC1Y 1SP
United Kingdom

SAGE Publications India Pvt. Ltd.
B 1/I 1 Mohan Cooperative Industrial Area
Mathura Road, New Delhi 110 044
India

SAGE Publications Asia-Pacific Pte. Ltd.
33 Pekin Street #02-01
Far East Square
Singapore 048763

Printed in the United States of America

Library of Congress Cataloging-in-Publication Data

Doel, Mark.
Contemporary field social work: integrating field and classroom experience / Mark Doel, Steven M. Shardlow, Paul G. Johnson.
     p. cm.
Includes bibliographical references and index.
ISBN 978-1-4129-8719-6 (pbk.)
    1. Social work education. 2. Social service—Fieldwork. I. Shardlow, Steven, 1952- II. Johnson, Paul (Paul Gordon), 1959- III. Title.

HV11.D635 2011
361.3071'55—dc22   2010005921

This book is printed on acid-free paper.

10   11   12   13   14   10   9   8   7   6   5   4   3   2   1

Acquisitions Editor:	Kassie Graves
Editorial Assistant:	Veronica K. Novak
Production Editor:	Astrid Virding
Copy Editor:	Gillian Dickens
Typesetter:	C&M Digitals (P) Ltd.
Proofreader:	Charlotte Waisner
Indexer:	Will Ragsdale
Cover Designer:	Bryan Fishman
Marketing Manager:	Stephanie Adams

Contents

Introduction   1

PART I. FOUNDATIONS OF PRACTICE   13
    Context: Where Does Learning Take Place?   13

1. LEARNING ABOUT SERVICE USERS
    AND THEIR COMMUNITIES   27
    About Activity 1: *Permission to Learn*   27
    Notes for Instructors   27
        Purpose   27
        Method   28
    Notes for Students and Instructors   28
        Variations   28
        Use by Other Professions   28
        Educational Policy Accreditation Standards   29
    For Students and Instructors   29
        Activity 1: *Permission to Learn*   29
    Notes for Instructors   32
        Teaching About Service Users and Their Communities   32
    Notes for Students   33
        Learning About Service Users and Their Communities   33
    Assessing Your Learning   37
    Further Reading   37

2. LEARNING ABOUT YOURSELF   39
    About Activity 2: *Points of View*   39
    Notes for Instructors   39
        Purpose   39
        Method   40

Notes for Students and Instructors   40
 Variations   40
 Use by Other Professions   40
 Educational Policy Accreditation Standards   41
For Students and Instructors   41
 Activity 2: *Points of View*   41
Notes for Instructors   43
 Teaching About Points of View   43
Notes for Students   45
 Learning About Yourself   45
 Use of Self   47
 Worldviews   48
 Worldviews of Service Users, Providers,
  and Other Professionals   50
Assessing Your Learning   50
 The Extracts   50
Further Reading   51

3. LEARNING ABOUT YOUR ROLE   53
About Activity 3: *Boundaries*   53
Notes for Instructors   53
 Purpose   53
 Method   53
Notes for Students and Instructors   54
 Variations   54
 Use by Other Professions   55
 Educational Policy Accreditation Standards   55
For Students and Instructors   55
 Activity 3: *Boundaries*   55
Notes for Instructors   58
 Teaching About Boundaries   58
Notes for Students   62
 Learning About Your Role   62
Assessing Your Learning   65
Further Reading   66

4. LEARNING ABOUT VALUE CONFLICTS
AND ETHICAL DILEMMAS   67
About Activity 4: *The Myth of Sisyphus*   67
Notes for Instructors   67
 Purpose   67
 Method   67

Notes for Students and Instructors 68
    Variations 68
    Use by Other Professions 68
    Educational Policy Accreditation Standards 69
For Students and Instructors 69
    Activity 4: *The Myth of Sisyphus* 69
Notes for Instructors 74
    Teaching About Values and Ethical Dilemmas 74
Notes for Students 76
    Learning About Values and Ethical Dilemmas 76
Assessing Your Learning 79
Further Reading 80

PART II. DIRECT PRACTICE 81
    Context: Interdisciplinary Learning
    and Practice 81

5. PREPARATION 89
About Activity 5: *Starting Out* 89
Notes for Instructors 89
    Purpose 89
    Method 89
Notes for Students and Instructors 90
    Variations 90
    Use by Other Professions 90
    Educational Policy Accreditation Standards 90
For Students and Instructors 91
    Activity 5: *Starting Out* 91
Notes for Instructors 92
    Teaching About Preparation 92
Notes for Students 94
    Learning About Preparation 94
Assessing Your Learning 98
Further Reading 98

6. GENERATING OPTIONS 101
About Activity 6: *Open Ends* 101
Notes for Instructors 101
    Purpose 101
    Method 101
Notes for Students and Instructors 102
    Variations 102

	Use by Other Professions	102
	Educational Policy Accreditation Standards	103
	For Students and Instructors	103
	Activity 6: *Open Ends*	103
	Notes for Instructors	105
	Teaching About Generating Options	105
	Notes for Students	108
	Learning About Generating Options	108
	Assessing Your Learning	111
	Further Reading	111
7.	MAKING ASSESSMENTS IN PARTNERSHIP	113
	About Activity 7: *Hold the Front Page*	113
	Notes for Instructors	113
	Purpose	113
	Method	114
	Notes for Students and Instructors	114
	Variations	114
	Use by Other Professions	114
	Educational Policy Accreditation Standards	114
	For Students and Instructors	115
	Activity 7: *Hold the Front Page*	115
	Notes for Instructors	117
	Teaching About Making Assessments in Partnership	117
	Notes for Students	119
	Learning About Making Assessments in Partnership	119
	Assessing Your Learning	123
	Further Reading	123
8.	WORKING IN AND WITH GROUPS	125
	About Activity 8: *No One Is an Island*	125
	Notes for Instructors	125
	Purpose	125
	Method	125
	Notes for Students and Instructors	126
	Variations	126
	Use by Other Professions	126
	Educational Policy Accreditation Standards	126
	For Students and Instructors	126
	Activity 8: *No One Is an Island*	126
	Notes for Instructors	128
	Teaching About Working in and With Groups	128

Notes for Students 132
    Learning About Working in and With Groups 132
Assessing Your Learning 134
Further Reading 135

PART III. AGENCY PRACTICE 137
    Context: Creative Practice and
    Procedural Requirements 137

9. **MAKING PRIORITIES** 145
    About Activity 9: *Home Truths* 145
    Notes for Instructors 145
        Purpose 145
        Method 145
    Notes for Students and Instructors 146
        Variations 146
        Use by Other Professions 146
        Educational Policy Accreditation Standards 147
    For Students and Instructors 147
        Activity 9: *Home Truths* 147
    Notes for Instructors 150
        Teaching About Making Priorities 150
    Notes for Students 152
        Learning About Making Priorities 152
    Assessing Your Learning 158
    Further Reading 158

10. **MANAGING RESOURCES** 159
    About Activity 10: *Travel Agent* 159
    Notes for Instructors 159
        Purpose 159
        Method 159
    Notes for Students and Instructors 160
        Variations 160
        Use by Other Professions 160
        Educational Policy Accreditation Standards 161
    For Students and Instructors 161
        Activity 10: *Travel Agent* 161
    Notes for Instructors 165
        Teaching About Managing Resources 165
    Notes for Students 167
        Learning About Managing Resources 167

	Assessing Your Learning	174
	Further Reading	174
11.	**ACCOUNTABILITY**	**175**
	About Activity 11: *Held to Account*	175
	Notes for Instructors	175
	Purpose	175
	Method	175
	Notes for Students and Instructors	176
	Variations	176
	Use by Other Professions	176
	Educational Policy Accreditation Standards	177
	For Students and Instructors	177
	Activity 11: *Held to Account*	177
	Notes for Instructors	180
	Teaching About Accountability	180
	Opportunities for Accountability	180
	Notes for Students	181
	Learning About Accountability	181
	Assessing Your Learning	185
	Further Reading	186
12.	**CHALLENGING SITUATIONS AND RESOLVING CONFLICTS**	**187**
	About Activity 12: *Dial "D" for Danger*	187
	Notes for Instructors	187
	Purpose	187
	Method	187
	Notes for Students and Instructors	188
	Variations	188
	Use by Other Professions	188
	Educational Policy Accreditation Standards	189
	For Students and Instructors	189
	Activity 12: *Dial "D" for Danger*	189
	Notes for Instructors	193
	Teaching About Challenging Situations	193
	Opportunities for Challenging Situations	194
	Notes for Students	194
	Learning About Challenging Situations	194
	Assessing Your Learning	203
	Further Reading	203

PART IV. THEMES OF PRACTICE   205
    Context—Social Worker as Researcher:
      Evaluating Practice   205

13. MULTICULTURAL PRACTICE   217
    About Activity 13: *The Drawbridge*   217
    Notes for Instructors   217
      Purpose   217
      Method   217
    Notes for Students and Instructors   218
      Variations   218
      Use by Other Professions   218
      Educational Policy Accreditation Standards   218
    For Students and Instructors   219
      Activity 13: *The Drawbridge*   219
    Notes for Instructors   220
      Teaching About Multicultural Practice   220
      Opportunities for Multicultural Practice   222
    Notes for Students   226
      Learning About Multicultural Practice   226
    Assessing Your Learning   231
    Further Reading   231

14. LAW-INFORMED PRACTICE   233
    About Activity 14: *A–Z of the Law: Spirit and Letter*   233
    Notes for Instructors   233
      Purpose   233
      Method   233
    Notes for Students and Instructors   234
      Variations   234
      Use by Other Professions   234
      Educational Policy Accreditation Standards   234
    For Students and Instructors   235
      Activity 14: *A–Z of the Law: Spirit and Letter*   235
    Notes for Instructors   237
      Teaching About Law-Informed Practice   237
      Opportunities for Law-Informed Practice   240
    Notes for Students   242
      Learning About Law-Informed Practice   242
    Assessing Your Learning   246
    Further Reading   246

15. GENERALIST AND SPECIALIST PRACTICE   247
    About Activity 15: *Essence of Social Work*   247
    Notes for Instructors   247
        Purpose   247
        Method   247
    Notes for Students and Instructors   248
        Variations   248
        Use by Other Professions   248
        Educational Policy Accreditation Standards   248
    For Students and Instructors   249
        Activity 15: *Essence of Social Work*   249
    Notes for Instructors   254
        Teaching About Generalist and Specialist Practice 254
        Opportunities for Generalist and Specialist Practice 256
    Notes for Students   257
        Learning About Generalist and Specialist Practice 257
    Assessing Your Learning   263
    Further Reading   263

16. COMPARATIVE SOCIAL WORK   265
    About Activity 16: *View From Another Place . . . Another Time* 265
    Notes for Instructors   265
        Purpose   265
        Method   266
    Notes for Students and Instructors   266
        Variations   266
        Use by Other Professions   266
        Educational Policy Accreditation Standards   267
    For Students and Instructors   267
        Activity 16: *View From Another Place . . . Another Time* 267
    Notes for Instructors   271
        Teaching About Comparative Social Work   271
        Opportunities for Comparative Social Work   271
    Notes for Students   272
        Learning About Comparative Social Work   272
    Assessing Your Learning   278
    Further Reading   279

References   281

Index   297

About the Authors   311

Introduction

This book is about social work practice, with a particular focus on teaching and learning social work in field settings. We hope that readers will find it a useful and entertaining guide to becoming a social worker.

As the authors, we cannot presume exactly who you, our reader, is. If you are a student of social work, you may be using this book independently to support your fieldwork learning or, more likely, with a person who is guiding and supervising your learning in the agency setting. If you are the person who has responsibility for helping a student learn about social work, you may be a practitioner, a manager, a service user, or a provider of care. Your location may be in the state social services, in a voluntary not-for-profit organization, in a private agency, in an organization or community group that is managed by service users, or, indeed, a place in which social work is not the main activity, such as a school, a hospital, or a prison. Whatever the site for the learning, it is important to remember that if you are the field instructor, your task is to help the student learn about social work, not to train him or her to do your job. In other words, the specific work that you do is just one example of practice. Your perspective as the student's guide, teacher, and instructor is hugely valuable, but it needs to be set in the broader context.

Helping students to move from the specifics of your location to the general of social work practice, then back to different specifics (not just yours), is a demanding skill. You may not officially be "the learner," but this is going to be a learning experience for you, too, no matter how experienced you are.

CONTEMPORARY FIELD SOCIAL WORK: THE MORE THINGS CHANGE . . . THE MORE THEY STAY THE SAME?

Writing a book of this kind is an occasion to make a statement of what constitutes "contemporary field social work." What should social workers know? How should they be able to "do" it? The modern curriculum for social work reflects current political as well as professional concerns; above all, it should reflect the concerns of the people who use these services, the clients or service users. It has been an interesting exercise to decide what the book's coverage should be.

The content of the social work curriculum arises, of course, from the expectations of government, employers, and regulators, as well as from those who practice social work and those who use it. Social work is a highly contextual form of practice; in particular, the organizations in which social work finds itself have a significant impact on the shape of that practice, especially the rapidly changing contexts for this practice, politically, economically, and professionally.

Yet, amid the whirlwinds of change, there is much that endures. We might transform our clothes with increasing frequency, but the body beneath hardly alters. One constant is the mission of social work to combat social injustice and oppression by working with people who are at the margins of society and the commitment of practitioners to that mission. Almost a century ago, Clement Attlee (1920), a social worker who was to become British prime minister in 1945, claimed that social workers will always be agitators. Of course, we cannot expect to receive thanks for our ability to remind the wider society of the effects of inequality and poverty. No change there. Competent social work practice continues to depend on an unusually broad and often contested repertoire of knowledge, values, and skills—not just in direct work with individuals, families, groups, and communities but also in negotiating complex organizations. Capable social workers continue to need qualities that help them cope with dilemma and doubt on a daily basis and to maintain their intellectual curiosity.

So, whatever the current closet of accreditation standards, the fundamentals change only very slowly. Indeed, in those aspects of life where real change would be most welcome (poverty and structural discrimination, for example), the pace of change is imperceptible. Service users continue to experience poverty, injustice, and distress—and many continue to survive these experiences with resourcefulness and determination. It is important to remember these constants in the midst of the frenetic activity that is sometimes mistaken for purposefulness.

Speaking in 1981, Eileen Younghusband reviewed several decades of social work education, training, and practice. In addition to looking back over several decades, she also looked forward, to the year 2001:

> There will be some things which won't change. What really matters, in the last resort, what people in perplexity, sorrow or disgrace really want is commitment to them as people—staying on the job, being "for them," being understanding and determined to help them, and having the imagination, the knowledge, the confidence and the resources to do so. It is that, more than anything else, that I hope will be alive and active in the year 2001.

Her 1981 vision for the year 2001 is just as true for the year 2021 and beyond.

So, it is crucial that we find ways of making social work attractive to those who are not yet committed. In a careers choice survey of more than 1,000 students conducted by the Careers Research Advisory Committee in 2003, 17 out of a hundred students favored management as a career choice, 13 chose banking and financial services, and 12 chose sales and marketing. Careers in the public sector were the least popular, with only 3 out of 100, and just 1 out of 100 choosing "social healthcare" (*Times Higher Educational Supplement,* June 13, 2003).

The U.S. Department of Labor Statistics (2009) expects employment for social workers to grow much faster than the average for all occupations through 2016:

> Job prospects are expected to be favorable, particularly for social workers who specialize in the aging population or work in rural areas. Employment of social workers is expected to increase by 22 percent during the 2006–16 decade, which is much faster than the average for all occupations. The growing elderly population and the aging baby boom generation will create greater demand for health and social services, resulting in rapid job growth among gerontology social workers. Employment of social workers in private social service agencies also will increase.

However, the U.S. Department of Labor Statistics (2009) also expects to see some changes in the kinds of employment for social workers:

> For example, agencies increasingly will restructure services and hire more social and human service assistants, who are paid less, instead of social workers. Employment in State and local government agencies may grow somewhat in response to growing needs for public welfare, family services, and child protective services, but many of these services will be contracted out to private agencies. Employment levels in public and private social services agencies may fluctuate, depending on need and government funding levels.

Recording support from political sources is also important, such as this homage to social workers from a member of the House of Representatives:

> Social workers affect our lives in so many ways. . . . Their work touches all of us as individuals and as whole communities. They are dedicated, highly trained, and committed professionals. They work in family service and community mental health agencies, schools, hospitals, nursing homes, and many other private and public agencies. They listen, they care. And most importantly, they help those in need. (Representative Bob Etheridge [D-NC] in Vallianatos, 2001, p. 1)

Any literature that captures the imagination of possible social workers is to be welcomed, and we hope this book will be a contribution to the mission to explain social work more widely. Although the employment opportunities for social workers are very encouraging, it is also imperative that those seeking employment are well prepared for social work. This requires an understanding of the social and organizational context of their work—the constants and the changes.

CONTEMPORARY FIELD INSTRUCTION AND PRACTICE LEARNING

One of the purposes of the practical training for social work students is to ensure that graduates are confident and competent to practice once they have qualified. The emphasis of training must be on practice and the practical relevance of theory. This means that students need a plentiful and varied supply of good opportunities to practice and to learn safely.

Students have long reported favorably about their placements. Historically, there has been a strong dependence on social work agencies to provide social work placements for both undergraduate and graduate students. The Council on Social Work Education (CSWE) stipulates the number of hours that an undergraduate and a graduate student is expected to be placed in a fieldwork agency over the course of an academic year. There are also numerous stipulations regarding the qualifications and expectations of the fieldwork instructor. Schools and departments of social work are reliant upon social work agencies in their locality, and it must be a partnership for the educational experience to work well for the student.

In 2008, CSWE implemented its new *Educational Policy and Accreditation Standards (EPAS)*. In that document, CSWE explained the notion of a "signature pedagogy," rather like a chef has a signature dish:

> Signature pedagogy represents the central form of instruction and learning in which a profession socializes its students to perform the role of practitioner. Professionals have pedagogical norms with which they connect and integrate theory and practice. In social work, the signature pedagogy is field education. The intent of field education is to connect the theoretical and conceptual contribution of the classroom with the practical world of the practice setting. It is a basic precept of social work education that the two interrelated components of curriculum—classroom and field—are of equal importance within the curriculum, and each contributes to the development of the requisite competencies of professional practice.

Field education is systematically designed, supervised, coordinated, and evaluated based on criteria by which students demonstrate the achievement of program competencies. (Educational Policy 2.3—Signature Pedagogy: Field Education, CSWE, 2008, p. 8)

If we see field education as equivalent to a top chef's signature dish, we can begin to understand not just the huge significance of placements but the crucial fit that is necessary with the "menu" as a whole. So, we must be vigilant that the emphasis on practical skills that characterizes much of fieldwork learning does not become detached from the critical thinking and theoretical aspects of social work as a discipline. As one student commented about theory-less practice, "It's like a model airplane kit without the instruction book." We hope this book provides both the kit and the instructions, a practice rooted in its theoretical foundations, and theories that draw from the experiences of their practical application.

These themes continue to be explored in greater detail throughout the book, especially in the introduction to Part I.

CONTENT, STRUCTURE, AND PURPOSE OF THE BOOK

Contemporary Field Social Work builds on features from *Modern Social Work Practice* (Doel & Shardlow, 2005), which was written from the British context. It is interesting to reflect on the similarities and the differences of social work in general and field instruction from country to country. The four parts to the book—Foundations of Practice, Direct Practice, Agency Practice, and Themes of Practice—define a curriculum for field instruction and practice learning. However, the chapters that introduce each of the four parts reflect the changing context of practice, across time and place. The topics in this book, *Contemporary Field Social Work*, reflect the current areas of significance for social work practice. In particular, we relate each topic to the relevant *EPAS* (CSWE, 2008). These standards have been established by the CSWE to help to ensure the quality of social work education and training across the United States.

ACTIVITIES

The book uses the technique of having one substantial activity to introduce the theme of a chapter. These activities have been tried and tested so that the suggested method that is presented before each activity is based on experience—hence the ideas for variations on the method. In addition, we give consideration to how students from other related professions could use the activity, either together with social work students or independently, and we link the theme of the chapter to the *EPAS*.

Although individual activities can be used on a one-off basis, it is better to become acquainted with the whole beforehand and to return to activities at different stages in the student's learning. The topics in Parts I, II, and III are in no strict chronological order, and the themes in Part IV run through the whole of social work practice. A knowledge of the whole curriculum for general practice will help when searching for the right activity for the occasion. A "teachable moment" happens when the learner is particularly receptive to the teaching, and a well-timed activity can help these moments to occur.

The activities that introduce each chapter in this book are designed to help participants to explore issues in practice as well as enhance technical skills. The activities develop an ability to learn, which we believe is a necessary condition to develop a competence to practice. Field instructors and student supervisors need to make links between the learning that takes place via these activities and the student's direct practice with people using the agency's services.

Sometimes it is helpful to translate an activity into circumstances that reflect the particular practice setting. This has its value. However, it is also true that it is easier to "think outside the box" if you are not actually in it! In other words, new kinds of situation are less likely to rely on established patterns of thinking and doing. We return to this theme later in the section on simulated learning.

The activities can be used to *assess* students' learning on placements as well as to develop it. In particular, revisiting an activity toward the end of a period of a placement is a good way to measure changes in their understanding of practice. However, students should always be clear about the purpose of any activity and what uses may be made of it.

Following each activity are two main sections, one about teaching (primarily for student supervisors and instructors) and the other about learning (primarily for students); each relates to the theme of the chapter. The teaching notes consider likely opportunities for the topic of the chapter and explore the topic in greater detail. The learning notes conclude with a section about how the learning might be assessed, with pointers to further reading. Although each set of notes addresses the reader as the instructor and the student respectively, you will nevertheless find it helpful to read both sets of notes, whatever your role, because there is considerable overlap between teaching and learning. Occasionally there is a suggestion in the guidance for the activity that you do not read the notes until *after* the activity has been completed.

TERMINOLOGY

Developments in practice have their parallels in changes in terminology. In general, we have used the term *service user* for "client." The term used to describe the person who facilitates the student's learning in practice settings is generally a field instructor or a student supervisor. In the United Kingdom, for instance, the term *practice teacher* or *practice educator* is often used. In the United States, *practice teacher* is a term generally used to describe a person who teaches social work practice in the college setting.

LEARNING

. . . AND PARTICIPATION

The kind of activity-based learning advocated in this book is participative in a number of ways. Students and instructors, learners and teachers, are undergoing a similar process while recognizing their different roles. The instructor is not a repository of knowledge who fills the student's empty vessel but rather a person with considerable experience who is prepared to look at practice critically and reflectively. This applies to the instructor's own practice as well as the student's. Activity-based learning acknowledges that students bring knowledge, beliefs, values, and skills that will have a vital impact on their practice and, perhaps even more crucial, on their ability to learn practice.

Those who use these activities must, therefore, be prepared to be open about their own practice and experience. Learning flourishes in a creative and energetic climate, but conjuring this environment in a busy day is not easy. The activities can add spice to student learning and staff development, and we would be surprised if they did not have an impact on everyone's practice, "teacher" or "learner."

In summary, the activities are participative in two ways: as a method of learning that is engaging and active but also as a process in which all participants (whether they are styled teachers or learners) are learning.

. . . AND SIMULATION

There are different ways of learning. *Learning by doing* is one, and it has been used heavily by student supervisors in the past. The student experiences direct practice with people and learns "on the job," with some preparation beforehand and discussion afterwards with the supervisor. The student gets an authentic experience of the coalface, but this method of learning tends to perpetuate existing practices—good and bad—and often fails to highlight the learning that may have taken place. When learning opportunities come solely via direct practical experiences, it is difficult to pace them in a way that can match the individual student's needs and abilities.

Live teaching in the same room uses direct practice with people as a learning opportunity. The field instructor can give direct feedback to students about their work, and this has an immediate impact on the students' practice in a way that is not possible when the instructor is absent. The advantages of such immediate feedback are clear, but the presence of the instructor has to be carefully managed (Doel, 2010).

Another way of learning, illustrated by the activities in this book, is by using materials that *simulate practice situations*. These can be very close approximations to practice, like flight simulations used to train pilots, or activities that, by their very distance from direct practice, help to cast it in a new light. Sometimes an interesting mix of distance and proximity can be achieved by using metaphors, and a number of activities in the book are based on metaphor.

Simulated practice is a relatively safe environment for learning because the pace of action can be controlled and the consequences of taking risks are not serious (Doel & Shardlow, 1996). In these circumstances, the learner can feel free to experiment and be open to new approaches. The learner can also take the time to reflect on the issues that underlie the practice, especially the assumptions and values that might otherwise remain hidden or unchecked. The supervisor can regulate the degree of challenge facing the student, so that it is sufficiently stretching to break new ground, but not so demanding that it breaks the student's confidence. Activities that simulate or represent aspects of social work practice can *accelerate* learning by encouraging risk taking.

Placements in some areas of the United States can be in considerable demand, so there are economic as well as educational pressures to consider how opportunities for simulated learning might be constructed independent of the actual placement site. However, activities such as the ones in this book are not a substitute for direct practice. Direct practice is essential to put the learning from simulation into action, to test it out, and to experience a sense of imminence and of responsibility.

One of the best-known examples of a successful simulacrum are city subway maps. These design icons help millions of people to navigate large cities, and their success lies in their ability to distort the places they portray, both in terms of relative distance and position. For the original modern subway map (the London Underground in the 1930s), the powers-that-be initially complained that it was an inaccurate and misleading guide to London's real complexities. However, we—the traveling public—know the diagram's success lies in its emphasis on connections and linkages because it provides *a mental map* of a city, and one that works.

The subway map is an excellent analogy for the difference between social work practice "on the ground" and the ability to present that practice in an accessible way. The task of the teacher of practice, the instructor, is to create a design that is based on confidence that an element of distortion can actually help learning rather than hinder it because the missing parts and the chaotic aspects can be fitted into the student's mental map sooner or later once the basic linkages have been absorbed.

To illustrate this point, we can choose to present the contents of this book in the conventional linear fashion (see the Table of Contents) or as a subway-style design (see below).

Figure 1	The Contents of *Contemporary Field Social Work* in the Style of a Subway Map

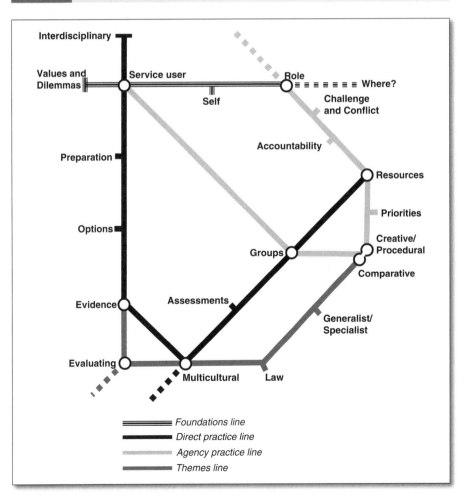

Do you prefer the conventional sequential layout (in the "Contents" of the book) or the subway presentation of the contents in Figure 1? Some readers will prefer the former, others the latter. Some might be attracted to the idea of the design but find its execution wanting (for instance, the reliance on gray shading rather than color is too obscure). Ask yourself why you are more attracted to one format than another and what implications this might have for your learning style or teaching style in placements.

It is important to reflect on your own response to these different approaches because, collectively, they mirror the different responses to styles of learning social work practice. The search for variety is a vital ingredient of effective teaching and learning. The topics in this book, as well as their attendant activities, should provide a lively and diverse experience, but it is necessary to use them alongside other methods as well, such as live teaching. It also helps to think of different *arrangements* for the practical learning: one-to-one; small groups, and so on. In addition to an understanding of preferred approaches to learning, it is useful to broaden these preferences. Students should not cut themselves off from certain kinds of learning experience—even if, for example, the "subway approach" is not immediately attractive, it is important to make efforts to broaden your style.

Making use of the opportunities to link simulation and live practice, learning and doing, is part of the art and science of teaching social work practice. The simulated activities provide a common frame of reference to make sense of what happens in direct practice and a chance to rehearse professional dilemmas. We hope this will make the live practice a more coherent experience for the student.

. . . AND UNLEARNING

Perhaps the biggest blocks to learning are the patterns of belief and behavior that have become so habitual that they are second nature. The opportunity to be a teacher of social work practice is an opportunity to question your own practice and reflect on it. This can be a difficult process because, as we become more "experienced," we face greater demands to appear competent and to deny the need for renewed learning. We can become so good at preventing ourselves from learning that the consequence can be *skilled incompetence*— "people who are incredibly proficient at keeping themselves from learning" (Senge, 1990). If making mistakes is not acceptable, we spend so much time covering up our mistakes that there is no time to learn from them.

. . . AND REFLECTION

The notion of supervision and practice learning in social work needs to be informed by ideas of professional education in general. With reference to this wider canvas (which, for instance, includes musicians and architects), Schön (1987) described the notion of a practicum and characterizes it as "a setting designed for the task of learning a practice. In a context that approximates a practice world, students learn by doing, although their doing usually falls short of real-world work. They learn by undertaking projects that simulate and simplify practice; or they take on real-world projects under close supervision" (p. 37).

The view that existing professional knowledge cannot fit every case and that not every problem has a right answer led Schön (1987) to the notion of reflection-in-action, by which "students must develop new rules and methods of their own." It relates to a central tenet of social work education—the concept of the transferability of knowledge; in other words, learning is not about experiencing every possible contingency (clearly an impossibility) but about making links and connections from one situation to another and by creating a greater whole out of the sum of the parts.

Practice learning for professional education transcends both the placement site and the educational establishment, but it must not become divorced from them. Schön (1987) went even further, suggesting that "in order to be credible and legitimate, a practicum must become a world with its own culture, including its own language, norms and rituals. Otherwise, it may be overwhelmed by the academic and professional cultures that surround it" (p. 170). This moves a long way from the notion of professional education as an apprenticeship, in which supervision is primarily concerned with regulating the student's behavior to fit the requirements of work tasks. In this vision of practical learning, the student enters a distinct world created for the purpose of learning reflective practice, described by Doel (2010) as *Socialworkland*. This is essential in order to establish professional practitioners rather than merely skilled technicians.

Crucially, supervision that nurtures the reflective student guarantees a future for the reflective practitioner.

IN CONCLUSION

In *Contemporary Field Social Work*, we aim to provide a comprehensive guide for all those engaged in teaching and learning social work practice, an aid to understanding and doing social work in the contemporary U.S. landscape.

There are already comprehensive texts for fieldwork learning, such as Barsky (2006); Birkenmaier and Berg-Weger (2007); Danowski (2005); Garthwait (2008); Rothman (2000); Royse, Dhooper, and Rompf (2007); and Wayne and Cohen (2001), and we make reference to other readings in each chapter as appropriate. *Contemporary Field Social Work* differs in its specific focus on the learning that takes place in the placement via a practicum based on the Educational Policy Accreditation Standards, as well as in its aim to include all of those who are likely to be involved in this endeavor—students, field instructors, faculty liaisons, service users, and providers of care—in active, participatory learning.

ACKNOWLEDGMENTS

Over the years there are many friends and colleagues who have contributed to, and commented on the ideas and activities we have presented in this book. Our thanks go to all those students and supervisors who have been willing guinea pigs in trying out exercises and new simulations. We would like to thank the book's reviewers for their helpful comments:

Eileen A. Arnold, Western Kentucky University

Marcia B. Cohen University of New England

Wayne C. Evens, Bradley University

Roy R. Fowles, Purdue University North Central

Bruce L. Hoem, Chadron State College

Patricia Magee, Pittsburg State University

Peggy Pittman-Munke, Murray State University

We have had the unstinting support of our Editor, Kassie Graves, to whom we are very grateful. Our sincere thanks to Veronica K. Novak, Editorial Assistant, and Astrid Virding, Senior Project Editor, for their help with the manuscript.

The book is adapted from *Modern Social Work Practice: Teaching and Learning in Practice Settings* (Doel & Shardlow, 2005) and is reprinted with the kind permission of Ashgate Publishing Limited. Our warm thanks in particular to Caroline Wintersgill and Claire Jarvis.

Part I

Foundations of Practice

Social work students learn much of their practice in field settings. In the United States, baccalaureate programs are required to provide a minimum of 400 hours of field education and 900 hours for master's programs. This amounts to 50% of the student's learning located in field education.

In 2008, the Council on Social Work Education (CSWE) implemented new *Educational Policy and Accreditation Standards* (*EPAS*). According to Educational Policy 2.1—Core Competencies (p. 3), competency-based education is an outcome performance approach to curriculum design. Competencies are measurable practice behaviors that comprise knowledge, values, and skills. The goal of the outcome approach is to demonstrate the integration and application of the competencies in practice with individuals, families, groups, organizations, and communities. *EPAS* identifies 10 core competencies (EP 2.1.1–EP 2.1.10d) as follows:

2.1.1 Identify as a professional social worker and conduct oneself accordingly.

2.1.2 Apply social work ethical principles to guide professional practice.

2.1.3 Apply critical thinking to inform and communicate professional judgments.

2.1.4 Engage diversity and difference in practice.

2.1.5 Advance human rights and social and economic justice.

2.1.6 Engage in research-informed practice and practice-informed research.

2.1.7 Apply knowledge of human behavior and the social environment.

2.1.8 Engage in policy practice to advance social and economic well-being and to deliver effective social work services.

2.1.9 Respond to contexts that shape practice.

2.1.10 (a)–(d) Engage, assesses, intervene, and evaluate with individuals, families, groups, organizations, and communities.

In addition to the above, CSWE (2008) also identified field education as its Signature Pedagogy. According to Educational Policy 2.3,

> In social work, the signature pedagogy is field education. The intent of field education is to connect the theoretical and conceptual contribution of the classroom with the practical world of the practice setting. It is a basic precept of social work education that the two interrelated components of curriculum—classroom and field—are of equal importance within the curriculum, and each contributes to the development of the requisite competencies of professional practice. Field education is systematically designed, supervised, coordinated, and evaluated based on criteria by which students demonstrate the achievement of program competencies. (p. 8)

This approach reflects the view that students should focus on learning competences, which in turn centers on the teaching function of placements. This view also emphasizes what social workers *do* rather than what social work *is*.

However, during this same period, the notion of the reflective practitioner also gained ground. Here, learning about social work practice was based on principles of adult learning, with an emphasis on the education of students, rather than the training, and a greater awareness of context and meaning. The tension between these two approaches led many to polarize the debate. However, a holistic view of this apparent conflict emerged, which enabled students and practice teachers to find ways to synthesize competence and context (Doel, Sawdon, & Morrison, 2002).

Baccalaureate and graduate social work education programs operate under the auspices of accredited colleges and universities. These education institutions vary by emphasis and size. With diverse strengths, missions, and resources, social work education programs share a common commitment to educate competent, ethical social workers.

The baccalaureate and master's levels of social work education are anchored in the purpose of the social work profession and promote knowledge, values, and skills of the profession. Baccalaureate social work education programs prepare graduates for generalist professional practice. Master's social work education programs prepare graduates for advanced professional practice in an area of concentration (i.e., a specialism).

This distinction, although conceptually admirable, in reality is difficult to implement. The CSWE considers that baccalaureate and master's levels of educational preparation should differ—for example, in terms of conceptualization and design, content, program objectives and depth, breadth, and specificity of knowledge and skills. While this can be achieved in courses offered by departments or schools of social work, when students are placed in their field work settings, numerous variables have an impact on this process.

If an agency takes both BSW and MSW students, how can one ensure that students are doing similar things but are being held to different standards? If an agency agrees to take an MSW student and another agency a BSW student, how can one ensure that the MSW student is achieving more advanced learning by experiencing more advanced work? There are also agency limitations: How many students can they take, what are the services the agency provides, and how many MSWs or BSWs are employed at the agency? How invested is the agency and/or the supervisor to the students' growth and development? We have also witnessed over the past few years financial constraints, with a number of agencies downsizing because they are no longer guaranteed federal and state funding and are becoming more and more reliant on grants, which is not a constant form of funding (Levitt, Beckerman, & Johnson, 1999).

Hence, although the CSWE has established criteria and standards, departments and schools of social work are totally dependent on agencies in their community, and without their support and cooperation, there would be no fieldwork education. This begs the question, *where does social work take place?*

WHERE DOES SOCIAL WORK TAKE PLACE?

It may seem strange to ask where social work takes place, but in the United States, there is a wide range of settings in which social work is carried out. For example, social workers practice in hospitals, nursing homes, day treatment centers, foster care and adoption agencies, residential programs, family and children's clinics, substance abuse programs, schools, community centers, and domestic violence programs; also, some social workers in the United States have their own private counseling practice. Indeed, one of the strengths of social work is its diversity and breadth.

Although there is a vast array of settings, one can categorize these as follows: First, there are those agencies that are staffed primarily by social workers such as child protection, foster care, and adoption agencies. One advantage of these settings is that they offer a sense of professional identity for social work students. Second, social workers work in settings that can be regarded as "host" organizations such as schools, hospitals, and nursing homes. These are settings where the main work of the organization is not social work; in these examples, it is education and health maintenance. Usually social workers comprise a small proportion of the organization's staff and are required to work with teachers and nurses to meet the goals of the organization. Students get an experience of working alongside other professions. Third is a hybrid of the two. A number of human service organizations, such as mental health centers, educational programs for teenage parents, adult day care programs, and programs addressing loss and bereavement, employ staff from a variety of disciplines. In these settings, there is an expectation that all professionals can work together as part of a multidisciplinary team and provide a wide array of services for clients.

Another major distinction is the division between public and private organizations. For example, at the federal level, there are veterans' programs, and at the state and local government level, there are Departments of Health and Human Services. Alongside these are numerous privately funded programs, which have emerged through historical circumstances and been sponsored by religious denominations. Even though one can point to these three categories, it also should be noted that there is a high degree of interdependence between the public and private agencies. Today, many public agencies contract out their services to private agencies. Finally, many practice settings differ in terms of whether their programs are mandatory or voluntary for clients. Although many social work students would like to believe that all services are freely chosen by clients, in reality many settings are required by law to constrain clients and mandate their involvement in particular programs.

While this diversification opens the way for more flexibility, there are indications that the search for practice learning opportunities is widening. In the state sector, practice learning sites are likely to extend from the traditional base of social work and social care settings into health, education, prisons, police, and so on; in the voluntary, independent and private sectors, these opportunities could extend to the wider world of social welfare, including small community projects and user-led organizations. Social work students will therefore have more opportunities to learn about social work processes in settings that are not primarily social work agencies, even to theater groups (Billington & Roberts, 2002). The practice learning opportunity should therefore do exactly what it says on the container and not be seen as "work experience."

Students will need to be broad-minded and creative in their approach, too, which means not being "concerned that unless they have a certain type of placement their employment prospects following the course will be hampered"

(Billington & Roberts, 2002, p. 31). Employers, too, will need to be less restrictive in their selection criteria for interviewing newly qualified social workers.

TEACHING AND SUPERVISING THE STUDENTS' PRACTICE LEARNING

There is a difference between being a good practitioner and being able to help somebody learn about good practice. There are already a number of excellent texts to guide this transformation (Barsky, 2006; Birkenmaier & Berg-Weger, 2007; Bogo & Vayda, 1998; Brown & Bourne, 1996; Caspi & Reid, 2002; Chiaferi & Griffin, 1997; Danowski 2005; Gardiner, 1989; Garthwait, 2008; Hawkins & Shohet, 2006; Rothman, 2000; Royse et al., 2007; Shardlow & Doel, 1996; Sheafor & Horejsi, 2008; Shulman, 2006).

However, despite the growing literature on practice learning, Brodie's (1993) verdict still stands—that we know very little about what actually takes place within the supervision process generally or the practice tutorial (supervision session) specifically: "Much of what occurs in supervision goes on behind closed doors, leaving all involved unsure whether the [student] is receiving quality education" (Caspi & Reid, 2002, p. 177). By and large, what happens between students and supervisors remains a very private affair. We hope that using the activities in this book, students and their field instructors will open up these processes. They can, after all, remain *confidential* without being hidden.

There is no specific code of practice for field instructors (although see the National Organisation for Practice Teaching [NOPT], 2000, for a British code of practice). The National Association of Social Workers (NASW, 1996) in the United States lists the following six core values that are relevant to social work learning in field settings as well as the classroom:

- Service
- Social justice
- Dignity and worth of the person
- Importance of human relationships
- Integrity
- Competence

In addition to a knowledge of any codes of ethics relevant to student supervision, it is important that everyone involved in the students' learning asks themselves, "What will make for a good practice learning experience?" Those who need to ask this question are not just the student, supervisor, and teacher but also other team members and agency managers involved in helping the student to learn about practice.

Clarke, Gibb, and Ramprogus's (2003, p. 110) findings with respect to the three key factors that help to create a positive placement experience for student nurses in Britain are relevant to social work students in North America:

- the hospital was prepared for them and had some structure to support the learning of the students [i.e., workgroup, in the case of social work students];
- staff were interested in them and they felt valued in their role;
- students were able to work with their mentor.

It is always important to discover what an individual considers important in the context of *this* particular experience. This is increasingly significant as opportunities for practice learning are sought outside traditional "placements," in sites where the experience of social work students is limited, perhaps because it is a host setting in which social work is not the dominant profession. Hence, there also needs to be agreement about how the aspirations for a good practice learning experience will be transformed into concrete reality.

Some state that there has to be a "fit" between student and supervisor. However, "the establishment of a positive supervisory relationship is not solely based on the 'fit' between supervisor and supervisee personalities" (Caspi & Reid, 2002, p. 124), whatever the term *fit* might be taken to imply. It is erroneous to assume that people with the same kind of biography (gender, ethnicity, age, etc.) are bound to have a better fit or that aiming for similarity is automatically beneficial to learning. If a core social work value is concerned with the celebration of diversity, let this be modeled in the student-supervisor relationship.

In the excitement about the possibility of new learning opportunities, we must not overlook the potential pitfalls, too. This is likely to become most transparent when it comes to making assessments of the student's performance. Of the common mistakes noted by Kadushin (1992, pp. 365–368), "contrast errors" may be the commonest. This refers to the mistake of comparing the student's performance to other workers or to the supervisor's own standard rather than to criteria that have been mutually agreed upon (see the section on Learning Agreement later) and that reflect the fact that this is a *student,* not a practitioner.

In particular, new supervisors and assessors need access to support and consultation from experienced field instructors; otherwise, the following findings are likely to be replicated:

[I] asked colleagues about their supervisory approaches and received two [kinds of] response. One group said that they drew upon their own experiences as supervisees, attempting to do (or not do) what their supervisors did with them. The second group said that they worked extemporaneously, "winging it" and learning through trial and error. (Caspi & Reid, 2002, p. 173)

Current and future students deserve better.

BENEFITS OF SUPERVISING STUDENTS

There are many benefits to supervising students. A study by Shardlow, Nixon, and Rogers (2002) found that field instructors regarded supervision as an opportunity for reflection on their own practice, which brought increased confidence and motivation to acquire more knowledge of research and theory. Students were seen as providing a challenge, in the best sense of the word.

Experienced practitioners can drift into automatic decision making, in which service users "are assessed as only needing services that the agency currently provides within its mission and area of expertise" (Wayne & Cohen, 2001, p. 18). Teaching and supervising a student encourages practitioners to slow down, in order to explain the thinking behind their actions. This helps not just the student but also the practitioner to consider fresh approaches and new perspectives, questioning any automatic tendencies in their own practice.

What are the economics of a student placement? Busy teams are often reluctant to offer a placement to students because of the pressure of work, but the balance of input and output can work in favor of the agency (Shardlow, 1988). The memory of an individual student who has been the center of concern, as well as perhaps much angst, sadly lives on well beyond the fonder remembrance of the 20 students who gave the agency a good experience. In reality, the benefits to an agency or project of those 20 students far outweigh the resources allocated to the one failing student.

A mind-set change is needed to perceive students as a potential resource, able to develop innovative services for the agency. The power of student placements to create and support new placements is evident from the examples in Box 1.

BOX 1   STUDENTS AS A RESOURCE

- Students have worked directly with children, which otherwise would not have happened.
- Students have started a reminiscence group in an older people's home, a service that is rarely provided to residents by existing staff members.
- In a medical practice, a student produced an information booklet for survivors of suicide attempts, which was widely distributed locally.
- The student designed a questionnaire about the team's knowledge of the law about cultural competency and led team discussion.
- A student placed with a nonprofit homeless organization accompanied members to Washington, D.C., to appear before a congressional hearing on homelessness.
- A student went to Venezuela with members of the National Poor People's Economic Human Rights Campaign and testified about the conditions of poverty in the United States.

(Continued)

(Continued)

- Several students were placed at a community resource center, which was established by a former member of the faculty of the school of social work. While at this yearlong placement, the students worked with many individuals who were homeless; ran breakfast programs, health care programs, and a teen center; and held an electoral registration drive. They also attended state hearings about homelessness and proposed legislation that would address this issue.

- A student placed at a community setting for the "mentally ill" was involved in a support program whereby the agency would receive a call from the local hospital, informing the student that a member from the organization was at the hospital and needed someone to accompany him or her.

- A student at the same program was involved in a cemetery program. This student helped identify through death records many individuals who had died in a state mental health facility. These individuals' deaths were never publicly recognized. The outcome was that the agency had a memorial service in which the names of more than a thousand people were read out, and the state acknowledged that these individuals had indeed died in their care.

- A student placed at a community mental health facility that provided day care services for senior citizens ran a reminiscence group. One of the gentlemen talked about graduating from school in the 1930s and never having received his diploma. The student, in conjunction with the local library, found pictures of the gentleman's school and put together a photo album for him. She also found school records, which indeed had his name and graduating class.

- A student placed at a residential group home for adolescent boys ran basketball and other recreation programs for these young boys. In the past, there had been limited recreation events after school and on weekends because staff were unwilling or unable to run such programs.

These are all examples of how students can be a tremendous asset not only to the agency but to the individuals with whom they are working. Perhaps students tend to be more creative and willing to try new approaches. They are likely to have a reduced case load compared to the full-time employees of the agency.

Of course, it is important that students do not fill the gaps of staff vacancies since they are not in the agency as a trainee employee; if a student is being used to reduce a pile of referral applications, this is exploitation. With this caveat, there is no reason why students cannot create or support services that might not otherwise have been available. For example, a team might agree that its work would be improved with more information about the way its services are experienced by the users, or there might be recognition that a group for certain service users would be a valuable addition to current activity. Indeed, students can be a major and positive force for change, and there is evidence that this kind of proactive practice learning project is welcomed by the students as well as the users and providers who experience it (Butler, 2004; Dent & Tourville, 2002; Muzumdar & Atthar, 2002; Underhill, 2002).

LEARNING AGREEMENT

Although many schools and departments of social work use the term *learning contract*, perhaps the term *agreement* is more appropriate. *Contract* has pseudo-legal connotations, while the term *learning agreement* suggests a joint undertaking by both the supervisor and the student to consider possible learning opportunities in each particular placement site.

In other words, the key to a successful practice learning opportunity is a clear understanding of expectations. That is not to say that every *t* must be crossed and every *i* dotted, for there will be plenty of learning that is serendipitous. However, the basic ground rules should be agreed on beforehand. These include practical details, such as expected times of attendance and resources available (desk, computer, etc.), and should also cover lines of accountability, as well as expectations of the frequency and kind of supervision and the kind and quantity of work available.

The following seven points provide some examples of the purposes of the learning agreement (University of Southern Maine, 2009, p. 29):

- To provide a planned approach to student learning in the field setting
- To promote effective linking of field agency goals and objectives with those of the student and college
- To promote clear and continual overall communications between all parties involved in the student's total learning program: student, field instructor, field agency, and college
- To clarify college expectations of field agencies, field instructors, and students
- To promote effective integration of students' classroom learning with practical application by identifying tasks or activities specifically designed to meet students' learning objectives
- To encourage student self-awareness through identification of learning strengths and deficits and through negotiation of the content of the agreement to meet identified needs
- To promote effective delivery of services to clients

The agreement should outline expectations around assessment, with examples of how the students will gather and present their practice and what will count as evidence of their abilities. There needs to be agreement about how the students' practice will be observed. This will be important not just for their learning and the assessment of their practice but also to monitor the quality of service to the clients.

Most important of all is agreement about what would happen if there are difficulties, with concrete illustrations. Although there is a cultural reluctance to discuss what might go wrong ("tempting fate," etc.), rehearsing potential issues makes them less, not more, likely to happen.

Examples of objectives that may be negotiated as part of the learning agreement are as follows (University of Southern Maine, 2009, p. 30):

Objective 1: Develop basic practice skills with clients.

Objective 2: Identify and be sensitive to ways in which cultural, economic, racial, ethnic, sexual orientation, disability, religious, and gender issues have a direct impact on the client's access to services and perception of them.

Objective 3: Demonstrate the ability to use the strengths perspective and systems model within the context of generalist practice perspective.

It is also beneficial to ask students to reflect on their experience so far, and this is assisted if the students have already prepared for the learning agreement (West & Watson, 2002). The following account is taken from a graduate's portfolio, reflecting back a number of years on the first weeks and months on her social work course:

When I started my education in social work I was very naïve and knew very little about social work. As a consequence, to begin with, the course proved to be very difficult. I attended every lecture with enthusiasm, taking in the knowledge provided like a sponge taking in water. The hardest part to understand initially was the legal and theoretical framework. With perseverance and a lot of background reading, alongside support from lecturers and a close friend reinforcing that I could do it, I grasped the fundamental issues in this area and never looked back.

It is important to remember that the student might be in the midst of this stage, "the course proving to be very difficult," and that your expectations should be of a *student,* not a qualified practitioner. The following "escalator" indicates a range of responses from novice (toward the bottom of the escalator) to expert (toward the top). Although progress is not linear, it is expected that the overall direction will be upwards; indeed, some students may well show natural abilities to operate relatively far up the escalator.

The Learning-Practice Escalator

Strategy taught to others
Strategy fully integrated
Strategy repeated, refined
Strategy tried and successful
Strategy tried and failed
A hypothetical response
No developed response
Awareness of dilemma or issue
Unaware of dilemma or issue

"Of course, assessing professional practice is not such an exact science that we can quantify the precise proportion of examples at each step [of the escalator]. The notion of a dilemma or practice issue is itself equivocal, as is the relative significance of any two such quandaries. . . . [However], this is a more authentic reflection of the shifting reality of professional practice than the illusion of fixed competencies" (Doel et al., 2002, p. 148).

Teaching social work practice is more than a technical skill, and the context of supervision has a significant impact. The supervisory process is influenced by your perspectives, whether supervisor or student, man or woman; it is influenced by your age, ethnicity, class, sexuality, faith, ability, and so on. It is crucial that issues of power are addressed openly to achieve practice learning that is anti-oppressive. In some circumstances, it is appropriate for students to have access to other resources—for example, consideration of an African American mentor for an African American student or a Hispanic supervisor for a Hispanic student in a predominantly White agency. It is crucial that these questions are addressed at the time of the learning agreement and not in the heat of any later moments.

The students' experience needs to be integrated not just across class and field but also between the various placements that they experience. The current field instructor needs to know about the students' *past* practice learning and help them to prepare for future learning. The development of new, nontraditional settings suggests that students will need even more assistance in transferring their learning from one situation to another (Cree & Macaulay, 2000).

SUPPORT FOR PRACTICE LEARNING

We have noted that students learn about practice from direct placement for half of their time on the course. In their attempts to integrate the learning in class and the learning in the field, they will rightly expect assistance from the field instructor and faculty instructor and, indeed, from any other people involved in their learning. As different kinds of opportunity are found for students, it will be important that the supports are reviewed, especially for people who are new to the role. Perhaps group supervision in the form of college-based seminars and workshops will become more appropriate than the traditional tutor visit (Fortune & Abramson, 1993). The role of e-support systems is also likely to increase; although most experiments in this area have been with students (Quinny, 2004), it is likely that we will see an extension to practice educators.

Other examples of support are monthly training sessions and workshops with supervisors on topics such as getting started, the significance of supervision, writing the learning agreement, working with challenging students, completing the end of term evaluation, and so on. In addition, training can be focused on more theoretical concepts. For example, many supervisors have commented that they would like more training on research (University of Southern Maine, 2009) and how to undertake program evaluations. At these trainings, both qualitative and quantitative research can be considered. Supervisors and agency personnel report the need to undertake grant writing (University of Southern Maine, 2009). Increasingly, agencies are dependent on grants for continual funding of programs, so this has become an additional expectation (Levitt et al., 1999).

Another benefit from undertaking these trainings is that supervisors can obtain Continuing Education Credits, which they require to renew their licenses in their respective states. It should be noted that supervisors also enjoy attending trainings and meetings to meet with colleagues from other agencies, with an important social component to these meetings. Finally, it is imperative that institutional support from universities and colleges include staff with dedicated time to student supervision, such as a fieldwork coordinator, fieldwork associate, and other faculty and field liaison staff. In other words, what we are proposing here is a radical departure from the traditional model of a "once a semester site visit" to a far more comprehensive and involved approach.

The faculty liaison role has been somewhat neglected in the literature (Degenhardt, 2003). Fortune and Abramson's (1993) study concluded that faculty liaison can offer more by helping, advising, and consulting with field instructors and less by monitoring the individual student. In a later study, the experiences of more than 300 field instructors were analyzed in relation to two models of liaison between college and field: the "intensive model" and the "troubleshooting model" (Fortune et al., 1995). Surprisingly, the evidence suggested that the field instructors preferred neither model over the other, suggesting that the troubleshooting model might, therefore, be a better use of scarce resources. The practice wisdom that the student's placement should be supported by consistent contact with a faculty liaison perhaps needs to be reconsidered in favor of more systematic methods of supporting placements. Certainly, we need more evidence about what kinds of support for practice learning are most effective.

At a strategic level, the partnerships offering the social work degree in the United States will need to consider how a wide variety of smaller agencies and projects can be best represented on formal bodies such as the Partnership Committees, which advise and support social work programs.

THE TIDE

In *The New Social Work Practice*, Doel and Shardlow (1998) noted,

> It is possible to discern a number of "tides" in the way the various aspects of the activity we call supervision has, and continues, to progress. Currently, there is a pull between the educative function, with an emphasis on the student as a learner and the use of a variety of teaching methods; and the assessment function, with an increasing concentration on the student's ability to demonstrate competencies. In this latter case, there is a danger that the processes of teaching and learning become buried beneath the weight of minutely detailed competencies.

We would like to keep the spotlight on the placement as a learning experience, not a work experience. As Thomlison and Collins (1995) note, "The primary responsibility of the [field instructor] is to facilitate the student's . . . educational plan through the service delivery system of the agency" (p. 225). The agency is primarily a service organization, and the education of students for professional practice is not a core concern. In these circumstances, field instructors have a crucial role to mediate the needs of the student with the requirements of the agency.

In this respect, the tide flows in the same direction as over 10 years ago. However, the widening of opportunities for practice learning and the increase in the amount of time in field settings means that the tide carries a larger and more diverse flotilla, with different support and service needs. It is a great opportunity for social work to widen its experience and also to influence the work of other professions.

Chapter 1

Learning About Service Users and Their Communities

Permission to Learn emphasizes the educational function of practice learning by allowing students to focus on the potential learning opportunities available from their respective placement settings.

PURPOSE

Your role as field instructor is highly significant in the educational and professional development of students, and we hope that, through the activities in this book, there can be an improved relationship between the learning in the classroom and that in the agency setting. As a field instructor with a responsibility to help a student's learning, *Permission to Learn* helps you to focus on the student as a learner and not as an employee.

A social work student might state a preferred agency or population he or she wishes to work with. How do you harness the student's commitment while broadening his or her ambitions? Moreover, the department or school of social work may not be able to place the student in the student's setting of first choice and—more significantly—can the student know at this early stage what the most appropriate fit is, when he or she has not yet worked in a setting in a professional capacity? What is more significant at this juncture is the fit between

---

[1]See the Introduction to the book for suggestions about how instructors and students can, separately and together, use the activities in this book.

the student and the field instructor—a field instructor who can support and, indeed, challenge the student's learning needs and styles.

Asking students to consider what they think they can *learn* from these situations (rather than what they can *do* or what their role is) puts the focus squarely on learning rather than practice. There will be plenty of time for that later.

METHOD

- Give the student a copy of the activity perhaps a week before the supervision session.

- Ask the student to follow the guidance that comes with the activity, answering the questions as and when indicated and making a written note of his or her deliberations.

NOTES FOR STUDENTS AND INSTRUCTORS

VARIATIONS

Most of the exercises in this book benefit from group activity. However, it is the interplay of individual and group that usually works best. Groups are not always as challenging as we hope or imagine them to be; group consensus can subdue real debate and allow individuals to be intellectually lazy. For this reason, it is often better to have a student complete an activity individually before any group discussion is arranged, so that individuals come to the group with their own views, some of which they should be prepared to change and others to defend.

Permission to Learn is better completed singly and discussed with the field instructor/supervisor. However, it is also an excellent exercise for the students to use in their respective fieldwork seminars or practice classes. At some later stage, a group of students could meet, to be exposed to the different approaches they have each taken to what is a very open-ended exercise.

USE BY OTHER PROFESSIONS

Permission to Learn lends itself to completion by a range of different professions. Students from health visiting, housing work, community psychiatric nursing, environmental health, rehabilitation work, education welfare, community work, town planning, policing, medicine, architecture, and others can learn from some or all of these situations. You could consider returning to the exercise later with a multiprofessional group of students to see how they would interpret the notion of interprofessional learning in this neighborhood.

The final question in the activity—*How do you think people might be helped by social work in these situations?*—would need to reflect the professional group in question: *How do you think people might be helped by policing in these situations?*

EDUCATIONAL POLICY ACCREDITATION STANDARDS

The topics in this chapter relate to the following *Educational Policy and Accreditation Standards* (*EPAS*) 2008 Primary Core Competencies (Council on Social Work Education, 2008):

1. Identify as a professional social worker and conduct oneself accordingly.

2. Apply critical thinking to inform and communicate professional judgments.

3. Engage diversity and difference in practice.

4. Apply knowledge of human behavior and the social environment.

5. Engage in policy practice to advance social and economic well-being and to deliver effective social work services.

FOR STUDENTS AND INSTRUCTORS

ACTIVITY 1: *PERMISSION TO LEARN*

Green Hill apartments were built as public housing in the 1960s to provide decent housing for people then living in slums. However, many of these "streets in the sky" acquired a bad reputation, partly because of the subsequent housing policies of the local housing authority, which used to concentrate people with problems in certain blocks. Even so, many of the Green Hill residents are loyal to the estate and have lived there for two and even three generations. It has an active tenants association. It has a community room. Security doors, CCTV, and intercoms have all been put in place, and the housing authority has had a policy for some time of mixed habitation, so that families, young couples, and older people live side by side.

Derby Street is one of the ground floor streets in Green Hill apartments. It consists of nine apartments:

At Number 1 is **Zoë Benner,** a single parent who was in public care for much of her childhood but is now reconciled with her mother, who lives on another street in Green Hill apartments. Zoë has a 14-year-old son (Jackson), a 12-year-old daughter (Kylie), and a baby daughter (Kara) age 11 months. Jackson was cautioned for shoplifting earlier in the year and has just been arrested on a charge of criminal damage. Kylie has not been to school for several weeks. She has few friends and is reluctant to leave the family's apartment. Kylie has been referred for help with her bedwetting problem. Kara is Zoë's daughter by another man who is attempting to gain custody of her. Kara has asthma and seems to suffer from unspecified allergies. Zoë has another child, Tilly, a 7-year-old girl currently living with foster parents on the other side of the city.

At Number 2 live **Jason Dean** and his partner **Sam Weiner.** Jason, a 28-year-old, has a previous drug-related charge and has just completed a rehabilitation program. Jason is unemployed but volunteers at a local drop-in center for homeless people. Sam is 46 years old and is on long-term disability, experiencing occasional periods of depression. He relies on Jason for much of his care. Sam is a leading light in the tenants association for the block of apartments.

Avis Jenkins lives at Number 3. She is 84 years old, and her only son lives in another part of the country. Jason Dean gives her quite a bit of support, calling in and checking in on her several times a week. Mrs. Jenkins has home care twice a week. Charging policies for home care services have changed recently, and Mrs. Jenkins is finding it difficult to cope financially. Her memory is deteriorating, and she is a regular member of a group called Memory Joggers at the local day center. Avis has lived in the area all her life and worked on the local newspaper until she retired.

Number 4 houses a young couple, **Loretta and Luke Carter.** They both work in low-paid jobs but put enough aside to run an old secondhand van. Luke also plays in a band, which sometimes comes to Number 4 to practice. The band play gigs most weeks and about once a month at a local bar.

Jim Rafferty lives at Number 5. He used to work in the steel industry in quite a well-paid job until he retired. He is now 72 years old and was widowed 3 years ago. Over the past 5 years, he has been losing his sight gradually through macular degeneration. His daughter lives a short bus ride away. Jim has written to the housing authority to complain about the noise from Number 4.

In Number 6, two Kurdish brothers, **Gregor and Stefan Kiyani** from Iraq, have recently been housed after successfully seeking political asylum. They are both trained as engineers. They are currently unemployed but are actively seeking work and are in regular touch with a local Kurdish support group. Gregor has good English, although Stefan's is more faltering. They get on well with the others on the street and have gone out of their way to say hello and invite people round to their apartment. However, they have recently been very distressed by an incident in which dog feces was posted through their mailbox.

Shama and Gary Homes live at Number 7. Shama works part-time in the kitchens of one of the local schools. Gary is a full-time homemaker. Shama and Gary provide respite care for children with learning disabilities. They have an adult daughter with learning disabilities who now lives independently in a program run by United Cerebral Palsy (UCP).

Ernie and Catherine Minkie live at Number 8. Ernie is a former Navy veteran and served in the Navy for 20 years from 1967 until 1987. During the time he was in the Navy, he visited many parts of the world. Catherine has chronic emphysema. Ernie works as the maintenance man at United Cerebral Palsy, where Shama and Gary's daughter lives. He enjoys working at the group home and gets along well with all of the staff and the 15 residents who reside at the group home. Ernie also likes going to the American Legion club, although recently due to Catherine's poor health, he has not been able to go as frequently. He enjoys "hanging out" with the guys and reminiscing about old times in the Navy.

Number 9 used to be a small corner store, but it closed 4 months ago and is currently boarded up. The nearest shop is a supermarket, which opened 6 months ago but lies across a busy highway.

Derby Street and a number of other streets on the north side of Green Hill apartments have a recurring infestation of ants. There are also difficulties with mildew from excessive damp. Green Hill apartments were owned by the local housing authority but were recently transferred for redevelopment to a not-for-profit housing association. Tenants will be involved in decisions about the coming changes, which will result in some tenants moving from the block while extensive refurbishments are made.

1. What do you think you might learn from working in the situations described above?

Avoid stating obvious generalisms, such as "I would learn how to work with someone losing their sight" and aim for learning that is more specific, such as "I could learn how an older person copes with the practical difficulties of losing their sight and how it affects them emotionally."

2. Prioritize a list of 10 possible learning points and make a written note of these.

When you have considered what you might learn from these situations, consider the next question (Q3).

3. How do you think people might be helped by social work in these situations?

Again, make a written note of your thoughts.

NOTES FOR INSTRUCTORS

TEACHING ABOUT SERVICE USERS AND THEIR COMMUNITIES

Opportunities

One of the major functions of practice learning in an agency setting is the opportunities it provides students to work with the people who use social work services. However, just because these opportunities are readily available does not mean that they will automatically result in a good learning experience for the student. *Permission to Learn* is designed to help both you and the student focus on the learning potential.

To make the best use of *Permission to Learn,* we suggest you first complete the activity yourself. Resist answering the question by reference to what you know of the social work role, agency procedures, eligibility criteria, and so on in your own agency—you may find this surprisingly difficult to do. Answering the three *Permission to Learn* questions for yourself will help you to understand the difference between you and the student.

As the authors, we cannot presume exactly who you, the field instructor, is. However, if you have responsibility for helping a student learn about social work, it is safe to assume that you are probably an experienced practitioner, manager, service user, or provider of services. The location of your work may be a social services department (or its equivalent); a voluntary, nonprofit organization; a private agency; a user-led agency; or, indeed, a location in which social work is not a prime activity. Even so, what is important to remember and too easy to forget is that your task is to help the student learn about social work, *not* to train him or her to do your job. In other words, the specific work in which you are engaged is but one *example* of social work in practice.

Helping students to move from the specific of your location to the general of social work practice, as well as back to different specifics (not just yours), is a demanding skill and is going to be a learning experience for you, too, no matter how experienced you are.

The Green Hill situation in *Permission to Learn* is designed to help you give the student permission to focus first and foremost on *his or her own learning.* There will be time enough for the student to learn about your agency's policies and mission statements, the limits to your role, and the procedures that govern what can and cannot be undertaken. These policies, procedures, and roles may or may not have been formalized with Zoë Benner, Jason Dean, Avis Jenkins, and the other residents of Derby Street in mind. The people living on Derby Street do not spend their time reorganizing their problems and aspirations to fit neatly into the mission statements of the agencies that may or may not help them. It is right that the student has the opportunity to consider the whole picture of a community's life before the lines are drawn. After all, it is this whole picture that more accurately reflects the lives of real people.

This holistic, generalist person-in-the-environment approach is not a utopian whim. The person-in-the-environment approach is embedded in the *EPAS* of the Council on Social Work Education (2008). Where better to begin, then, than our community in Derby Street in the Green Hill apartments?

NOTES FOR STUDENTS

LEARNING ABOUT SERVICE USERS AND THEIR COMMUNITIES

Who Is the "Client"?

One of the learning points to note from *Permission to Learn* is that it is not clear-cut how and with whom you might work. This is a longstanding issue and has been characterized in the social work literature by the question, "Who is the 'client'?" (see, e.g., Davies, 1994; Hepworth, Rooney, Dewberry Rooney, & Larsen, 2006).

Client is a term whose usage has been changing. For a while, there was a flirtation with *customer,* but it was clear even to the most ardent supporters of market forces that people who use social work services do not have the economic freedom of choice that the term *customer* implies. Many do not want to purchase social work services and are forced to receive them as an unwelcome gift. *Citizen* is a worthy term but is now considered to exclude some people who are not yet citizens, such as political asylum seekers, who should nevertheless have access to services. *People* is the most inclusive term, but sometimes we need a term that is specific to people who are using social work services. The authors would propose that a more appropriate term is *service user*. There is also increasing recognition of the significant role that providers play and the importance of involving providers, the people who are involved in the care of service users, in the work.

We pose the question "Who is the 'client'?" in a very particular way. It was put some time ago by Pincus and Minahan (1975) as part of an attempt to help social workers think more widely about the various systems with which they worked. Rather than seeing the social work "client" as necessarily an individual person (or even family), Pincus and Minahan's work suggested there were client systems whose boundaries depended on different circumstances. Doel and Marsh (1992) suggested that the "client" is the conceptualization of the problem. In Green Hill apartments, for example, one client could be *the problem of the damp*. Dent and Tourville (2002) describe how a multiracial inner-city community became the students' client in an innovative project in which students worked alongside medical students and community development students in partnership with the local community. "The students also learned to develop and provide one-on-one services with residents" (p. 28). These social work students were working with physical, economic, and social issues simultaneously, and their client was much broader than any one individual.

Individuality of Service Users and Providers

As well as emphasizing your learning, *Permission to Learn* has helped you to understand the way in which people and their difficulties are interconnected. Social policy at central and local levels affects individual lives; structural racism and sexism limit individuals' potential and oppress them; neighbors have an impact on each other's lives. The people on Derby Street can be seen as members of larger social groups, women and men, African American people, Kurdish people, White people, gays, lesbians, straights, children, teenagers, adults, providers and cared-for, older people, blind people, able-bodied and disabled people, and so on. People are discriminated against and have dog feces put through their mailboxes because of these social labels. They also find strength in meeting together as groups, such as the support group that the Kiyani brothers attend, the Green Hill Tenants Association, and the Memory Joggers group for people with memory problems.

To what extent does it help to know Mr. Jenkins as a "visually impaired person" as opposed to someone who was a steel worker, someone with gray hair and brown eyes, or someone with a kind manner and soft speech? You might be able to use your previous knowledge of someone with a visual impairment to begin to understand how "people" respond to sight loss. However, you must also understand that each person's response is unique. The capacity to move between the general and the particular is an important part of becoming a social worker. This is the ability to comprehend the racism that the Kiyani brothers face at a personal and institutional level while understanding their individual circumstances of loss and likely trauma.

Strengths Perspective

A visit to the doctor usually occurs because something is wrong, although more and more insurance health plans are encouraging individuals to be more proactive and promoting wellness plans for regular and annual checkups. It is not surprising, then, that the doctor fails to comment on how well your legs are working when it is your broken arm that you are consulting the doctor about. Nevertheless, it was your legs (and various other working parts) that successfully took you to the doctor!

The strengths perspective means recognizing the strengths that are inherent in individuals, groups, and communities and using these strengths as building blocks for change. According to Saleebey (1992),

> A strengths perspective assumes that when people's positive capacities are supported, they are more likely to act on their strengths. Thus, a belief in people's inherent capacity for growth and well-being requires an intense attention to people's own resources: their talents, experiences, and aspirations. Through this active attention, the probability for positive growth is significantly enhanced. (p. 25)

It is understandable if your first knowledge of the service user is in reference to what is wrong, since it is these problems and difficulties that bring you into contact. However, there is a process in which the practitioner can dwell on these deficits to such an extent that the person is seen only as the sum of his or her inadequacies. This is sometimes referred to as pathologizing the person. At its very worst, users find themselves in a Catch-22 situation, in which their opposition to the attempts to pathologize them is taken as a sign that they are in denial, thus providing further "evidence" of their neediness.

Knowing the service user means knowing about his or her abilities and aptitudes, too—the two "A"s, if you like. This is often referred to in the social work literature as the strengths perspective (Graybeal, 2001). Looking back at your work on the *Permission to Learn* activity, to what extent did you focus on the deficits and on the strengths? "What strengths?" you may protest! Well, return to the activity and you will see that there are many indications of strengths, both in the lives of individuals and in the community at large. Moreover, most situations that become defined by the language of deficits (*single parent* Zoë Benner with a son who is *in trouble* with the police, a daughter who is *refusing* to go to school, and a *sick* baby) might be reframed as a *survivor* of public welfare, keeping a family *together* in dire circumstances. Usually the situation is a complex mix of both possibilities, but it is important not to lose sight of the strengths in people's lives. It is these strengths that will enable you to work together to make improvements.

You will also be developing theoretical perspectives that help in explaining some of the events or phenomenon that can influence your work with service users and providers (Dewees, 2006; see Part IV, this volume).

Relationship Between Social Workers, Service Users, and Providers

How do changes in the tasks and requirements of social workers affect the relationship with service users and providers? Some current commentators are concerned that a focus on the whole person is increasingly being replaced by a focus on his or her various needs. Lymbery (2000) argues that services are organized around specialized aspects of need (e.g., a person's mental health needs) rather than the person as a whole; it is important to understand how people's lives are joined, how individuals' lives are connected to others, and their problems are but one facet of their overall experience.

Lymbery (2000) describes three paradigms for the relationship between social worker and user:

- The traditional view: A relationship exists between a professional and a "client," in which there are differentials in power and knowledge and social distance between the two.
- The market view: The social worker is a purchaser (occasionally a provider), and the service user is a consumer, with a relationship that is supposedly commercial.
- The partnership view: This is a modified view of professionalism, in which social workers engage service users in an active participation, recognizing the expertise that the service user brings to the relationship.

The current rhetoric emphasizes the last of these, but you should observe which of these paradigms is the most characteristic of the relationships between practitioners and users of services in the agency where you are learning your practice. Sometimes there is a gap between the rhetoric and the reality; indeed, the rhetoric can be a barrier to recognizing and appreciating this gap. The increasing involvement of service users and providers in the education and training of social work students means that you will probably have the opportunity to meet people who use social work services in the class setting as well as the practice learning site. Participation by service users and providers in the full range of social work education—planning, delivery, and evaluation—is meant to ensure that the partnership view described above is transparent throughout your experience as a student.

Service User and Provider Control

Much of the discussion has moved on from notions of participation to ones of empowerment. In research and policy making, in particular, social work has been exploring how service users and providers can move from participating to initiating. This is a philosophy that moves beyond the satisfaction survey ("how did you find that service?") to more control of the nature of the service itself. There are some interesting examples of this in practice, including research projects in which service users and providers hold the budget.

We have discussed the importance of knowing the service user as an individual, as a member of a social group, and understanding him or her as a whole person in the context of his or her community. Turning this on its head, how might the service user know you and how, as individuals or in collaboration with others, can he or she acquire more control over the kinds of service that are available?

ASSESSING YOUR LEARNING

It will be important for you to demonstrate an understanding of the whole person, that is, the service users in their wider context and not just in their relationship to the agency where you are studying. This understanding needs to include an appreciation of people's strengths as well as their problems and an ability to engage with them, even when their circumstances and their biographies are very different from your own. Your ability to identify and work with people's strengths will be part of your assessment as a social work student.

FURTHER READING

Dewees, M. (2006). *Contemporary social work practice.* New York, NY: McGraw-Hill.

Graybeal, C. (2001). Strengths-based social work assessment: Transforming the dominant paradigm. *Families in Society, 82*(3), 233–242.

Hepworth, D. H., Rooney, R. H., Dewberry Rooney, G., & Larsen, J. (2006). *Direct social work practice, theory and skills.* Belmont, CA: Brooks/Cole/ Thompson.

Saleebey, D. (1992). *The strengths perspective in social work.* New York, NY: Longman.

CHAPTER 2

Learning About Yourself

Points of View takes a look at social work from several perspectives. Brief quotations present examples of different views about social work, and students are invited to consider their responses to the various statements.

NOTES FOR INSTRUCTORS[1]

PURPOSE

The reasons why people come into social work are numerous. Some have clear, well-rehearsed positions, and others have difficulty identifying their motives and beliefs. Some subscribe to an "-ism" or two, and others have muddled views with no obvious guiding principles. Some may have had personal experiences, such as having used social services or being a provider (Parker & Merrylees, 2002), and there may be differences between the motivation of men and women entering social work (Cree, 1996).

We all have some kind of personal philosophy, ways of looking at the world and explaining it, but how aware of them are we? The purpose of this activity is to help students to acquire a better understanding of how the way they view the world influences their work—in other words, how beliefs interact with actions.

---

[1]See the Introduction to the book for suggestions about how instructors and students can, separately and together, use the activities in this book.

METHOD

- This activity is best undertaken by a student and fieldwork instructor jointly; even better with a group of three, four, or more students. Give a clear explanation of the purpose of the exercise, emphasizing the exploratory aspects and making sure the student knows that there is no pressure to take up any particular position.

- The students read the various statements in the *Points of View* activity and write down responses to each of the statements. Arrange a time when you can exchange comments (probably the next fieldwork or class seminar) and suggest that the student makes a few notes ready for this discussion.

- Encourage the student to enter a dialogue about the statements and your mutual preferences. It is important to avoid preaching or trying to enforce a consensus; the discussion is an opportunity to share the ways you each view the world and, if these are not clear, an attempt to articulate previously unspoken worldviews.

- Help the student to relate worldviews to professional practice. What are the implications of each of these statements for practice? How do different beliefs affect the choices social workers make about what they do?

NOTES FOR STUDENTS AND INSTRUCTORS

VARIATIONS

You can substitute different statements from a wide variety of perspectives. Alternatively, you can use different viewpoints about particular aspects of practice (e.g., child care, work with older people). In many respects, it is irrelevant which views are discussed with the student; the purpose of the activity is for students to become aware of their own views by looking at the world as others see it.

You can use this activity at an early stage in a student's practice learning. It is also the type of activity that can be revisited using either the same or different extracts later to help students identify how their worldview has or has not changed.

USE BY OTHER PROFESSIONS

The extracts in *Points of View* put social work behind the prism, but other professions have these kinds of different perspectives, too. Should medicine focus on ill health or well-being? Just as advances in environmental health (drains and fresh water) had the greatest impact on public health in the 19th century, should medicine focus more on health promotion than hi-tech laser surgery? Is occupational therapy a radical, political activity (Kronenberg, Algado, & Pollard, 2004) or a skills-based profession that should focus on individual rehabilitation? Instructors can gather examples from the literature or articles in the professional journals that illustrate a wide range of belief about the mission of their profession.

EDUCATIONAL POLICY ACCREDITATION STANDARDS

The topics in this chapter relate to the following *Educational Policy and Accreditation Standards (EPAS)* 2008 Primary Core Competencies (Council on Social Work Education, 2008):

1. Identify as a professional social worker and conduct oneself accordingly.

2. Apply social work ethical principles to guide professional practice.

3. Apply critical thinking to inform and communicate professional judgments.

4. Engage diversity and difference in practice.

5. Advance human rights and social and economic justice.

6. Apply knowledge of human behavior and the social environment.

FOR STUDENTS AND INSTRUCTORS

ACTIVITY 2: POINTS OF VIEW

Consider the following four brief extracts about social work and ask yourself the following:

- Which of these extracts do you feel most attracted to? Why?

- What are the ideological beliefs that underpin each of these extracts?

Extract 1: The Social Work Relationship

In much contemporary social work practice, the chief concern is not with causation, but with the practical consequences of given sets of circumstances. Howe (1996) has defined this as a move away from the "depth" that characterized much traditional social work literature to a concern with the "surface," based on eligibility criteria, standard service responses, and a concern with the classification of needs. He states that "it is the category into which the client's behavior or condition fits which increasingly determines the response required" (*ibid:* 91). It could be argued that, given this priority, it is unnecessary—even distracting—for a social worker to seek to establish a relationship with the service user. The social worker's purpose is defined more simply, as the need to secure sufficient information on which to make the categorization, on which a subsequent purchase of services within the market is based.

Extract 2: The Messiness of Practice

The emphasis on cognitive-behaviorist approaches and positivist methods of evaluation go hand in hand with a contemporary view of social work as a rational-technical activity, characterized by management, systems of audit, procedures, legalism, and a concern with outcomes. These characteristics derive from a view of practice dependent on the application of knowledge emerging from objective, testable, replicable techniques. What becomes lost in all of this is an acknowledgement that social work is also a moral, social, and political activity, one in which discretion and judgment cannot be discounted. The blunt instruments that measure changes in client behaviors often cannot capture the dilemmas confronted by practitioners, which lead to uncertainty and confusion, and which are key elements in decisions made in everyday situations affecting their clients' lives. To leave these motives, meanings, doubts, and influences—the messiness of practice—unavailable to examination is to have an incomplete and distorted picture of the patterns of action in concrete situations.

Extract 3: Social Workers' Constructions of Power

A major assumption [in the group of ten social workers] was that the power resided either with the managers, supervisors, recalcitrant colleagues and, in some cases, the community groups with consumer voice. In no instances did workers see themselves as powerful. Either each person had exercised what power they thought they had and it had proved inadequate, or they felt they did not possess enough power to bring about any change. The common themes in the stories we shared showed that we had each constructed ourselves as powerless, denying or minimizing the influence of different types of power we might possess. Sometimes we identified as powerless with individual clients for whom we were acting, but in other instances we also invested these people with power we did not have. A major assumption there-fore was that *other people had the power, workers did not.* There was almost a sense in which workers saw themselves as victims.

Extract 4: Empirical Practice

In general, empirical practice draws, as much as it can, on scientific atti-tudes, knowledge, and processes. In empirical practice one gives primacy to research-based theories and interventions. Due to the emphasis placed on research, empirical practitioners make an effort to become familiar with studies relating to populations, problems, and interventions they are work-ing with. In treating individual clients, families, or groups, the targets of intervention are specifically stated, and devices such as direct observation and standardized tests are used to collect assessment data. Intervention methods are defined in terms of specific actions by the practitioner, and they are used as systematically as possible. . . . The practitioner monitors change and evaluates outcomes in relation to the interventions used.

The sources of these extracts can be found at the end of the chapter. It is strongly suggested that you do not consult this until you have completed the activity and had the opportunity for discussion.

NOTES FOR INSTRUCTORS

TEACHING ABOUT POINTS OF VIEW

Opportunities

There are as many worldviews as there are people to hold them. What we know as "-isms" (socialism, feminism, etc.) are worldviews that are so cogent that we often refer to them as theories. A theory is a coherent explanation of why the world is as it is. According to Rubin and Babbie (2008, p. 47), a theory is a systematic set of interrelated statements intended to explain some aspect of social life or enrich our sense of how people conduct themselves or find meaning in their daily lives. As such, a theory provides an analysis of some aspect of the world, and sometimes it gives prescriptions about how the world might be changed to rectify wrongs that are evident in the analysis, which is made evident in a particular theory.

There are, therefore, almost infinite opportunities to help the student to develop his or her self-knowledge. However, if you were to ask students "cold" about their personal philosophy, you would probably get an equally cold response. It is a very personal matter to look at the way in which we view the world and the beliefs we hold, and there may be many reasons why we have learned to be careful about how and whether to reveal them. It can help to start from a less personal position and to move at the student's pace to a more subjective point.

Points of View helps students to open up about professional values and the beliefs they have to explain the world. It is difficult to remain disengaged, and the activity triggers sympathies, antipathies, and discussion of general issues and perhaps sometimes reveals confusion on the student's part. For example, how does the use of language differ from one statement to the next, and is this significant? How are meanings construed? What does the student make of the similarities and differences between aspects of the extracts?

It is important to be open about your own beliefs, too. It may be difficult to avoid dispute with an opinionated student or to avoid providing answers for one who is diffident, but your aim is to open up a genuine dialogue. At this stage, you are not making a judgment about the student's own world-view; you are helping the students to explore how it is likely to influence their work.

Examples

Molly was eager to discuss *Points of View*. She had read it carefully before-hand as requested and had made notations on the extracts. However, she was quickly critical of the crude representation of one of the viewpoints and claimed that the others were irrelevant in the face of a feminist critique. Molly gave a forthright and articulate account of her views and referred her practice teacher to Langan and Day (1992) and Orme (2002) for some perspectives on different feminist positions. The field instructor suggested that it might be a good idea for Molly to write a specifically feminist position and commentary to use as part of the exercise, but this was met with short shrift on the grounds that a caricature would debase feminism and that there wasn't "a feminist worldview," just differing interpretations. The field instructor's views were, in fact, similar to the student's, but she was unhappy that Molly's manner prevented her (the field instructor) from sharing her own beliefs.

"How do I feel?" the field instructor asked herself 15 minutes into the activity. The answer came, "like a hurricane is blowing me away." She decided that it was time to turn the session into a more reflective mode and gently shared her impressions with Molly, who was initially surprised. When Molly began to reflect on her approach to the session, she realized that she had assumed that she would be expected to give a good account of her own views. Although she had denied it to herself, she had been nervous but was determined "to get it right—to my own satisfaction." This explained her earnest single-mindedness. "I suppose I've played the good little girl to your school-teacher and I resented it, but I realize that wasn't what you were looking for."

Molly's approach could easily have been interpreted as rigid, and in part, it did point to a tendency to get hold of the wrong end of the stick. However, Molly's honesty and intelligence proved an asset to her work. She had no doubts about the rightness of her philosophy, but she increasingly understood that what motivated her did not necessarily motivate other people.

James was very quiet during the discussion of *Points of View,* tending to follow his field instructor's lead. When he was asked more directly for his views, he suddenly became dismissive of issues that he had been nodding at earlier. He felt that people were trying to make social work out to be more than it was and that he "just gets on with the job, finding people as they are." He didn't think it mattered with which statements he agreed or disagreed. In his opinion, it was much more important to learn about social work skills and to get on with the business of just doing your best for people.

The practitioner should not make assumptions about James's practice from this one reaction but discover what these views indicate. For reasons that are not yet clear, abstract discussion with James has not been successful. Perhaps it would be helpful to introduce a concrete example from practice familiar to James. If this is constructed to illustrate a practical dilemma, the practice teacher can help James find the principles that lie behind his practice, by teasing out the reasons for the choices he makes in the face of the dilemma. James will need reassuring that he is not being asked to adopt an "-ism" but to look at the approaches that he uses, perhaps instinctively, in his own practice and how these pull together. Revisiting *Points of View* later in the placement would show how much James had developed; if he is still unable to conceptualize, this would lead to questions about his competence in this area.

NOTES FOR STUDENTS

LEARNING ABOUT YOURSELF

Social work is a profession that draws people from a broad range of backgrounds. For some, social work is a second or third career. In fact, many educational programs, particularly at the graduate level, view prior educational and career experience as an advantage for students entering studies. These prior life experiences help prospective social workers by providing them with greater sensitivity and understanding of people and various social issues.

"Others enter the field to reciprocate for help they themselves once received" (DuBois & Miley, 2005, p. 5).

As a profession, social work has been closely associated with individuals who have been discriminated against historically—for example, African Americans, Native Americans, people with disabilities, gay men, lesbians, people who are transgender, immigrants, people living with physical or mental disabilities, children, and the elderly. In contemporary fieldwork practice, the concept that we would use to categorize these individuals would be populations at risk. Social work is a profession that values and embraces diversity and respects individuals (Kirst-Ashman, 2007).

Populations at risk are groups of people who are at greater risk of social and economic deprivation than those in the mainstream. Because social work practice involves finding resources and helping solve problems, social workers frequently work with populations at risk of such deprivations. It follows that social workers need information and insight concerning these populations' special issues and needs.

It is highly likely that the experience of being a member of one of these groups, or working or volunteering with them has had a profound impact on you—perhaps instrumental in your decision to become a social worker, because at some level you wanted to make a difference. While you were volunteering at a program for the mentally and physically challenged, you realized that these programs needed more trained staff to work with them and that mentally and physically challenged individuals could accomplish a great deal. While you were working or volunteering at the elderly person's home, you realized that these elderly individuals were not all the same and needed to be regarded as individuals with fascinating pasts; many of them were grandparents, had raised families of their own, and had made substantial contributions in their lives. While you were working or volunteering at the homeless shelter, you realized that the population was diverse—families as well as homeless alcoholic men—with some people working two or three jobs yet still dependent on the program. In other words, you started to question or disregard the stereotypes that were associated with this program.

These personal experiences can have a tremendous impact on your decision to enter the profession of social work. So, one aspect of learning about yourself is knowing why you wanted to become a social worker and how this motivation can be sustained. One practitioner described her own rather rapid experience in her post-graduate portfolio: "I went to a job fair where a computer program indicated that I should consider social work. I applied to several Universities and was accepted into the BSW/MSW program on a full-time basis at the school of social work close to my home."

Life experience is a significant aspect of motivation to enter social work, although we know very little about these connections, and it is currently "a neglected form of knowledge in social work education and practice" (Christie & Weeks, 1998, p. 55). How have your life experiences led to your decision to become a social worker, and in what ways are they likely to influence your practice?

USE OF SELF

When people are asked for their views about what makes a good social worker, the responses tend to focus on qualities such as friendliness, warmth, kindness, sincerity, reliability, and so on. There are other qualities that may not be named but that we might also, on reflection, feel are important, such as optimism and a sense of hope (Trotter, 1999, p. 116). These basic qualities are fundamental to good practice, although there is much debate about whether you just have them or whether they can be learnt. It is also important to develop competent skills to put these good intentions into practice. Training and education help you to make conscious decisions about your behavior; this does not make the behavior insincere, but it does mean that you are more aware of yourself and how you use yourself.

There is much talk of the "conscious use of self" in social work practice (see, in particular, Minuchin & Fishman, 1981). What does this actually mean? Caspi and Reid (2002) claim that "the 'self' consists of all facets of the person . . . including feelings, thoughts and ways of behaving as well as fixed attributes such as age, sex and physical characteristics" (p. 129). The fixed attributes do not change, or only slowly, while the other facets might not even be visible to ourselves. If you want to explore different notions of yourself, download "Tree 1" of The Virtual Placement (Doel & Cooner, 2002) and work through each of the Word Photos in the program.

Why might it be particularly important to know yourself in social work? Make a list in the box below and share this with your field instructor.

"Self-awareness enables deliberate choices about how to behave" (Caspi & Reid, 2002, p. 215), whether this is in your professional role as a social worker or, indeed, in your personal life. One significant aspect of self is the way in which you construe the world, as mediated by your beliefs and understandings. In your studies for the social work qualification, you will come across terms such as *postmodern* and *constructionist,* and these refer to the idea that meanings are not rigid dictionary definitions but are constructed socially (Parton, 2000). In turn, the term *reflective practice* is one that builds on this idea that it is important to know yourself to better understand your professional practice (Lishman, 2002).

WORLDVIEWS

Everybody has a worldview, even if it is not very clear or consistent. A worldview is just another way of saying how we make sense of the world, including personal theories we use to explain what goes on around us. Problems can arise if we have views that exclude other interpretations to such an extent that we are unaware of other people's worldviews, whether they are colleagues or service users. Problems can also occur if we are not aware of the personal beliefs that lead us to act as we do.

Take an example from your current period of practice learning. This may be someone you have been working with, or perhaps one of your colleagues can provide an example. Think of the *case path* for this person (a case path is a way of describing the person's contact with the organization from start to finish). Look at the case path from the different perspectives of the writers of the four extracts in the *Points of View* activity.

- How does each point of view affect your explanation of the person's situation?

- How does this influence what you do?

- What effect might this have on the case path?

You might want to consider how the beliefs in each of the four extracts might influence your work with the various residents of Derby Street in Activity 1, *Permission to Learn* (Chapter 1, this volume). It may help if you begin to color in some additional information, perhaps relating to people's faiths; for example, that the Kiyani brothers are devout Moslems and that Shama and Gary Homes are Adventists.

You have been looking at different worldviews, but how about the view that you carry all the time—what does that look like? We get so used to looking at the world through our own particular spectacles that we often forget that we have a distinctive point of view, not necessarily shared by others. The statements below should help to trigger your thoughts about this. Which statements do you feel attracted to or repelled from?

1. Blood is thicker than water.

2. Behind every cloud is a silver lining.

3. Women are unpredictable.

4. Under the skin we're all essentially the same.

5. People don't like being reminded of their responsibilities.

6. In general, people respond to reason.

7. Gay men understand women.

8. There's a lot of untapped goodwill in the community.

9. The more things change, the more they stay the same.

10. Men can't do more than one thing at a time.

11. Childhood—the best years of your life.

12. Never judge a person until you've walked in their moccasins.

Compare your responses to those of other students. What do the differences and similarities in your responses tell you about yourself?

The way we make sense of the world is influenced by the sum of our experiences to date, but our worldview is not static. Indeed, the experience of your professional training is likely to have a major impact on your understanding of yourself and your perspective on the world, even if it is not so dramatic as, say, that of Ebeneezer Scrooge[2] in Dickens's *Christmas Carol*. So, remember to make a note of how your experiences both in class and in the practice learning sites have changed your worldview and how these changes have in turn influenced the way you have worked with someone in a practice setting.

---

[2]A fictional character who has a life-changing, overnight conversion from mean businessman to kindhearted philanthropist.

WORLDVIEWS OF SERVICE USERS, PROVIDERS, AND OTHER PROFESSIONALS

We have so far been considering your own worldview, but it is important to remember that the people you work with have their own worldviews, too. For instance, their belief in the possibility or impossibility of change is a strong factor in the success or failure of your efforts with them.

Do you think it is important to find out about the worldview of the service user? If so, how can you do this? One approach is to review the range of research about users' views of the world (see regular bulletins from J. F. Rowntree's *Findings,* for example www.jrf.org.uk/publications). You may discover that users' and providers' worldviews are in sharp contrast to yours, perhaps even in strong disagreement, and you need to consider whether you would disclose this. Can you think of occasions when it would be appropriate to challenge these worldviews?

Differences between your worldview and that of other professionals with whom you are working can sometimes explain the sense of not pulling together. These differences can crystallize into stereotypes, so that we do not see a particular person who is a police officer but our own caricature of a police officer. The lawyer does not see you but his or her own stereotype of a student social worker. It is users and providers who pay the price of this stereotyping, so it is important to learn how to challenge these assumptions effectively.

ASSESSING YOUR LEARNING

Although this particular chapter appears early in the book, we recognize that it is a process that continues throughout your practice learning and beyond. It is the *outcome* of this process that is assessed: in other words, how your growing self-knowledge influences your values and practice. Moreover, in addition to the intellectual self-knowledge that *Points of View* helps to put into focus, there are other equally important facets to self-knowledge, such as emotional intelligence, in which emotions and thoughts are harmonized (Goleman, 1996). This, too, has a strong influence on your developing practice.

THE EXTRACTS

The extracts in Activity 2, *Points of View,* are taken from the following sources:

Extract 1: The Social Work Relationship

Lymbery, M. (2000). The retreat from professionalism: From social worker to care manager. In N. Malin (Ed.), *Professionalism, boundaries and the workplace* (pp. 133–134). London: Routledge.

Extract 2: The Messiness of Practice

Humphries, B. (2003). What *else* counts as evidence in evidence-based practice? *Social Work Education, 22*(1), 83.

Extract 3: Social Workers' Constructions of Power

Fook, J. (2002). *Social work: Critical theory and practice* (p.109). London: Sage.

Extract 4: Empirical Practice

Reid, W. J. (1992). *Task strategies: An empirical approach to clinical social work* (pp. 7–8). New York, NY: Columbia University Press.

FURTHER READING

Adams, R., Dominelli, L., & Payne, M. (2009). *Social work: Themes, issues and critical debates* (3rd ed.). Houndmills, Basingstoke, UK: Palgrave.

Payne's chapter in this book considers the relationship between social work theories and reflective practice. Other individual chapters consider different theories for practice in social work, such as feminist social work, psychosocial approaches, and cognitive behavioral practice.

DuBois, B., & Miley, K. K. (2005). *Social work: An empowering profession* (5th ed.) Boston, MA: Allyn & Bacon.

Kirst-Ashman, K. (2007). *Introduction to social work and social welfare: Critical thinking perspective* (2nd ed.). Pacific Grove, CA: Brooks/Cole/Thompson.

Rubin, A., & Babbie, E. (2008). *Research methods for social work* (6th ed.). Pacific Grove, CA: Brooks/Cole/Thompson.

CHAPTER 3

Learning About Your Role

Boundaries consists of a number of questions designed to expose practice dilemmas. These dilemmas focus on the distance social workers place between themselves and the people who use their services.

This activity gets best results with four to eight participants, but it can be undertaken by a single teacher and learner.

NOTES FOR INSTRUCTORS[1]

PURPOSE

It can be difficult to know what a professional relationship means in practice and how it differs from a personal relationship. This activity is designed to highlight the differences between *friendships* and what we might call *workships* (professional working relationships between practitioners and other people). It helps students become more skilled at deciding where and how the boundaries between the personal and professional should be drawn. It also encourages students to reflect upon how they might be perceived by others, according to how these boundaries are defined.

METHOD

- Arrange a time to meet and outline the purposes of the activity, but not the details, since you want spontaneous responses.

---

[1]See the Introduction to the book for suggestions about how instructors and students can, separately and together, use the activities in this book.

- Give each person a copy of *Boundaries* and take each of the 23 sections in turn to trigger discussion. It does not matter if you are unable to finish all categories in the time available. Kick off the first item yourself with a *never, always,* or *it depends* and invite others to join in with their responses.

- Relate the discussion to actual experiences in order to avoid idealized replies; encourage dissent and try to tease out any general principles that have come out of the discussion.

- Summarize the main areas of consent and dissent and write down any general principles that have come out of the discussion. Ask for feedback from everyone about the usefulness of the exercise.

NOTES FOR STUDENTS AND INSTRUCTORS

VARIATIONS

This activity has been used successfully in many different settings, usually in the early stages of the practice learning and even as part of a meeting before the practice learning begins. It also has been used successfully as part of the selection process for a social work course, as the focus of group discussions between candidates. Alternatively, the exercise could be used at different points during the student's practice learning.

A particularly useful variation is to ask students to complete the activity, then to present the activity to a group of service users and/or providers and ask them how they think social workers ought to behave. Some agencies provide excellent opportunities for this—for example, those already working with users and providers in groups, such as residential programs for children and older people, day care programs, and group projects for young people. The comparison between the views of students, users, and providers can prove very interesting and highly informative in helping students to define the boundaries of professional behavior.

You can use *Boundaries* to highlight a particular dimension of practice. For example, students can be asked to consider how issues of race, gender, or age would alter their responses. You could cross-reference to Activity 1, *Permission to Learn,* to ask how students would vary their responses if the service user or provider were Zoë Benner, one of the Kiyani brothers, Shama and Gary Homes, and so on.

USE BY OTHER PROFESSIONS

The general principle of *Boundaries* can be readily transferred across professions and countries. The situations in the *Boundaries* exercise can be modified to ensure that they reflect common dilemmas in the profession in question. It is enlightening for groups of students from differing professions to discuss a *Boundaries* exercise together, exploring similarities and differences in their views. The exercise can also be modified so that it considers the boundaries between different professional and vocational groups in relation to their mutual roles in work with patients, clients, and service users (Doel et al., 2010). In a hospital, it may be the boundaries between the health care staff and the social work staff that you wish to highlight. There are dilemmas, too, in the patient-doctor relationship that you could compare with user/patient-worker activities.

The *Boundaries* exercise is just as provocative when used with experienced workers as with students. Interprofessional teams can use a *Boundaries*-style exercise to consider the ways in which roles overlap and are discrete.

EDUCATIONAL POLICY ACCREDITATION STANDARDS

The topics in this chapter relate to the following *Educational Policy and Accreditation Standards (EPAS)* 2008 Primary Core Competencies (Council on Social Work Education, 2008):

1. Identify as a professional social worker and conduct oneself accordingly.

2. Apply social work ethical principles to guide professional practice.

3. Apply critical thinking to inform and communicate professional judgments.

4. Engage diversity and difference in practice.

FOR STUDENTS AND INSTRUCTORS

ACTIVITY 3: *BOUNDARIES*

Where do we draw the boundary between personal and professional relationships?
  How should social workers present themselves to service users and providers?
  Can you answer "always" or "never" to any of the questions below?
  If your answer to a question is "it depends," what does it depend on?

Reciprocation

1. Do service users and providers call you by your first (given) name?

2. Do you call them by their first (given) name?

3. Would you accept a service from a user or provider:
   - Let them bake you a cake?
   - Knit you a sweater?
   - Advise you what is wrong with your car?
   - Mend an electrical fault in your home?

Phones

4. Would you give your cell phone number to a service user or provider?

5. Would you send a service user or provider a text message?

6. Would you turn your cell one off while interviewing a service user or provider?

Self-Presentation

7. Do you wear:
   - Jeans and sneakers to meet with service users and providers?
   - A bare midriff?
   - Body piercings or visible tattoos?
   - Formal dress for a case presentation?

8. Would you think it OK for someone to wear a badge when meeting with service users and providers:
   - "Stop the war"
   - "Help the aged"
   - "Proud to be gay"
   - "Black is beautiful"
   - "Support Obama"

Interview Culture

9. On a home visit, would you accept:
   - A cup of coffee?
   - A snack (such as a cookie)?
   - An alcoholic drink?
   - A meal?

10. In the unit, hospital, or group room, would there be circumstances in which you would:
    - Talk about personal matters with other people present?
    - Make a cup of coffee for the service user or provider?

Social Contact

11. Would you accept from a service user or provider:
    - A wedding invitation?
    - An invitation to a party?
    - A request to attend a funeral with them?
    - Offer a ride in your car?

12. Would you avoid frequenting a place where a service user or provider worked?

13. Would you lend money to a service user and provider?

14. Would you take the children of service users to McDonald's on their own?

Self-Disclosure

15. Do you compare life experiences with service users and providers:
    - Let them know how you feel about their circumstances?
    - Let them know what sort of day you've had?
    - Talk about your work with other service users or providers in similar circumstances?

16. Do you share personal information with your users and providers:
    - Good news, such as your partner has been promoted?
    - Bad news, like your father suffers from Alzheimer's?
    - That you have just booked a vacation?
    - That you have prayed for them?

17. Would you give your home address or a personal phone number?

18. Would you disclose how much you disagree with one of your agency's policies?

Touch

19. When you meet a service user or provider, would you:
    - Shake hands?
    - Kiss socially on the cheek?

- Embrace?
- Make a physical gesture?

20. Would you touch a service user or provider who is upset:
    - On the arm?
    - Round the shoulders?
    - On the knee?

21. When with a services user's family:
    - Would you play with their children?
    - Romp with them on the floor?

Looking the Other Way

22. Do you ignore the illegal activities of a service user or provider:
    - The presence of a cannabis plant in their home?
    - Claiming benefit when they are working?
    - Electricity that has been reconnected by the user?
    - Receiving stolen goods?
    - An absconder who is being harbored?
    - Unlawful sexual activity?
    - Working as a prostitute?

Sexuality

23. Would you:
    - Flirt with a service user or provider?
    - Discuss your HIV status with a service user or provider?
    - Consider having sexual intercourse with a service user or provider?
    - Help a severely disabled person find a prostitute?
    - Disclose that you are gay, lesbian, or transgender?

NOTES FOR INSTRUCTORS

TEACHING ABOUT BOUNDARIES

Opportunities

To talk of opportunities for learning about the role is like looking for opportunities for breathing: Every moment of the student's practice learning will relate to the question of role. However, you *will* need to create opportunities to help the student consider role dilemmas. For example, guidance about how to behave with people is often paradoxical:

You must be engaging, personable, and able to step into people's shoes.	You must be purposeful, objective, and able to stay outside the situation.
Act natural.	Be professional.
Be warm.	Keep your cool.

It is not surprising if students feel that making a successful professional relationship is like squaring a circle. Asking somebody to be detached and connected at the same time is confusing. Students need to consider how the way they present themselves to people can influence the nature of the professional relationship.

This paradox should be discussed early on with the student. It gives you both a reference point later, when things happen in the student's work that illustrate these dilemmas. It might help to avoid the kind of experience illustrated by the following quote from the portfolio of a licensed social worker:

One parent where I was involved in assessing the family due to neglectful and poor home conditions misunderstood my role. Although I had carefully explained my role at the beginning of my involvement with the family, my assistance and friendly manner and social work approach with the mother was interpreted by her as friendship. When it came to completing reports for court, my assessment of the situation was interpreted [by the mother] as being negative and "backstabbing" due to the information she had volunteered to me. She stated that she would never of *(sic)* discussed some issues with me if she knew that I would use that information as part of my assessment.

Different Expectations

Students behave now as they have learned to behave in previous settings, which may have been very different from the current one. A student who has been working in a residential setting with disabled people may be used to a lot of physical contact and informal relationships; this student may not understand the different expectations of a formal office setting and vice versa.

Students are at an early stage in their careers and may have a strongly felt desire to help people, perhaps resulting in close identification with the user and an emphasis on personal friendship. In practice, this could mean an interview in a restaurant, intimate talk by a resident's bedside, or activities like bowling with groups of young people in the evenings. This may be fine in some circumstances but not in others; professionals exercise considerable power in their work, and students need an early appreciation of the dimensions of their power (Hugman, 1991).

On questions of professional standards, the difference of opinion about what is acceptable is striking. For example, Jayaratne, Croxton, and Mattison (1997) point out that "virtually no empirical studies of professional standards exist . . . in effect, practitioners and those who judge practitioner behavior are making decisions with relatively little guidance from the profession" (p. 187). Their own exploratory study in Michigan of 826 practitioners found that hugging or embracing a client was commonplace, but the acceptance of expensive gifts and lending or borrowing money was rare. There were no clear majorities either way for commenting on clients' physical attractiveness, cursing or swearing during sessions, discussing one's religious belief, and providing a home telephone number. In other words, social workers said these were acceptable and not acceptable in roughly equal numbers.

The primary reference for the professions value base is the National Association of Social Workers (NASW) Code of Ethics. The code establishes a set of clear beliefs that define ethical social work practice and thus act as unifying force among all social workers. The way we work with and behalf of others, how we view social issues, and the remedies we consider for individual, group, or community concerns are all firmly rooted in our value base.

The following example shows how students who have been used to keeping service users and providers at arm's length might respond to the prospect of practice learning where the users or providers of the agency are not kept at such distance. We also see how *Boundaries* can be used to judge the suitability of a period of practice learning before it is planned.

Example

Yusef, a South Asian student, and Jim, an African American student on the same social work program, were interested in a placement in a user-led neighborhood family resource center. So far, they had experienced field social work, which was their intended career, and they wanted the chance to have a placement together to run groups for young people. The field coordinator thought that the style of the center would be a contrast with previous placement experience and arranged for a meeting for Yusef, James, and the two field instructors from the center.

The field instructors, Carmen and Nalini, began by emphasizing that the people who came to the center were called users, not clients. They had chosen five specific dilemmas from *Boundaries* that they felt highlighted the work at the center, and they invited Yusef and James to add any others. The subsequent discussion revealed that the boundaries that the practice teachers drew around their relationships with the users were more permeable than Yusef or Jim had known.

Yusef queried some of the boundaries drawn by the field instructors, but he said that the center's relationship with its users would be a new experience for him, and he was interested in the contrast. He had reservations about the effects on his family life, especially the policy of letting users have a personal phone number.

Jim answered all the questions with "It depends," complaining that the circumstances in each case needed elaborating before he could give an opinion on the basis of the information available. When the field instructors asked him to explain what he thought *it* depended on, Jim said that he would have to meet each situation as it came. "It would depend on what felt right at the time."

After the meeting, the field instructors and the students reflected separately on what had been said. Rejoining the meeting, Carmen and Nalini said they thought Yusef would have an interesting placement, and his past experience would be a stimulating challenge to their own work. They understood the strain this work places on domestic lives, and they would respect whatever decision he and his family came to.

They had concerns about Jim's inability to state his position on any of the dilemmas. They had no problem with "It depends" as an answer, but they would expect James to be able to say what it depended on. More to the point, the users of the center would expect that, too; an answer that relied on whatever "felt right at the time" would not be acceptable to them.

The activity gave everybody a chance to find out about the expectations at the agency and whether they would be acceptable. It was also a useful assessment for the field instructors to find out how willing the students were to question their own judgments. For example, giving your personal phone number is neither professional nor unprofessional, but failure to question the principles behind the decision *is* unprofessional.

Developing a Style

The task is to create a climate that enables the student to make conscious choices in terms of style, which might be defined as the unique way in which each student defines and expresses the boundaries between himself or herself and users.

Perhaps an analogy will illustrate this: The Norwegians have a saying that there is no such thing as bad weather, just bad clothing. In other words, what is appropriate in one circumstance is inappropriate in another. It is the same with style and personal presentation. It is not that a particular style is right or wrong in itself but that certain styles might suit particular occasions (although there are some styles, it is true, that suit no occasion). Students need opportunities to try on different clothing and to experiment to find the style that suits them and is consistent with agency expectations.

Finally, there is another role that students need to begin to understand: your role, whether as practice teacher, practice assessor, work-based supervisor, and so on. It is important that you and the student know what you each expect of supervision, especially since the word *supervision* has different resonances for different people. Keep the focus on student learning and service user welfare, not on a student's personal problems.

NOTES FOR STUDENTS

LEARNING ABOUT YOUR ROLE

"The key to the profession's identity lies in the recognition that what makes something social work is not what is done but *how* it is done" (Davies, 1994, p. 155).

Boundaries places you in the position of a professional person. It reflects some of the dilemmas you will face when making working relationships with people. Let's turn this situation on its head and think about times when it is *you* who receives a service. This helps you learn about what you think shows professional behavior. Make some notes in relation to each of the following:

As a patient with toothache, what would you describe as professional behavior by the dentist?

As a borrower with debts to pay, what would you describe as professional behavior by the bank manager?

As a householder with three inches of water in your basement, what would you describe as professional behavior by the plumber?

As a parent of a child experiencing problems at school, what would you describe as professional behavior by the teacher?

As a buyer seeking to change a product and being referred to a call center, what would you describe as professional behavior by the customer service representative?

Think of your positive and negative experiences as a user of services. You can do this on your own or with a small group of other students. Use the examples above, or choose different ones. Use flipchart paper to make two lists: one for the positive experiences and the other for the negative ones.

From the lists, draw up a number of guidelines for professional practice and prioritize them into four or five main principles. How do these principles relate to professional social work practice? How do they compare with the NASW Code of Ethics?

Process and Outcome

An important theme in social work practice is the extent to which outcome is important when evaluating this question of professionalism. In other words, does the relief of pain by the dentist indicate professional behavior, or is it possible to think of situations when the pain was relieved but the behavior was unprofessional or when the pain was not relieved but the behavior was professional? The section on the social worker as researcher will return to this theme (see page 205).

Occupational Control and Status

Who defines the social work role? A number of commentators have reflected that the social work profession is losing control over what social work is and what social workers do; Jordan (2003) claims that the factors that used to give the social work profession a strong identity are now its weaknesses, particularly its close association in the United States with the social welfare system. The relative lack of occupational control has sometimes called into question the right of social work to be considered a fully-fledged profession. Occupational control is certainly limited by the location of social work in welfare bureaucracies, with constraints on the use of professional discretion and the requirements for standardized responses to people's needs. Is good practice "defined as being the ability to follow rules and procedures competently, rather than the ability to make individual professional judgments" (Lymbery, 2000, p. 131), or is it possible to define it as both?

The fact that the knowledge base of social work is contested (i.e., there is no consensus about what constitutes this knowledge base) and shared with others (i.e., it draws from other disciplines) is often cited as another limitation to its right to be considered a profession, although these factors are by no means limited to social work. Certainly, you should consider how the practices of social work are "different from those of ordinary social intercourse" (Howe, 1996, p. 117). In many respects, it is these differences that make your work that of a professional rather than a well-meaning amateur.

Some aspects of the social work role have attracted more status than others. For example, work with children and families has been seen as "offering most opportunity to engage in high status casework activity," while work with adults and older people "has had a greater focus on indirect tasks concerned with the arrangement of services" (Lymbery, 2000, p. 124). It is paradoxical, then, that as work with children and families has become increasingly dominated by procedures, it could be argued that it is in some of the less fashionable areas of practice that "real" social work is still possible, if "real" is to be understood as less bureaucratic and more direct contact.

As a student, it is understandable if you narrow your focus on the here and now of the work of the agency. Even so, it is important to find time to understand your role in its wider context. How do social policies have an impact on the day-to-day practice of social workers and the everyday lives of people? How will you retain and make best use of the motivation that brought you into social work, protecting it from the effects of the compromises you will make as a routine part of your learning and work? (Occasional dips into Sheppard's [2006] *Social Work and Social Exclusion* will provide a refresher.)

Metaphors for the Social Work Role

Before you arrive at your first placement learning site, you might like to think about a metaphor that, for you, epitomizes the social work role. Make a note of the metaphor and any others that come to mind during your social work education and training. Return to the metaphor at various points during your learning and see how your view has changed or not. Is the metaphor you chose at the beginning of your course the same as the one at the end?

As a start, you might consider this metaphor from Howe (2003): A social worker is "like the sculptor who frees the sculpted form from the marble: the worker recognizes the potential of their client and enables him to realize that potential" (p. 113).

Role as a Student

So far we have been considering the role of professional social worker. You are also coming to terms with another role, that of student. The *Boundaries* exercise could just as easily be modified to consider appropriate boundaries between student and field instructor. For example, there is now general agreement that the boundary between supervision and therapy is important to maintain. Support in supervision is different from helping in therapy, not least because of the power that supervisors have with respect to students' professional lives.

Caspi and Reid (2002, pp. 105–106) suggest that knowing the reasons why this boundary is sometimes crossed is probably the best way of preventing it. They suggest four reasons:

- supervision and therapy processes are quite close, so there are overlaps;
- many supervisors are promoted from clinical positions and may fall back on their clinical expertise when confronted with the experience of new challenges as a supervisor;
- some supervisees may prefer the focus to be on their personal life rather than their work performance, as a way of avoidance, conscious or not;
- supervisees may well be in positions of stress (poverty, etc.).

The crucial question is the extent to which any life stresses impede your ability as a student to learn and to practice. There are times when practice teachers must address these issues but as a supervisor of your learning, not as a personal therapist.

Just as student drivers carry signs on the car saying "student driver," as a student social worker, you are officially permitted to learn. In some respects, this allows you more discretion than those who have already undertaken their training. Despite the rhetoric of lifelong learning, it can be very difficult for qualified workers to be seen, or allow themselves to be seen, as continuing learners. So, although it may feel a relatively powerless role, there are also aspects of the student social work role that are relatively privileged.

As someone who is permitted to learn, you may be in a better position than the qualified and permanent staff in the agency, in terms of experimentation and openness to considering a wider variety of "hows" of social work practice.

ASSESSING YOUR LEARNING

Your ability to define professional boundaries is an important part of your assessment. For example, if most interviews seem to take place in street settings or if every user is told to attend the office for appointments, there may be concerns about your ability to respond flexibly to the different needs of people. A preferred style may have become one that is fixed.

You will need to become aware of any unintended messages of how you present yourself. For example, warmth and friendliness can be interpreted in the wrong way, perhaps as a willingness to give more than you can or should offer. Sexual attraction does not respect user-worker boundaries. A dress code often carries different messages from one situation to another. Style is one of those personal issues that affects your ability to work as an effective professional. Although these may not be part of your formal assessment, they do show your *suitability* for social work practice.

FURTHER READING

Lymbery, M. (2000). The retreat from professionalism: From social worker to care manager. In N. Malin (Ed.), *Professionalism, boundaries and the workplace* (pp. 123–138). New York: Routledge.

Loewenberg, F. M., & Dolgoff, R. (2000). *Ethical decisions for social work practice* (6th ed.). Itasca, IL: Peacock.

You can find out more by looking at the various codes of practice for social workers. These include the following:

- National Association of Social Workers, Code of Ethics. Approved by the 1996 NASW Delegate Assembly and revised by the 1999 NASW Delegate Assembly. www.naswdc.org
- International Federation of Social Workers (2003). www.ifsw.org
- International Council on Social Welfare (2007). www.icsw.org

For a comparison of codes of practice, see Banks, S. (2006). *Ethics and values in social work* (3rd ed.). New York, NY: Palgrave Macmillan.

See also Jayaratne et al.'s (1997) comment on the limitations of the standards in the NASW's Code of Ethics, which "contains no historical or case references, interpretative guides, or formal or informal opinions' (p. 188).

CHAPTER 4

Learning About Value Conflicts and Ethical Dilemmas

According to Greek mythology (Homer), Sisyphus was the wisest of mortals who disclosed to the public that the god Zeus had abducted and raped Aegina, the king's daughter. For this act, Sisyphus was condemned by the gods to perpetual punishment in the underworld. This punishment was to roll a large boulder up a hill, only to have to watch it roll down again and endlessly repeat the cycle. Encapsulated in this myth are all the fears, worries, and potential consequences for those who contemplate the disclosure of information.

The activity, *The Myth of Sisyphus,* has been designed to provide students with an opportunity to explore some of the types of situations that could be construed as a value conflict that leads to an ethical dilemma.

This chapter should be read in conjunction with Chapter 11.

NOTES FOR INSTRUCTORS[1]

PURPOSE

The activity, *The Myth of Sisyphus,* is designed to help students think about some of the pressures that might impinge upon their practice and present them with a value conflict or ethical dilemma.

METHOD

The Myth of Sisyphus is an exercise that could be completed in the fieldwork seminar, in a practice class, or in advance of a supervisory session.

---

[1]See the Introduction to the book for suggestions about how instructors and students can, separately and together, use the activities in this book.

Students should be asked to read this chapter in the week before completing *The Myth of Sisyphus* activity.

NOTES FOR STUDENTS AND INSTRUCTORS

VARIATIONS

The situations used in *The Myth of Sisyphus* can be readily amended to fit any other specialist practice contexts. However, there is considerable virtue in encouraging social work students to think broadly and outside of their developing specialist interests. It is interesting to explore the extent to which tolerance for a particular behavior is engendered by familiarity with or proximity to the performance of that behavior.

Given the increasing importance of interprofessional practice, a highly desirable variation is to employ the activity within a mixed group of students from different professions. Such a context allows for the exploration of conflicting expectations among professions; as Hewison and Sim (1998) suggest, professional codes of ethics that apply to different professional groups may tend to foster professional distinctiveness and exclusivity and may form a barrier to effective interprofessional working in areas such as disclosure of information.

USE BY OTHER PROFESSIONS

Concerns over values and ethics are universal and affect all professional groups. At your placement, you usually have contact with a number of other professionals such as teachers, guidance counselors, principals, nurses, doctors, psychiatrists, psychologists, lawyers, occupational therapists, physical therapists, and so on. All of these individuals are, like you, accountable to professional organizations, a professional set of values and standards, and licensure boards. They are also likely to have a different perception of the individual, family, or community than you, influenced by their different professional perspectives.

This is apparent not only in your professional environment but also in your social environment. Think about times that you have been to a concert, a movie, or a sporting event. When you have talked to friends about the event afterwards, no doubt each of you saw the movie a little differently or thought that a particular song was preferred or that a particular play in the game was the best.

Similarly, at your placement agency site, the school principal is likely to view the students and teachers differently, to some extent, than yourself. The psychiatrist's focus is more likely to center on the diagnosis, while the lawyer focuses on his or her duty to get the children back to their biological parents. In other words, professionals have different responsibilities.

If you look at the five boulders, you will see that different individuals have various interpretations of what to do in each situation. There are competing choices, and the participants are being pulled in different directions. What is the right course of action? What choices should be made? What are the potential consequences?

Educational Policy Accreditation Standards

The topics in this chapter relate to the following *Educational Policy and Accreditation Standards (EPAS)* 2008 Primary Core Competencies (Council on Social Work Education, 2008):

1. Identify as a professional social worker and conduct oneself accordingly.

2. Apply social work ethical principles to guide professional practice.

3. Apply critical thinking to inform and communicate professional judgments.

4. Respond to contexts that shape practice.

5. Engage, assesses, intervene, and evaluate with individuals, families, groups, organizations, and communities.

FOR STUDENTS AND INSTRUCTORS

Activity 4: *The Myth of Sisyphus*

The intent of the activity, *The Myth of Sisyphus*, is an opportunity to examine the competing values and ethical dilemmas that confront professional practitioners. Read the description of each *boulder* and consider all the competing values. What are the possible scenarios in each of these examples? Having identified the value conflicts, what are the ethical dilemmas in each example? In addition to these particular boulders that are "rolling down the hill," think about your own practice setting—what are some of the value conflicts and ethical dilemmas you are confronted with? Write *key words* in each of the boulder boxes on the activity sheet. When you have written all of the "push" and "pull" factors that come to mind, do the following:

1. Weigh the relative strength of the push and pull factors and decide which is the strongest.

2. Decide which action you would take with respect to each boulder.

3. Compare each of the five boulders and consider the different push and pull factors and consider if there are any differences in the way that you would respond to each boulder.

4. What are the reasons for these differences in behavior?

Boulder 1

The parent of a person with learning difficulties informs you that people with learning difficulties are being systematically abused in a residential unit owned and managed by your employer. You bring this to the attention of senior managers, who seem unwilling to take action. Some 6 months later, you are visiting the unit and you witness an incident of a person with learning difficulties being verbally abused. You inform senior management, who thank you for your information. A further 6 months later, you learn from a friend that nothing has happened.

Boulder 2

Your supervisor "jokes" that it is very easy to claim for expenses that have not been made. About a week later, you hear him in the kitchen area saying much the same to another colleague. You think you hear him say that he has claimed several hundred dollars over the past few years. He sees you come in and notices your expression. At the next supervision session, he explains that over the years, he has run a number of user groups and has been completely unsuccessful in getting the agency to fund them, so he "robs Peter to pay Paul."

Boulder 3

The social work agency that you are placed at is desperately short of placements for children, despite a widespread and expensive advertising campaign. Consequently, the agency has entered into an agreement with a private company that provides care in several locations throughout the state. These homes provide group living for children who are ages 8 to 14 years old. Each home is run as a "family group home" with a small number of staff working long hours but who provide a "constancy of care." You have visited two of these homes and over a period of a year and notice that the physical conditions in which the children are cared for have significantly deteriorated. You are particularly concerned about one of these homes where there seems to be many more children than the physical accommodation can cope with: It seems there are possibly eight children sleeping in one room in bunk beds—the house only has three bedrooms, and two are used for staff. The quality of physical care is poor, and there are appear to be rather "scratch" meals and not much change of clothing. You have mentioned this to your immediate manager and to the services manager for children and families services. On both occasions, they have assured you that they are aware of the difficulties and that this is only a temporary problem.

Boulder 4

You witness a colleague from another profession who appears to be unwell while conducting a joint assessment with you and a service user. However, you smell his breath and suspect he is under the influence of alcohol. The behavior of the colleague was rude and demeaning toward the service user; his seniority, your newness to the team (you have only just started your placement), and your embarrassment in front of the service user meant you felt unable to act there and then. You mention your concerns to your work-based supervisor who says that he is "a bit of a maverick" but is really well respected. Another says she's heard he has some personal problems at present and tells you that it was probably a one-off. However, a third colleague tells you it's about time something was done about him, but she's not going to stick her neck out because he's got friends in the right places. Despite reservations, you decide to follow the advice to sit on it. In the final weeks of your placement, you go on three separate visits with this colleague. On the first two visits, he is fine, but he turns up drunk to the third (4 days before you leave the placement) and is offensive toward the service user.

Boulder 5

You have just been appointed to your first post as a licensed social worker. It is early June and your new supervisor informs you that you must perform a certain number of assessments before June 30 (the end of the financial year); otherwise, the department is liable to lose a large amount of grant. Indeed, if the department does not meet its target, it is likely to be penalized by $1 million, which would have a devastating impact on services. The supervisor explains that staff vacancies and the inadequacies of the person you are replacing have led to this situation. She realizes that you will not be able to complete the assessments together with the service user, but as long as they are filled in before the 30th, "you can do the proper work and do joint assessments together with the service users and providers of care after then, when there's more time." She realizes that this is not good practice, "but we are all between a rock and a hard place."

Figure 4.1   *The Myth of Sisyphus:* Push and the Pull

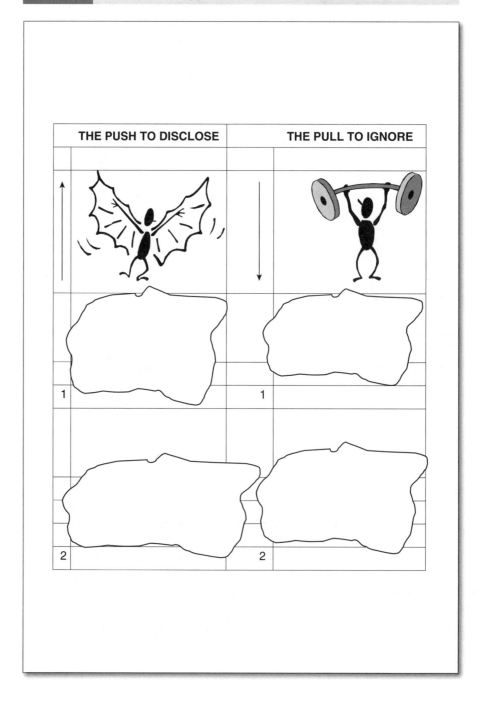

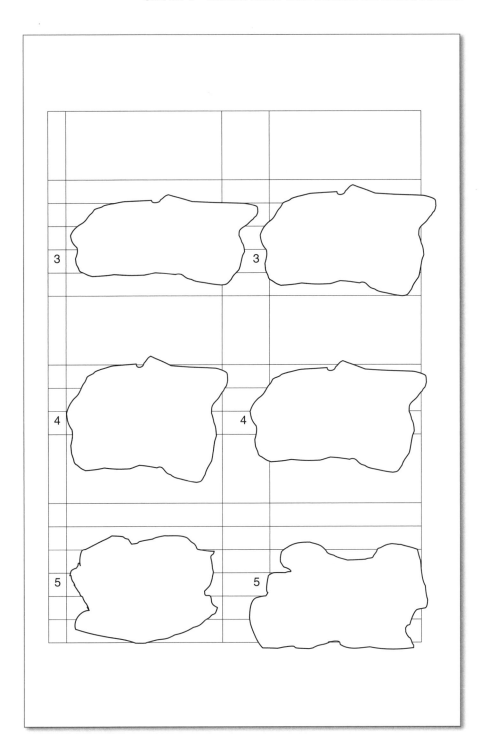

NOTES FOR INSTRUCTORS

TEACHING ABOUT VALUES AND ETHICAL DILEMMAS

Opportunities

Values and ethics are constantly referred to in schools of social work. Indeed, the Council on Social Work Education (2008) states the following:

Educational Policy 1.1—Values. Service, social justice, the dignity and worth of the person, the importance of human relationships, integrity, competence, human rights, and scientific inquiry are among the core values of social work. These values underpin the explicit and implicit curriculum and frame the profession's commitment to respect for all people and the quest for social and economic justice.

Educational Policy 2.1.2—Apply social work ethical principles to guide professional practice. Social workers have an obligation to conduct themselves ethically and to engage in ethical decision making. Social workers are knowledgeable about the values of the profession, its ethical standards, and relevant law.

- recognize and manage personal values in a way that allows professional values to guide practice,
- make ethical decisions by applying standards of the National Association of Social Workers/International Association of Schools of Social Work's Statement of Principles,
- tolerate ambiguity in resolving ethical conflicts, and
- apply strategies of ethical reasoning to arrive at principled decisions.

Professional Social Work Values

Social work practitioners' values need to take account of the general societal values—that is, values that are held by the larger society in which they practice. However, they need also to reflect critically on these values. The Code of Ethics of the National Association of Social Workers (1999, pp. 5–6) summarizes the core values of the social work profession as follows:

1. Social workers elevate service to others above self-interest. (Service)

2. Social workers pursue social change, particularly with and on behalf of vulnerable and oppressed individuals and groups of people. (Social justice)

3. Social workers treat each person in a caring and respectful fashion, mindful of individual differences and cultural and ethnic diversity. (Dignity and worth of person)

4. Social workers understand that relationships between and among people are an important vehicle for change. (Importance of human relationships)

5. Social workers are continually aware of the profession's mission, values, ethical principles, and ethical standards and practice in a manner consistent with them. (Integrity)

6. Social workers continually strive to increase their professional knowledge and skills and to apply them in practice. (Competence)

The principles of practice in social work are connected directly to the values of the profession. Levy (1976) stated that people trust that they will receive adequate and decent treatment and this serves as a central ingredient in the relationship between worker and service user.

Professional values serve as "a guide to the perplexed" but are worthless without their implementation in practice. They must serve the immediate needs of the worker in making and accepting ethical decisions; therefore, they can be regarded as values only when they are followed by the appropriate action, and only then can they serve as ethical guides in practice and be of value to the social worker.

How to move from values to behavior is a problem that is not limited to social workers. It is a more general challenge that has become the focus of attention of ethicists.

Ethical Dilemmas

"The principles of social work ethics derive from values that are simply declarations of, or that represent, a consensus about preferences which may or may not coincide with approaches to the successful fulfillment of professional responsibility" (Levy, 1976, p. 233). In other words, ethics are based on values; an ethical dilemma is defined as a choice between two actions that are based on conflicting values. Another way of describing this is that the values are the thinking component of this process, and the ethics are the doing/action part of the process.

Using Boulder 3 and the scenario of the group home, we might observe that the social worker and the private agency have very different interpretations about what qualifies as appropriate standards for running the group home. For example, the social worker appears very concerned about the number of children in the home, the physical care of the children, and the lack of food. On the other hand, the personnel running the group home seem to be under the impression that this is only a temporary issue and is being addressed. Why, then, is there such a discrepancy, and how does one arrive at a decision about what to do? Do questions of power, and relative power, have a bearing on the situation?

How to Address Ethical Dilemmas

Reamer (1999) asserts that seven steps in the process assists the social worker in dealing successfully with ethical dilemmas and arriving at a conclusion:

1. Identifying the ethical issues that are controversial, including the values of social work and the obligations in conflict with one another

2. Identifying the individuals, the groups, and the organizations that would be affected by the decision

3. Temporary identification of all the possible means of action

4. A thorough investigation of the reasons for and against an action

5. Discussion with colleagues and with experts

6. Documenting the process of decision making

7. Follow-up and evaluation

Summary

Using the five boulders, the Green Hill apartments, or a case the student has at the agency, guide the student's exploration of the issues in a sequential way. What does the student identify as the presenting value conflicts? Why are there so many diverse views and opinions on this issue? Once the student has attempted to identify the competing values, ask him or her to use Reamer's (1999, p. 72) seven-step process. Keep focused that you are not looking for the correct answer but rather helping the student to investigate the situation in a logical, step-by-step manner. This may well also help the student not feel overwhelmed by the case.

NOTES FOR STUDENTS

Learning About Values and Ethical Dilemmas

Social workers, like so many other professionals, often fail to distinguish between the terms *values* and *ethics*. They use them interchangeably as if they have the same meaning. Maslow (1962) once observed that values are like big containers that hold all sorts of miscellaneous and vague things. John Dewey used the term in a more precise way by noting that it must include some element of appraisal or preference. Kupperman (1999) suggested that a value refers "to what is worth having or being." Values enhance a life or the world and define "those conceptions of desirable states of affairs that are utilized in selective conduct as criteria for preference or choice or justifications for proposed or actual behavior" (R. M. Williams, 1967, p. 23).

According to Levy (1973, p. 38), as root premises of social work, values may be conceived along three basic dimensions that, while perhaps not exhaustive of all possibilities, would account for the major value orientations that are or ought to be shared by all social workers and related to them to all elements of their professional practice:

1. Values as preferred conceptions

2. Values as preferred instrumentalities for dealing with people

3. Values as preferred outcomes for people

Preferred Conceptions

There are likely to be numerous different interpretations of the way in which you view each scenario (the five boulders in *The Myth of Sisyphus*). According to Levy (1973), these are our *preferred conceptions,* and they have a direct impact on the way you view the presenting problem. The situation becomes even more complex when we start to consider other professionals who may also work in these cases and what their conceptions might be.

Preferred Instrumentalities

How you view the problem will have a direct impact on the way in which you address each of the problems. For example, in Boulder 1, regarding the person with learning disabilities, do the social worker and senior management have a different view of the situation? Are they both looking at the same issue, or do they have different priorities and agendas? If there are major differences, how might this lead to different outcomes?

Preferred Outcomes

Your preferred conceptions and preferred instrumentalities will determine the likely outcome. Using the example in Boulder 1, it would appear that the social worker and senior management have different roles. The social worker appears rightly concerned about the individual's rights, whereas management seems more concerned with the overall functioning of the program.

Hence, there are different outcomes. If management shared the social worker's concerns for the well-being of the individual resident, one could propose that they would speak to the individual concerned or perhaps offer a training session on how to speak to residents in the program. Instead, it appears that management is more concerned with the running of the program. Perhaps they are having difficulty getting staff to work at the program. Is the program understaffed, or have there been financial cutbacks, leading to staff working extra hours? In other words, management's concern is centered on an array of other issues.

Ethical Dilemmas

According to Joseph (1989), ethical decision making is based on a logical process in which various steps are shown in a predetermined sequence. In other words, the ethical dilemma is expressed by comparing one benefit with another competing one. The model requires that the social workers be aware not only of their own personal values but also of their personal bias in their professional practice. In using Joseph's model, one should pay attention to the background of the ethical dilemma and to the relevant facts pertaining to it, and one should weigh these for both their positive and negative aspects.

For example, let us use Joseph's (1989) model to tease out the relevant facts in Boulder 4, where a colleague appears to be acting under the influence of alcohol and the student considers him to have been offensive toward a service user.

1. Colleague is under the influence of alcohol, perhaps even drunk on one occasion.

2. Colleague is rude to a service user (what did he actually do or say?).

3. Colleague has seniority (what is the relative power balance?).

4. Supervisor informs you to ignore issue (what reasons might explain this?).

5. Another supervisor states that this is a one-off situation (again, what might explain this perception?).

6. Another colleague states that this behavior has been ongoing (why is this different from other colleagues' perceptions? How can you know which reflects the situation most accurately?).

7. Behavior should be reported (what behavior should be reported, when, why, and to whom?).

8. Concerns about reporting behavior and how agency administration will respond (what are the possible consequences of reporting the behavior for each of the parties concerned, including you?).

Based on these observations, what are the push and pull factors? How do they weigh against one another? Using your fieldwork seminar or supervision with a field instructor, discuss what course of action you might take.

Summary

Social workers and other similar professionals are influenced by more than just their professional roles and obligations. They are also influenced by their own personal motivations, attitudes, and preferences in making their decisions (Doel et al., 2010). Rules against basic harm to the necessary preconditions of human action, such as life itself, health, food, and so on, take precedence over rules against harm such as lying or revealing confidential information or threats to goods such as recreation, education, and wealth (Reamer, 1999, p. 72).

ASSESSING YOUR LEARNING

Over the course of your social work career, you will repeatedly hear the terms values and ethics. As we have noted, these terms get intertwined and are often used interchangeably. However, values and ethics are the keystone of the profession. The founders of social work invested a great deal of effort in developing rules of ethics and professional conduct that could stand against even very strict social criticism. The challenge that faces you in attempting to identify what are the value conflicts and how to operationalize these is complex. If you are able to examine your practice as we did with the boulders in a systematic manner, this not only will be of great benefit to you but will also have a profound impact on your service users. There is no doubt that this approach is painstaking and difficult in today's fast-paced "technological" world. However, if you can slow down the process and use a systematic approach to your practice, which considers many different perspectives and alternatives, you are well on your way to becoming an excellent social worker.

Are values assessed on placement? Are there "right" and "wrong" values? How can or should values be assessed? It can feel very unfair if your values are inferred from your behavior, so how are you and the field instructor going to consider how your values might be assessed? Discussing dilemmas such as those in the boulders activity and, of course, real ones that arise during the placement is a good place to start.

FURTHER READING

Guttman, D. (2006). *Ethics in social work: A context of caring.* Binghamton, NY: Haworth.

Kupperman, J. J. (1999). *Value . . . and what follows.* New York, NY: Oxford University Press.

Levy, C. S. (1976). *Social work ethics.* New York: Human Sciences Press.

Reamer, F. G. (1999). *Social work values and ethics* (2nd ed.). New York, NY: Columbia University Press.

Part II

Direct Practice

CONTEXT: INTERDISCIPLINARY LEARNING AND PRACTICE

There is a growing emphasis in contemporary field social work on the need to remove the barriers between different professional groups to provide a more coherent service for people. These barriers allow professions to protect their own territory and prevent them from working together with other professions. Unfortunately, it is only when social work makes the nightly news due to some tragic event, such as the death of a child in foster care, that the general public starts to question why there is not better communication between all these various disciplines. For example, why didn't the school notice that the child was excessively absent? Why didn't the medical profession notice the bruises on the child? Why didn't the social worker make more home visits? The usual conclusion is, Why weren't all these disciplines working in collaboration?

Even so, social work practice is increasingly organized around or within other professional disciplines. Whereas social workers in the last part of the 20th century were more likely to be employed together in a social work team, at the beginning of the 21st century, we see social workers increasingly employed in multidisciplinary teams. These teams usually have a "client group" focus (people with learning disabilities; people with mental health problems; young offenders), and the team is designed to bring together people with different skills to encourage collaborative working, to the benefit of the people who are served by the team.

However, these changes in the field are not reflected at the college, where the education continues to be broader and generalist, for good reasons. Undergraduate students are required to take a number of liberal arts classes, such as human growth and development, human biology, macroeconomics, psychology, criminology, and sociology. At the master's level, social work students are able to take several electives, some of which may be from another discipline such as education, counseling, or law. Yet, in the United States, there is no formal learning with other professional disciplines; departments and schools of social work operate in isolation from other university departments, and there is no systematic information sharing. This stands in contrast to social work education in countries such as the United Kingdom (Doel & Shardlow, 2009).

One of the challenges facing professional programs in the new millennium is the need to create interdisciplinary classes to develop the kind of interprofessional collaboration that is needed to improve the experience of service users. This may occur due to economic necessity rather than the desires of the departments or schools themselves. For example, state budget deficits are leading university administrators to consider merging departments or to reconfigure colleges. A school in New England where there is discussion about merging the school of social work with the college of education, the college of nursing, or the school of public service (or indeed merging all the professional degree programs be into one college) is typical of similar deliberations across the country. However, necessity might indeed prove to be the mother of creation, with economic forces providing the professional programs with an opportunity for students of different professions to learn together.

Another opportunity to bring about interdisciplinary learning is through continuing education. Student supervisors will be aware that, to renew their license, they are required to complete a number of continuing education courses. These courses are university led. Many universities offer continuing education programs with continuing education units (CEUs) for licensed professionals. These programs are offered to all professionals and therefore provide a further opportunity for social workers and other professionals to learn together.

DIFFERENT WAYS OF WORKING TOGETHER

The terminology to describe these developments varies considerably—multiprofessional, interdisciplinary, interagency, collaborative working, shared learning, and so on (Barr, 2002; Miller, Ross, & Freeman, 1999; Weinstein, Whittington, & Leiba, 2003; Whittingon, 2003). In some respect, these terms reflect the continuum of possibilities—from a team in which there are two professions who do very little or no joint working to a team in which there are many professions who are consistently working together directly with service users and providers.

Most social care and health professionals will have experience of working with people from a number of agencies and professions, but the distinctions between different types of interaction are frequently blurred. The terms multi-disciplinary, multi-agency and inter-agency tend to be used interchangeably to describe a variety of working relationships. A multi-disciplinary team, for example, may define itself as such in terms of the various skills required to meet the complex needs of a service user, but the team members and services may be provided by the staff of one agency, such as social services (multi-disciplinary) or by staff from several agencies including health, community services and the voluntary sector (multi-agency). Equally, the planning, funding and commissioning of services may be the result of joint initiatives by a number of agencies (inter-agency) with the provision of such services requiring the skills base of a number of disciplines and from a variety of agencies. (Central Council for Education and Training in Social Work, 2000, p. 10)

In developing a definition of what is meant by multidisciplinary working, it may be helpful, therefore, to consider it in terms of levels of modes of *cooperation* between professionals and agencies providing social and health care services.

Cooperative working can be identified within five modes of interaction:

- Communication
- Consultation
- Collaboration
- Bilateral working
- Joint working

Communication is defined as cooperation at its most basic level, involving one discipline or agency informing another of its actions or intentions.

Consultation involves activities where one discipline or agency approaches others for their opinions, information, and advice on a proposed course of action.

Collaboration involves a degree of mutual activity between disciplines or agencies with adjustments and agreement on the scope and level of participation in that activity but usually with the expectation that each agency or discipline will operate independently in the provision of services.

Bilateral working implies the recognition of an overlap in services provision between disciplines or agencies, which can give rise to both individual and collective operational planning and service delivery.

Joint working implies agencies working together to plan and operate a mutual course of action.

While recognizing these various intensities, we will use the word *interprofessional* as a convenient single term to cover all aspects of learning and practice between two or more professional groups.

ISSUES CONCERNING INTERPROFESSIONAL PRACTICE

Social workers are well placed to promote interprofessional practice because, in many ways, they have been doing it for a long time. It may have been called something else (joint working, working in partnership, or collaborative practice), but it is a central aspect of social work practice, sometimes also called *networking,* to be able to bring together a wide range of people who are significant to a particular purpose. Above all, social work is a peripatetic activity, physically and metaphorically. Its practitioners go far beyond a narrow technical skill to an understanding of wider systems, including the effects of social policy and agency procedure. In essence, then, much of the practice of social work is already interprofessional, and social workers are well placed to advance this approach.

Social workers work with a wide variety of other professional and vocational groups beyond the field of health—police, lawyers, judges, probation officers, psychologists, guidance counselors, teachers, principals, occupational therapists, physical therapists, dieticians, residential staff, direct care staff, and many others. So, interprofessional working is not just about health and social care. It refers to any situation in which two or more professions are collaborating to provide a better, more seamless service. For many, perhaps most, social workers, it is likely that there is more contact with professionals who are *not* health workers.

Interprofessional working is in danger of becoming entangled with notions of multiskilling and flexible working, all of which are often seen as euphemisms for loss of professional identity and care on the cheap. "As relationships became more flexible, risk of territorial disputes increased" (Barr, 2002, p. 11). Although there are specific areas of expertise that the different professions can contribute (see later in this chapter for a discussion of the social work role in a multidisciplinary team), we need to be open to the fact that there are areas of overlap, too, and that people benefit if we are able to make best use of these.

For example, if you are having an extension built to your house, you will employ builders, electricians, plumbers, plasterers, joiners, and decorators, each with their own area of expertise. You might reasonably expect each to have some knowledge of the others' work to understand how it all fits together. Moreover, the plumber should be able to take up a floorboard and nail it back down without calling for the joiner, the decorator to smooth a dint in the wall without the plasterer being recalled. While you would probably want to be in control of what the extension will look like (and details of where the sink, electrical sockets, etc. will be placed), you will also want advice about what is likely to work best, how long it is likely to take, and the relative costs.

You might also want to employ a project manager with oversight of the whole job, making sure it is properly coordinated and standards are met. This seems a reasonable analogy for the kind of interprofessional working that users and providers of care should expect from their human services.

Effective interprofessional working requires each profession to value the contribution of the other. Different professions may not share the same value systems, but they must at least have a mutual respect for each other's differences and an understanding of how they might complement one another. Different value systems have very practical consequences, such as how confidentiality is interpreted, whether record systems will be communal or separate, and the terms used to describe the people with whom the professions work (Øvretveit, Mathias, & Thompson, 1997).

POWER AND STATUS DIFFERENTIALS

There are considerable differences in power, status, income, and working conditions among the various professions; indeed, the term *profession* is in dispute for some groups (nurses, social workers) but not for others (doctors, lawyers). "Inter-professional working can only successfully take root when there is mutual respect for the *differences* as well as the similarities between the professions, especially where there are notable power differentials" (Doel, 2002a, p. 170).

Students need preparation for these complex issues so they can understand the intricacies of interprofessional working before they are exposed to them. Indeed, there is a need for much more research into interprofessional practice, although what is available is well summarized by Barr (2002). As with other areas of practice that become "favored sons," the dash to interprofessional working is in danger of trivializing the complexities and failing to build on existing good practices. Perhaps we could learn more from public inquiries into examples of good practice?

INTERPROFESSIONAL COLLUSION

In the uncritical rush to break down perceived barriers between the professions, there has been little analysis of a quite different risk to good practice arising from the relationship between different professionals. Research evidence is hard to come by, but anecdotal evidence suggests that professionals' commonly held stereotypes of clients and patients are as great a barrier to good practice as any interprofessional rivalry. In other words, a collusive consensus about individuals or families, reinforced by different professionals, can be discriminatory and excluding. It is relatively covert and implicit, but perhaps the problem of interprofessional collusion is the more pervasive. Taking our earlier analogy of the extension to your home, it is as though all those different trades (builders, plumbers, etc.) were in absolute agreement that you were a complete and utter troublemaker (they have seen your sort before), and they were all unified in their determination to build your extension as *they* saw fit because they know best for you.

In their advocacy role, social workers can find themselves frequently at odds with other disciplines and having to counter strongly held preconceived notions and assumptions about the service users with whom they come into contact. Challenging this perspective and helping other professionals to consider alternatives is a difficult but essential task. The social work perspective of the person-in-the-environment and the underlying values and ethics of the profession (see Chapter 4) place the social worker in an excellent position to question other agencies and their assumptions and conclusions.

Combating interprofessional collusion still requires working together, of course. However, it will often first be interpreted as not working together, as being different. A core value in social work is the celebration of diversity, but this is not necessarily a key value for other professional groups, where consensus may be valued over difference. Social workers need the skills to ensure that offering different perspectives is not seen as an obstinate desire to break consensus.

ISSUES AROUND INTERPROFESSIONAL LEARNING

If people from different professions are to work more closely together, the logic suggests that they should begin to learn about each other and from one another in their training. The joint education of students (shared learning) from different professions is an increasing feature of the curriculum.

Learning together in the classroom is an obvious place to start. However, there are a number of challenges to overcome to make this a reality, not least harmonizing complex timetables. The tendency for professional bodies to prescribe the curriculum and to add new content without extracting old means that there is little room for maneuver, although there are undoubted areas of overlap, such as communication skills. With respect to interagency working, health and social care professions do not share common standards that practitioners are expected to learn (Shardlow et al., 2004). Therefore, expecting these groups to work easily together is naive. However, there are some examples of courses offering joint awards—for example, for social workers and nurses working with people with learning disabilities, a feasibility study for the joint training of social workers and occupational therapists (Alsop & Vigars, 1998), and a postqualifying initiative for practice teachers and clinical supervisors in social work, occupational therapy, and nursing (Weinstein, 1997).

The quality of learning is an important consideration. In most U.S. university faculties (schools) where both nursing and social work are taught, the nurse students outnumber the social work students by anything up to 10:1, making balanced small groups of students difficult to achieve. There are risks that professional groups are taught together on the basis of convenience, because they happen to be in the same faculty or school, rather than the need to develop joint standards and collaborative practice.

It is important, too, that these experiences of interprofessional learning are properly managed. Throwing students together without group building and opportunities to practice honest communication can only serve to reinforce negative stereotypes. Tajfel's (1981) contact hypothesis suggests that mere exposure is not enough, and students will need to find these encounters rewarding if their perceptions of other professions are to shift. These formative impressions are important ones and need to be carefully considered as opportunities for learning. Coming together for common teaching on a shared topic is one way forward, but this will need to be supplemented by sessions that focus quite specifically on the skills and values of interprofessional learning and practice. The group work skills we explore in Chapter 8 are essential to this process.

THE SOCIAL WORK CONTRIBUTION IN MULTIDISCIPLINARY TEAMS

Social workers have long been located in multidisciplinary teams, and this is an accelerating trend. Rather than see it as a potential threat to social work's integrity, it is an opportunity to influence others and to learn from them, provided that social workers have a strong sense of their own professional identity. Social workers in multidisciplinary teams have a particular opportunity to consider what it is to do social work by considering what is different about their role in these teams. This "contrast effect"—defining social work by discovering what others perceive as the social work dimension—is an invaluable opportunity for social work students to learn about their profession.

In a small-scale study of a multidisciplinary team working with people with learning disabilities, Herod and Lymbery (2002) found that other professions did have a clear understanding of the social work contribution and that this was valued positively. A non–social work team member observed of the social work contribution,

> I think what is valuable is you just having a broader, all encompassing view of the community and the people and what's out there. A much wider picture than some of the other disciplines. (Herod & Lymbery, 2002, p. 21)

The health care workers on this team saw social workers as focusing on the importance of social models of disability. They appreciated the values and ethics of social work, the holistic perspective and strategic approach to organizations, and the coordinating abilities of social workers, and finally, they perceived a certain quality of relationship with service users that was somehow "closer." All in all, non–social workers were able to pinpoint what they would miss if social workers were not members of the team.

These are encouraging findings, and they are probably generalizable to many other multidisciplinary teams that include social workers. They suggest that, far from confusing students about what the social work role is, they may be able to gain an even sharper understanding by asking people who are not social workers. Replicating the Herod and Lymbery (2002) study, or something similar, would be an interesting and valuable project for the student and the team.

In summary, interprofessional learning and practice is essential to good communication between all the people who are working together to provide services. The political drive toward interprofessional working in the United States tends to focus on a negative view of professions as protecting their own corners and a desire to trivialize some of the very real practical difficulties involved. Social work is a profession long experienced in bringing together people with different perspectives and contributions to make, *including service users and providers*. Other professionals seem to value the holistic perspective of social work, although social workers may find themselves confronting examples of interprofessional collusion when this collusiveness is detrimental. Mere exposure to difference does not guarantee better understanding, especially when there are power and status differentials between different professional groups. More important than gathering people in the same room at the same time is the quality of that experience and a shared belief that other professions have a distinct and valuable contribution to make.

CHAPTER 5

Preparation

In Chapter 1, we explored preparation for learning, and this was the focus of the *Permission to Learn* activity. In this chapter, we consider preparation for practice, and this is the focus of *Starting Out*.

NOTES FOR INSTRUCTORS[1]

PURPOSE

As a student, it is expected that you will become increasingly able to reflect on your practice and your learning. This usually occurs either during or after the experience itself. However, *Starting Out* helps you to reflect *before* you have direct contact with people, so that you are reasonably prepared for the encounter.

METHOD

Students should be familiar with the *Permission to Learn* activity in Chapter 1, so that they can develop it further in *Starting Out*. Ask the student to follow the guidance, which includes writing notes of his or her responses. These can be used in supervision.

---

[1]See the Introduction to the book for suggestions about how instructors and students can, separately and together, use the activities in this book.

NOTES FOR STUDENTS AND INSTRUCTORS

VARIATIONS

Once students have completed *Starting Out* with one of the hypothetical situations from *Permission to Learn,* they can follow the same process to prepare for contact with an actual service user or provider. This activity can be used both at the beginning of the period of practice learning and toward the end, to see what changes there are in the quality of the student's responses.

USE BY OTHER PROFESSIONS

Starting Out can be adapted for use by students from different professional backgrounds, in the same manner as *Permission to Learn*. Students can be asked to consider whether the questions in the *Starting Out* activity are generic; that is, do they translate across professions, or are different kinds of questions relevant for different professional groupings? The commonalities across professional groups can come as a surprise to some students.

EDUCATIONAL POLICY ACCREDITATION STANDARDS

The topics in this chapter relate to the following *Educational Policy and Accreditation Standards (EPAS)* 2008 Core Competencies (Council on Social Work Education, 2008):

1. Identify as a professional social worker and conduct oneself accordingly.

2. Apply social work ethical principles to guide professional practice.

3. Apply critical thinking to inform and communicate professional judgments.

4. Engage diversity and difference in practice.

5. Advance human rights and social and economic justice.

6. Apply knowledge of human behavior and the social environment.

7. Respond to contexts that shape practice.

8. Engage, assesses, intervene, and evaluate with individuals, families, groups, organizations, and communities.

FOR STUDENTS AND INSTRUCTORS

ACTIVITY 5: *STARTING OUT*

Part 1

Look back to *Permission to Learn* (Activity 1, page 29). Choose one of the situations described in this activity and consider how you might prepare for the person or people involved, using the six clusters of questions below. Remember that your preparation should be tentative and that you would need to be open to very different possibilities when you actually come into contact with the people.

By way of an example, we have developed the following scenario concerning Jim Rafferty at 5 Derby Street. We know already that he

used to work in the steel industry in quite a well-paid job until he retired. He is now 72 years old and was widowed 3 years ago. Over the past 5 years, he has been losing his sight gradually through macular degeneration. His daughter lives a short bus ride away. Jim has written to the housing authority to complain about the noise from Number 4.

You now have this additional information:

Jim immigrated to the United States from Ireland in the 1950s. Until a year or two ago, he used to see two or three of his old friends from his days in the steel mill, but his deteriorating eye condition has made him feel less secure about going out. Age-related macular degeneration affects his central vision, but his specialist says it is unlikely to lead to total blindness. However, he cannot recognize facial features and gets little pleasure watching television. Seeing something directly ahead is a problem. He senses that other people do not know that he has a vision problem. He was very depressed after his wife died, and he is still feeling lost without her. His daughter visits as often as she can, and he gets a lot of joy from being with his grandchildren.

Clearly, there are potentially many kinds of work to do with Mr. Rafferty, some of which might involve people other than a social worker—for example, a rehabilitation worker from the sensory impairment team. For now, however, use the following six clusters of questions to consider his situation, and make a written note of your responses:

1. "Tuning in": How do you think that the persons might feel about their current situation? How do *you* feel about their situation? Do you have

any similar or parallel experiences you can relate it to, or is the situation very new to you?

2. Possible problems: What aspects of their current situation might the persons like to change? Who is involved in the problem and who would need to be involved to work on the problem to make changes? What aspects do you think are most likely to be amenable to change?

3. Strengths: What strengths might there be in the persons' situation? Thinking of the two "A"s (Chapter 1), what potential aptitudes and abilities can you identify?

4. Aspirations: What hopes do you think the persons may have for their situation? What changes would be necessary to realize these hopes, and what efforts would be required? Are these likely to be relatively long-term or short-term efforts?

5. Resources: What kinds of resources might be needed to help the persons with their situation? Where do you think these resources might be found? What other professionals may need to be involved?

6. Reviews: How would the persons know that they had accomplished what they wished to? What would indicate to other people that changes had occurred?

Part 2

When considering the question of resources in the list above, you were asked to consider what other professionals might need to be involved. In Mr. Rafferty's situation, we mentioned the sensory impairment team as a possible resource. In Part 2 of this activity, we suggest that you make contact with other professional groups who would be likely to have involvement in the scenario you have chosen and find out more about how they would see their involvement, as well as yours, in this kind of situation. Make a note of your contacts to discuss in the next supervision session.

If you have time, repeat the *Starting Out* activity with another situation taken from the *Permission to Learn* activity in Chapter 1.

NOTES FOR INSTRUCTORS

TEACHING ABOUT PREPARATION

Opportunities for Preparation

Opportunities for students to learn about preparation and to practice this aspect are likely to be plentiful. However, consideration needs to be given to the particular "career paths" of the people who use your agency. Are most people coming in a voluntary capacity or not? Will most people whom the student meets be new to the agency, or are they likely to know the agency already? The answers to these kinds of question will have an impact on the kind of preparation that the student will need to make.

Expectations

The first encounter with a potential service user can be like wandering onto a football field with few rules or "painted lines" for guidance. There are a whole host of expectations that each player brings onto the field. Students need to become acquainted with both the general kinds of expectation that people have of their agency and also the particular ones that each new contact brings. Students must begin to discover what the agency's mission is, so that they have an understanding of whether the agency will be able to respond to the potential user's concerns.

The encounter between the student and the service user or provider does not take place in a vacuum. Continuing the football field analogy, some agencies have very fixed rules that leave little room for maneuver; potential service users may think they are entering an open program, only to be met with a nonnegotiable response from agency staff. Students might discover themselves more restricted than they had anticipated; however, in some settings, they may also be surprised by the amount of flexibility in which they can exercise discretion.

The student must learn about the way boundary disputes between this and other agencies get resolved. Do people find themselves being referred back and forth? All agencies must also live with expectations in the wider society, which may be near or far from the reality of the work. In short, the student is learning to question whether there is "a mandate" for work and, if so, where the boundaries of this mandate lie (Marsh & Doel, 2005).

Existing Networks

Prior to making contact with professional services, the majority of people have usually considered other options such as seeking advice from friends and relatives. Unless they already have a history of contact, most people have been referred on to the agency, formally or informally, by friends, relatives, neighbors, or other professionals (Royse et al., 2007, pp. 69–70). It is rare, therefore, that the student will be the first person with whom the person has discussed his or her concerns.

Part of the process of introduction involves tracing the path that has led the person to knock at the agency's door. This may have entailed many "rehearsals," and it is worth asking the student to consider how many other people the potential user has been obliged to tell his or her story. These rehearsals may have changed the person's view of his or her situation or possibly made it more entrenched. All of this information is pertinent to the student's knowledge of how this person or these people have come into contact with the agency and how existing networks will help or hinder any future work.

The networks for some users are provided by the agency itself. Longstanding users, those who are very dependent, residents in the care of the agency—all of these groups of people are likely to know much more about the agency than the student. Even so, it is important that expectations and "rules" are checked out, just as they would be if the person were completely new to the agency. The fact that the student brings a new outlook can sometimes help longstanding service users to reappraise the service they are receiving from the agency.

Students need to consider the path that has brought the user into contact with the agency. This may extend backwards for some time, especially for longstanding residents and families with a string of social workers under their belt. Whatever the timescale, an understanding of the person's entry into the agency's orbit will develop the student's ability to focus the subsequent work. This ensures that the service user's time with the agency is not aimless and neglected.

Induction

As well as preparing students for contact with potential or actual service users, it is important to help them settle into the agency. In most cases, this should entail some form of induction program to help students become familiar with their new environment. Sometimes this can best be done by providing an orientation exercise that guides students to significant parts of the agency (Doel & Shardlow, 1998, p. 17). Although the induction is usually best organized by one person (the supervisor or field instructor), the process of induction is an opportunity to steer students toward other colleagues who will have some interest in, or impact on, their learning.

There is no doubt that students appreciate an agency that is well prepared for their arrival: "One [student] commented that the agency had added her name to the door of a shared office space. She said that this gesture made her feel welcome and that she belonged at the agency" (Caspi & Reid, 2002, p. 158).

NOTES FOR STUDENTS

Learning About Preparation

First Impressions

It is always difficult to know how reliable our first impressions are, and usually we forget them as we acclimatize to a new setting. Nevertheless, it is interesting to compare first impressions with later ones and to think about the ways the early impressions have changed or been confirmed.

Make a note of some of the impressions you have gained from your own experiences of being placed at an agency. These are your private impressions, so you should decide whether you want to share them with your faculty instructor, fieldwork supervisor, or peers in your fieldwork seminar when you discuss your responses to the activity. You may just want to write them down. These are some suggested headings:

- The ease of travel by public transport
- The directions to the agency and within it
- The access for disabled people
- The physical appearance of the unit or office
- The reception area and the responsiveness of reception staff
- The feelings that your new colleagues express about their work and about the agency
- The attitudes of your new colleagues toward service users and providers
- The opportunity for privacy or quiet space
- The pace of work (especially compared to what you are used to)
- The "climate" in the team or agency setting

Toward the end of the period of your fieldwork placement, it will be interesting for you to reflect on these first impressions. How do they look now that you know the setting and your colleagues better? In particular, which impressions have been confirmed by experience and which ones have been changed?

First Contacts

The first contact with a potential user sets the tone for the rest of your work. The initial contact may be a personal encounter or it may be a written introduction, such as a letter or, perhaps more common in the future, an e-mail. Whatever the means, it is important to make careful preparations and to consider the best form of introduction.

Introduction by Letter or E-mail. At some time during your education for social work, it is important to have experience in composing written appointments of introduction, especially if these have not been a central part of your practice learning so far. The ability to convey professional purpose in a friendly manner and to write clearly in a way that invites participation is one worth practicing. Letters and e-mails convey a particular style, and your choice of words will reflect this style, on a continuum from familiarity to formality

(Doel & Shardlow, 1998, p. 60). You could link this to the discussion of friendships and "workships" in Chapter 3. It takes practice to establish a style that conveys a sense of purpose in a friendly manner. You need to strike a balance between overfamiliarity, on one hand, and formal professionalism, on the other. It is helpful to discuss with your practice teacher how the particular context should influence this balance. You will need to consider whether the person is likely to be a nonreader.

Introduction by Phone. Let us assume that you have the phone number for a person who has been referred to the agency. In what circumstances would you consider making a first contact by phone rather than by correspondence? What do you feel would be the advantages and disadvantages of making a phone call to introduce yourself?

Introduction in Person. There are many settings for practice learning in which introductions are informal and unplanned. You are unlikely to write a letter to a resident for whom you are the key worker! However, you should think carefully about the means of the first contact and use whatever seems the most appropriate in terms of allowing both of you to be adequately prepared; remember, it is important to allow the service user or provider the opportunity to be prepared, too. If your first contact is in a group (e.g., in the residents' lounge), how might you plan a person-to-person session?

Attitude

A positive view about the possibility and desirability of change is an important factor in the success of any work, and it is important to think about how this is best conveyed. A naive optimism in the face of unremitting grief is not appropriate, and an overambitious agenda for change in the user's life can lead to disappointment and loss of confidence. However, cynicism about the prospect for change and a belief that changes are imposed from outside are unhelpful, too, even if they sometimes reflect the user's own feelings. At some point, a sense of realistic optimism should be conveyed. Should this be conveyed in an introductory letter or e-mail and, if so, how best to do this?

Taboo Topics

A clear, open message about the reason for your contact will tend to reduce any anxieties the user might have. However, there are some issues in which it is difficult to be open about. These taboo topics need careful discussion with your practice teacher or assessor. Return to the situations in the *Permission to Learn* activity in Chapter 1; what taboo topics might there be in these various situations?

The first contact with people should usually start with the topics on which they are likely to want to focus; these may or may not be the most pressing ones, but they are likely to be the ones that are most acceptable and help build confidence in order for any taboo topics to be addressed. On the other hand, there are times when it is obvious that the taboo topic is the one that brings you to the person's doorstep, and "beating about the bush" will seem dishonest or shifty. How might you decide at which point to point openly to a taboo topic?

Ad Hoc Contacts

In some settings, people make ad hoc and one-off contacts. In a citizens advice bureau, for example, people typically drop in and may not require further involvement beyond a one-off session. In these circumstances, it is still important and possible to be prepared, but more for the *kind* of problems that people are likely to bring to the agency rather than trying to prepare for a particular individual.

Preparing Your Learning

So far we have been considering your preparation for practice. It is also important to continue to prepare for your learning, as we emphasized in Chapter 1. How can you be best prepared to take care of your learning? An excellent way to develop your learning is to ensure you have opportunities for direct feedback. There are four main sources of direct feedback:

1. *You.* You are giving yourself continual feedback, but it is important for you to learn how to recognize this and reflect on it. What cues do you respond to? How do you feel to be doing, and what do you do with these feelings? How do you respond to challenges and difficult times?

2. *The service user or provider.* Much of the time, feedback from the user or provider is implicit and inferred, from reading his or her verbal and nonverbal behavior and from making assumptions on the basis of these readings. However, it is important to learn how to seek explicit feedback, so that you can question these assumptions.

3. *An observer.* The third source of feedback is from an observer, preferably one who knows what to look for and how to give feedback constructively. Your field instructor, the director, or assistant director of the division you are placed in is another possible source. There may be other

social workers at the agency who you have come to respect who are in a good position to be observers. You should be clear as to whether this is part of any formal requirement to observe your practice or whether this is additional, and you should prepare for any observation by agreeing to the ground rules for feedback. In some settings, such as group care and day care, practitioners are likely to be able to see you in direct work with people as a part of their own daily work. These settings are open, with the work taking place in full view of others. In other settings, opportunities for direct observation must be created.

4. *Audio-video feedback.* An audio or video recorder is a valuable "observer" of your work, providing a unique source of direct feedback.

An observer will need to be properly introduced, and the purposes of the observation explained, with every assurance that users and providers are able to exercise their right not to have an observer present. If audio or video equipment is proposed, it is important to obtain signed permissions from those involved and to ensure that people are given a proper opportunity to decline.

Making Your Learning Explicit

One aspect of your preparation is deciding how you will keep track of it. These arrangements should be included in your learning agreement (see page 21 in Part I), and they will be separate from the records you keep for the agency with respect to your work with people. One method is to keep a record of one of your first contacts from early in the placement; this will act as a "baseline" of your early practice. This record might be a letter of introduction or a brief description of a personal encounter in the agency or community. Toward the end of the placement, review this record. If it is a letter, how might you rewrite it now you have the experience of writing several letters of appointment? If it is a personal encounter, how would your preparation for the encounter differ now that you are more experienced? This review, taken together with the baseline from the beginning of your placement, will demonstrate the way your practice has developed and enable you to make your learning explicit. Making the learning explicit will enable you to transfer the learning from this specific experience to others (Cree & Macaulay, 2000; Garthwait, 2008).

ASSESSING YOUR LEARNING

Increasingly, the *portfolio* is the favored method to record your learning and to reflect on its impact on your practice (Baltimore et al., 1996; Swigonski et al.,

2006). This is true not just of social work but of many other professions (Doel et al., 2002). *Portfolio* is a term used to cover many different kinds of document, and it is crucial that you prepare yourself by becoming familiar with the structure of the portfolio so that you can make best use of it (Doel & Shardlow, 1995). As you make observations about your own learning, it is helpful to organize these observations using the structure of the portfolio, and you can only do this by becoming familiar with it.

FURTHER READING

Baltimore, M., Hickson, J., George, J., & Crutchfield, L. (1996). Portfolio assessment: A model for counselor education. *Counselor Education and Supervision, 36*(2), 113–121.

Garthwait, C. L. (2008). *The social work practicum: A guide and workbook for students* (4th ed.). Needham Heights, MA: Allyn & Bacon.

Royse, D., Dhooper, S., & Rompf, E. (2007). *Field instruction: A guide for social work students* (5th ed.). Needham Heights, MA: Allyn & Bacon.

Swigonski, M., Ward, K., Robin, S., Mama, R. S., Rodgers, J., & Belicose, R. (2006). An agenda for the future: Student portfolios in social work education social work. *Education, 25*, 812–823.

CHAPTER 6

Generating Options

Open Ends presents a brief transcript of a service user speaking. The student is invited to consider a number of options for a response to the person and to discuss the implications of choosing different lines of enquiry.[1]

NOTES FOR INSTRUCTORS[2]

PURPOSE

Helping service users to consider different options is an important element in social work practice. *Open Ends* is designed to aid students' understanding of their existing communication patterns, how these influence the way in which options are generated, and to consider possible alternatives.

METHOD

Both the field instructor and the student should read *Open Ends* and make a note of the two questions that most closely fit the line of enquiry you would each wish to take and the two questions that you feel would be most inappropriate. Each make your own brief notes to explain your choice.

---

[1]The difference between *enquiry* and *inquiry* is subtle, the former suggesting a more informal process than the latter; the meaning we seek in this chapter is somewhere between the two.

[2]See the Introduction to the book for suggestions about how instructors and students can, separately and together, use the activities in this book.

Compare these notes at the next supervisory session, opening up a discussion about different strands of enquiry and the likely consequences of taking different routes.

Subsequently, the student should use the *Open Ends* approach with an audiotape of an interview with a service user or provider. The student should choose one of the person's statements and make a note of three or four possible questions that *could* have been asked at that point. The student should then describe why he or she took that particular line of enquiry, with any suggestions for changes, having had time to reflect. The student should consider what options his or her line of enquiry opened up for the person and which ones were closed off.

NOTES FOR STUDENTS AND INSTRUCTORS

VARIATIONS

The *Open Ends* example can be adapted to different settings, using case material that is specific to the student's practice learning. On the other hand, we have found that the issues and the learning points transcend any particular example of *Open Ends*. Students do not have to be familiar with the specific aspects of Jason's situation in order to use the learning points, although they may need extra encouragement if they are not very confident or imaginative. Indeed, if the territory is too familiar, case material can sometimes be a block to new learning because of a natural tendency to rely on established patterns of thinking when the circumstances feel cozy. It is important to break free from any "rut."

You may also wish to introduce the student to a scenario that involves communicating with children. The manner of enquiry with children needs to reflect language that is appropriate to their age; indeed, students may need to consider different kinds of play as a substitute for language-based enquiry (Horwath, 2009; St. Thomas & Johnson, 2003, 2004, 2007). Consider developing the situation in the Benner family (see Chapter 1, *Permission to Learn*, p. 29) to help students practice communication skills with children.

USE BY OTHER PROFESSIONS

Open Ends refers back to Jason Dean, who we first met in the *Permission to Learn* activity in Chapter 1 (p. 29). A number of scenarios in that activity could be developed into an *Open Ends* activity for students from various professions. The opportunity for different students to hear each others' choices and to understand how they relate to their own is beneficial in developing understanding, to the benefit of all the people they work with.

EDUCATIONAL POLICY ACCREDITATION STANDARDS

The topics in this chapter relate to the following *Educational Policy and Accreditation Standards (EPAS)* 2008 Core Competencies (Council on Social Work Education, 2008):

1. Identify as a professional social worker and conduct oneself accordingly.

2. Apply social work ethical principles to guide professional practice.

3. Apply critical thinking to inform and communicate professional judgments.

4. Engage diversity and difference in practice.

5. Advance human rights and social and economic justice.

6. Apply knowledge of human behavior and the social environment.

FOR STUDENTS AND INSTRUCTORS

ACTIVITY 6: *OPEN ENDS*

In *Permission to Learn* you met Jason Dean, who lives with his partner Sam Weiner. At the moment, all you know is that Jason is a 28-year-old, with a previous drug-related charge, and he has just completed a rehabilitation program. Jason is unemployed but volunteers at a local drop-in center for homeless people. His partner, Sam, is 46 years old and receives long-term disability benefit, experiencing occasional periods of depression. Sam is a leading light in the housing association for the apartments.

After a bit of preamble, during which you smell alcohol on Jason's breath, this is what he has to say:

> I just want to talk to someone . . . I had my first drink when I was about 14, and one thing led to another and I was soon into drugs in a big way and it was all out of control. My dad died, I think in an accident, and my mother wasn't taking it too well . . . I was sickly as a boy, no brothers or sisters, and it was all too much. Dad was depressed before he died and I don't think they were happy with each other—Dad and my mother. I've been in trouble with the law, but I didn't get sent away, thank God. I've been out of rehabilitation a while now and it's felt good . . . but I've been finding it really hard these last few weeks. Sam and me have been arguing and it makes me feel bad and I know I'd feel better if I . . . well, the dealers are back in the area and it'd be so easy, but I've got it under control. . . . We're getting a lot of

abuse from people calling us queers and Sam's going into one of his depressions, not going out so much . . . I'm OK, but Sam worries and I just don't know how I'm going to see us both through it.

What lines of enquiry could you follow? The number of possible lines are infinite, but you are going to limit yourself to ones that begin with *how, what, when, where, who,* and *why.* These are interrogatives, and they introduce open-ended questions that can't adequately be answered with a yes or no.

Out of the 20 questions below, choose 2 that most closely fit the line of enquiry you would wish to follow with Jason after he has spoken, and choose 2 that you would most wish to avoid. Explain your choices.

1. How old were you when your father died?

2. How do you connect your first drink at 14 with your drug problem now?

3. How were you sickly as a child?

4. How do you feel about your parents' unhappy marriage?

5. Why did you get into trouble with the law?

6. What kind of help did you receive from the rehabilitation program?

7. How long did your addiction last?

8. Where are you most likely to come across the dealers?

9. Who did you do drugs with?

10. What do you think the future holds if you go back to the drugs?

11. What do you think is making Sam depressed?

12. When do you and Sam find yourself arguing?

13. Why do you feel responsible for Sam?

14. Why don't you go and see a couples counselor?

15. What feelings do you have for Sam?

16. How does Sam get to the housing association meetings when he's depressed?

17. Who's been calling you queer?

18. What have you done so far about the abuse you are getting as a gay couple?

19. What would you most like to change about your situation?

20. Where do you see things going from here?

The questions I choose are the following:

❑

❑

My reasons are as follows:

The questions I would most avoid are the following:

❑

❑

My reasons are as follows:

Some of the 20 questions are more open than others. Which are the less open questions?

NOTES FOR INSTRUCTORS

TEACHING ABOUT GENERATING OPTIONS

Opportunities for Generating Options

It will help the student if you begin by considering some examples from your own practice in which you have helped people to consider different options. This should enable you to identify likely areas of work in which the student will be able to practice generating options in partnership with people and to develop a realistic picture of how the student might prepare for this aspect of his or her learning.

Recognizing and Interrupting Patterns

Gaining an understanding of the way we communicate, the patterns of our communication, is the first step to understanding how these limit or expand the options for service users and providers. Recognizing these patterns can be surprisingly difficult, especially when people are unaware that they are indeed locked into a pattern. Moreover, if it is powerful enough, just one incident can determine our behavior in a subsequent similar situation. This is powerfully illustrated by the following extract from a portfolio written by a graduate social worker reflecting on her formative experiences at secondary school (as usual, names have been changed):

> A friend, Suzy, confided in me that she believed that her father had made her pregnant. He had, and when Social Services became involved, no adults appeared to recognize that she needed her friends more than ever, and she was moved out of school and placed in foster care with no way of us contacting her. When Antony [another friend] came into school after a long period of absence with his hair hacked off with a razor by his mentally ill mother, I supported Antony by keeping it secret and helping him financially and by washing his clothes, etc. This was due to the fear that we all had about informing the teachers following Suzy being taken away by the Social Services. (Social work postgraduate portfolio)

Open Ends is designed to help students become aware of the pattern of responses that they use when responding to people. The aim is to broaden the repertoire of these responses, so that students are making clear choices rather than relying on habit. In theoretical terms, this is close to a social constructionist approach, in which a critical stance is taken toward the taken-for-granted ways the student chooses to understand the world (Burr, 2003; Dewees, 2006, pp. 219–220).

Even if the student does not espouse a particular theory or approach, his or her choice of responses to the *Open Ends* activity signifies his or her "practice theory"; in other words, it helps the student to begin to understand how the leads that he or she picks up from people are guided by his or her own view of what is important. This is true of your choices, too! *Open Ends* can, therefore, be a useful way to return to some of the issues that we introduced in Chapter 2

("Learning About Yourself"), especially if the student experienced difficulties in understanding or identifying with any particular viewpoint.

The following three steps are designed to help students consider their present repertoire of responses and how they might expand these and to develop their role as *navigator* for service users and providers.

Step 1: Awareness

The student's first step comes with an understanding that each intervention (verbal and nonverbal) moves the work in a certain direction. The student needs to be aware of this process. It is not wrong to be directive, in terms of taking responsibility for the direction of a session; abdicating this responsibility is a little like sitting in a car with the handbrake off and wondering why and where the car is moving. The student's aim is not to take over in the driving seat (after all, it is the user's or provider's car) but to help with the navigation.

Ask the student to reflect how lines of enquiry beginning with Questions 1 to 4 in the *Open Ends* activity might come to different conclusions from inquiries beginning with Questions 18 to 20. The first set of questions points down the road to "current problems as a consequence of past traumas," while the second set of questions points down another route to "current problems as a basis for here-and-now change."

Step 2: Repertoire

Second, students need an understanding of any established patterns of enquiry that they bring to their work. Continuing with the metaphor of riding in a car, it may be that one student has a preference for navigating down main roads, while another has a preference for back routes. If this works and successfully helps people to go where they want to, that's fine. If, however, a student seems always to take right-hand forks or takes the car straightforward even when the road bends, the journey is likely to be unsatisfactory.

Self-aware practice means the student can develop a broader repertoire of enquiry skills and understand how the shape of questions now influences the outcome of work later. Students should be able to inspect their own practice to get this particular perspective. Audio- and videotapes are very useful ways for students to hear and see themselves.

Step 3: Discernment

The third step is to gain a greater feel for when different kinds of response are appropriate to use. *Appropriate* always seems unsatisfactory because it is so ill-defined, but there is no neat answer. The student's ability to reflect on successful and unsuccessful responses will help him or her approach the elusive definition of *appropriate*.

When Jason finishes his story in the *Open Ends* activity, enquiry is only one of a number of different responses that the student could give. Other kinds of responses would help generate a range of options for people to consider.

- An example of a *supportive* response would have been, "I want to do all I can to help you because I can see how difficult it is to make this kind of decision alone." Some students might feel drawn to a prescriptive response such as, "You ought to see a drugs counselor and I think you should encourage Sam to make contact with the community psychiatric nurse."

- Prescriptive responses are characterized by *ought* and *should*. Enquiry 14 in *Open Ends* is a prescriptive response disguised as an enquiry. Although there are occasions when a prescriptive response is appropriate, it often denotes an untutored "neighbor over the fence" approach.

- Students are less likely to employ a confrontational response, which requires confidence and needs particular care with timing and phrasing. However, confrontational responses can help someone consider an incongruity or a disparity of which they are unaware. For example, "Jason, you said you have things under control, but I can smell drink on your breath, and I'm wondering what that is about?"

Students need your help to consider the question, "Which kind of response would you choose—enquiry, support, prescription, challenge, or some other?" Usually, "it depends"; good practice is the ability to articulate what it depends on. Students need to discuss the factors that would lead them to choose a particular kind of response and to learn about as wide a range as possible. Generating options for themselves is an important step to helping generate options for others.

NOTES FOR STUDENTS

LEARNING ABOUT GENERATING OPTIONS

Spirit of Enquiry

As the *Open Ends* activity has shown, your choice of enquiry has a profound effect on the direction of the work with people, and even a brief piece of dialogue provides opportunities for enquiry in many different directions. It will, of course, be necessary to develop a repertoire of communication and interviewing skills that build on this spirit of enquiry (Trevithick, 2005).

There are circumstances when it is difficult to continue in a spirit of enquiry—for example, when you disagree strongly with the views of the person. Are there are times when it is right not to continue the enquiry?

You are visiting Avis Jenkins on the Green Hill estate (Chapter 1, *Permission to Learn,* p. 30). In the preliminary "social chat," Avis suddenly says,

Two immigrants have moved in at Number 6, you know. [She looks very disapproving.] They come here taking our own people's jobs, sponging off the state and expecting to be handed a living on a plate. I can't be doing with it and it's about time they put a stop to it.

How would you respond to Mrs. Jenkins? Would the purpose of your visit alter the way in which you might respond and, if so, how?

Positive Reframing

So far we have been considering the effect of your communication patterns on the choices for people. The detail of your discussion with them can have a significant impact on how they see their situation. Initially, it is important for the person to feel confident that you are able to listen to them and to understand what they are experiencing, even if it is outside your own personal experience. It is tempting to offer solutions at this point, such as, "Have you thought about . . . ? Why don't you . . . ?" or to offer reassurances like "I'm sure things will get better . . . it's quite natural to feel like this. . . ." Even if they make you feel better, these kinds of responses are not likely to be experienced as helpful and supportive. Take a moment to think why this might be the case.

Attempts to help a person feel better about his or her situation by offering solutions or normalizing his or her experience spring from good motives. However, assisting someone to begin to reframe his or her situation is a slow and skilful process. Positive reframing is one of the most powerful skills you can develop as part of your repertoire of communication skills. An example of this is provided by de Bono (2000) in terms of someone losing a tennis game: "Don't look at it as a defeat. Look at it as a powerful way of finding out the weaknesses and strengths of his tennis game" (p. 64). This kind of prescriptive reframing is usually less appropriate in social work communication, and of course, it is crucial that you do not use positive reframing as a way of glossing over real difficulties.

Indeed, the best reframing is that done by service users and providers themselves as a result of your enquiry with them. This is likely to take some time. People have often told their story many times and will have become familiar with the well-rehearsed trials and tribulations of their situation. Careful and sensitive enquiry can lead people to discover new aspects to their circumstances, opening up options that they have not had the opportunity to explore. Generating options is very much what de Bono (2000) has called an opportunity for speculative thinking. "People are forced to solve problems but no-one is ever forced to look for opportunities. However, every-one is *free* to look for opportunities—if they so wish" (de Bono, 2000, p. 108).

Nonverbal and Symbolic Communication

Only part of our communication is verbal and explicit. The way in which the words are spoken also reflects our meaning: The same phrase can sound sincere or sarcastic depending on the tone, gestures, facial expressions, body posture, and context of the spoken words. Sometimes the content of the verbal communication and the message conveyed can be contrary or ambiguous (Trevithick, 2005, p. 55).

Watching the television with the sound turned down is a good way to develop your recognition of nonverbal communication. It is also worth noting when you find the nonverbal communication unclear (silences are often difficult to interpret) and the way in which cultural norms influence the way we read situations. This is particularly evident when creating a physical distance between ourselves and other people; what is considered an acceptable social distance varies considerably.

You should also be aware of "symbolic communication" (Lishman, 2009, p. 18), such as punctuality and attention to detail, which can be symbolic of your concern or lack of it.

Action Techniques

We have considered the way in which the style and detail of your communication influence the choices open to people. In addition to your verbal and nonverbal communications, you also have a choice of actions that can be used to help people to generate options. Social work, particularly counseling, has been referred to as "talk therapy," but talk is only one way in which people may communicate. Children, for example, often use play as a means of developing understanding and communication (Horwath, 2009; St. Thomas & Johnson, 2007). It is through play that children wrestle with the emotional and intellectual challenges they encounter. Using action and art-centered activities, children are able to find authentic voice and are capable of transcending otherwise insurmountable realities. What is even more significant about these activities is that they are driven by the child's instinct (St. Thomas & Johnson, 2007, pp. 12–13).

As a student in the classroom, you will be familiar with the use of flipcharts to generate ideas and discussion. If these methods are effective in generating new pathways of thought and action for you and fellow students, why deny other people this opportunity? Restricting yourself and the service user to talk is to limit the possibilities, and there are many kinds of action technique that you can use with service users, either individually or in groups (Doel & Sawdon, 1999, pp. 130–159).

ASSESSING YOUR LEARNING

One of the most effective ways of capturing your ability to help people to generate options is for you to make a tape recording. We hear our interactions with other people very differently when they are not immediate, and there is much learning to be gained from listening to yourself in as objective a way as possible. However, tape recording must be processed very carefully. Of course, permissions are necessary, and you should always consult with your practice teacher about the agency's guidelines.

FURTHER READING

Dewees, M. (2006). *Contemporary social work practice*. New York, NY: McGraw-Hill.

Horwath, J. (2009). *The child's world: The comprehensive guide to assessing children in need* (2nd ed.). Philadelphia, PA: Jessica Kingsley.

St. Thomas, B., & Johnson, P. G. (2007). *Empowering children through art and expression: Culturally sensitive ways of healing trauma and grief*. Philadelphia, PA: Jessica Kingsley.

For a comprehensive account of social work skills, see Trevithick (2005), with specific reference to Chapter 4 (Basic Interviewing Skills).

CHAPTER 7

Making Assessments in Partnership

Hold the Front Page aims to help students consider making assessments from the point of view of the service user and provider. This may seem an obvious aim, but the proliferation of assessment frameworks can take the focus away from the person and on to the assessment process itself. *Hold the Front Page* should enable students to keep people's needs, wants, and problems at the forefront of their assessments.

PURPOSE

Finding out about a person's situation is not unlike investigating a story as a journalist. There may be a number of different, interrelated stories, each with its own headline and more detailed storyline. When listening to people's stories, it is important to listen for quotes from what they have to say; these quotes summarize the story and help to keep it authentic by using the person's own voice. This activity and the chapter that follows emphasize the skills of active listening as core to making assessments in partnership with people.

---

[1]See the Introduction to the book for suggestions about how instructors and students can, separately and together, use the activities in this book.

METHOD

The student should have a copy of *Hold the Front Page* well in advance of the supervision session or fieldwork seminar. Ask the student(s) to construct a draft "Front Page" that would consist of a main headline and four or five other headline stories, with a possible quote for each topic and some text by way of a storyline.

Discuss with the student(s) why the headline story and the other topics were chosen. Of course, it is crucial to emphasize that this is speculation for the purpose of the learning and that work with actual people will not be speculative.

NOTES FOR STUDENTS AND INSTRUCTORS

VARIATIONS

It is interesting to repeat *Hold the Front Page* later in the practice learning, in order to reflect work with an actual person. This is a technique that can also be used in direct work with people, as has been done very successfully by a number of students and practitioners. The *Hold the Front Page* technique is especially effective when used with flipchart paper and can unlock creativity in people's responses to assessment.

USE BY OTHER PROFESSIONS

This method of making assessments in partnership is relevant to all professionals who need to find out people's stories. Students from different professions could use the technique together, either speculatively or in practice. It would be interesting to see what differences there might be in the kinds of story they are likely to focus on.

EDUCATIONAL POLICY ACCREDITATION STANDARDS

The topics in this chapter relate to the following *Educational Policy and Accreditation Standards (EPAS)* 2008 Core Competencies (Council on Work Education, 2008):

1. Apply critical thinking to inform and communicate professional judgments.

2. Engage, assesses, intervene, and evaluate with individuals, families, groups, organizations, and communities.

FOR STUDENTS AND INSTRUCTORS

ACTIVITY 7: *HOLD THE FRONT PAGE*

In *Permission to Learn* (Chapter 1, Activity 1, p. 29), we met Zoë Benner and her family:

> At Number 1 is Zoë Benner, a single parent who was in foster care for much of her childhood but is now reconciled with her mother, who lives on another street in Green Hill apartments. Zoë has a 14-year-old son (Jackson), a 12-year-old daughter (Kylie), and a baby daughter (Kara) age 11 months. Jackson was cautioned for shoplifting earlier in the year and has just been arrested on a charge of criminal damage. Kylie has not been to school for several weeks. She has few friends and is reluctant to leave the family's apartment. Kylie has been referred for help with her bedwetting problem. Kara is Zoë's daughter by another man, who is attempting to gain custody of her. Kara has asthma and seems to suffer from unspecified allergies. Zoë has another child, Tilly, who is a 7-year-old girl currently with foster parents on the other side of the city.

If there was a newspaper just about Zoë and her family, what might the front page look like? (You will need to elaborate on Zoë and her family's situation.)

Construct a front page for Zoë Benner (see Figure 7.1). What might the main headline be? Fill in the storyline and a likely quote from Zoë to illustrate the story. As well as the problems and difficulties, what might she say that she *wants?* What other headlines and stories might there be? Construct the rest of the front page by adding four or five other headlines. Add the more detailed stories, and likely quotes, to summarize them in a nutshell. Include what Zoë or other family members might want to happen in relation to each particular storyline. Add your own "editorial" about how you see her situation.

Figure 7.1   *Hold the Front Page*

The FRONT

Headline:

The story:

The story continued:

Another headline and story:

Also:

More news:

And finally:

TEACHING ABOUT MAKING ASSESSMENTS IN PARTNERSHIP

Opportunities for Making Assessments in Partnership

According to Siporin (1975), assessment is the "differential, individualized, and accurate identification and evaluation of problems, people, and situations and of their interrelations, to serve as a sound basis for differential helping intervention" (p. 224). Meyer (1995) defines assessment simply as "knowing, understanding, evaluating, individualizing, or figuring out." Sheafor and Horejsi (2008) assert that "assessment is the thinking part of the process by which the worker reasons from the information gathered to arrive at tentative conclusions" (p. 239). All social work practice begins with some form of assessment. The social worker gathers data from the client and from the systems that affect the client (Hepworth et al., 2006). For our purposes, assessment is the investigation and determination of variables affecting an identified problem or issue. It refers to gathering relevant information about a problem so that decisions can be made about potential solutions.

When preparing opportunities for the student to learn about the assessment of people, it will be necessary to decide how much autonomy the student should have in this process. This, in turn, will depend on the risk factors associated with the assessments and the circumstances of the particular student; for example, does the current period of practice learning come early or late in his or her program of study? A helpful model is for the student to shadow others making assessments before taking supervised responsibility himself or herself.

Your Role in Teaching About Assessment

In the introduction to Part I, we touched on the difference between good practice and good practice teaching. The distinction is especially strong in this area of "assessment." The student is indeed *a student* and not a trainee, and it is important that the learning goes above and beyond the specific assessment frameworks used in your own particular agency or area of practice. Students are not learning to "do assessments" as a worker in your agency; they are learning "about assessment." However, doing assessments will be a tool for them to learn about assessment. So, they will learn how to do an assessment within a particular framework (depending on the opportunity in any particular setting) but also learn to generalize from this particular experience to learn about the notion of assessment.

During a period of practice learning, students should be enabled to understand the following:

- Philosophical principles that underpin the idea of assessment
- Practice skills that are needed to make a good assessment when working with service users, providers, and other colleagues in an interprofessional context
- Emphasize the importance of identifying and using a client's strengths in addition to focusing on problems

As part of understanding the idea of assessment, students should be encouraged to recognize what is *general* to all assessments, what is *specific* to an assessment protocol, and what is *particular* to the context in which the assessment is made (the agency context). Perhaps students should be encouraged to keep a journal of their practice, for example, by keeping a list of the numbers of assessments they have made using a particular assessment protocol, rather in the way that the medical profession keeps a record of the number of assessments made using a particular protocol (see below for a discussion of protocols).

The vagueness of the term *assessment* presents one of the greatest challenges to your practice teaching, not least the potential confusion because the same term describes the process to which students are submitted in relation to their practice abilities. Experience in doing assessments does not necessarily mean that you will feel confident in teaching about assessment, and you might want to familiarize yourself with Milner and O'Byrne (2002) and Parker and Bradley (2003), the suggested texts in the Further Reading section toward the end of the chapter. We discuss some of the issues around assessment in more detail later.

Assessment and Intervention

There has been a tendency for assessment to be seen as a separate activity from intervention. However, the student is learning both about social work practice and agency practice; social work practice emphasizes the close connection between assessment and intervention. Indeed, assessment in the sense of "finding out and making judgments together" continues throughout the intervention period.

By asking the student to include statements about what Zoë Benner and her family might *want*, you have also been encouraging the student to consider what kinds of intervention the assessment might lead to. This is crucial to social work practice since we doubt whether an assessment without an intervention is, in fact, social work. The assessment should be theoretically grounded and based on available evidence (see Part IV: Social Worker as Researcher: Evaluating Practice).

NOTES FOR STUDENTS

LEARNING ABOUT MAKING ASSESSMENTS IN PARTNERSHIP

Assessment: A Note of Caution

The term *assessment* is deeply embedded in the social work vocabulary at professional and organizational levels. We need to be honest about the reservations we have about the term. There are two good reasons to sound a note of caution.

First, it is a confusing term. Is it a process, a skill, an outcome, or all three? In addition to its principal use in this chapter in connection with judgments made with respect to service users and providers, you will find it used to describe the process and outcome of your own competence to practice social work.

Second, and more seriously, the term *assessment* has connotations that are contrary to the spirit of partnership. The preposition that most commonly follows *assessment* is *on* rather than *with* (e.g., "Have you completed your assessment *on* Mrs. Smith?" rather than "Have you completed your assessment *with* Mrs. Smith?"). This is not a semantic point, and it is one that lies at the heart of a fundamental dilemma: Assessments usually comprise professional judgments about people, their state of mind, their risks, their eligibility for resources.

Clearly, there are times when it is necessary to use professional judgment about a situation, in which case it would be more honest to use the term *judgment*. *Judgment* is more candid than *assessment* because the former recognizes the element of discretion (and room for mistake), whereas assessment makes a claim to objectivity that is not necessarily justified. Assessment is about making judgments based on information (Middleton, 1997). A professional judgment should, of course, be made that takes full account of the views of a range of stakeholders about needs and wants.

Feedback From *Hold the Front Page*

If we think of assessments as an "exploratory study" (Coulshed & Orme, 2006), it is possible to see links with a journalist's skill. The aim is to find out what is happening, who it involves, what people think about what is going on, what they have tried to do about it, and what their aspirations are. The journalist does this to sell newspapers, and the social worker does it to see what kind of help might be appropriate. Journalists often have their own agenda of what spin can be put on the story to sensationalize it (to sell *more* papers); social workers too often have their own agenda, too—what parts of the person's story fit into the proforma, the assessment criteria. Unfortunately, this can lead to one ear being closed to the person's story, as it is processed by the social worker for a "fit."

Of course, resources are limited and must be fairly allocated, so at some point, there has to be a process of assessing a person's *need* and not just his or her *wants*. However, in closing off discussion so that it only fits the agency's agenda, we are acting contrary to the spirit of partnership and, indeed, to the principles of good social work practice. The *Hold the Front Page* activity lays the foundations for "open book" listening, unguided by assessment structures, so that you know what an open assessment can, at least, look like.

Wide Range of Assessments

Social workers are involved in a very wide range of assessments, which include the following:

- Assessment of children in need and their families
- Assessment in child care, with three domains: the child's developmental needs, parenting capacity, and family and environmental factors
- Community care assessments
- Mental health assessments for admission to hospital or guardianship
- Assessment of appropriate discharge plans for hospital patients
- Diversity considerations when conducting assessments (e.g., age, class, color, culture, disability, ethnicity, family structure, gender, marital status, national origin, race, religion, sex, and sexual orientation). For each case, social workers should ask themselves whether any aspects of diversity may be significant.

Assessment and Government Guidance

Many assessments carry the authority of the courts, so they are exceptionally powerful, as is the whole notion of assessment. Although the format may be prescribed and limiting, McDonald (1999) acknowledges that assessments do carry statutory authority and legitimation. In particular, this impact has been to increase the "emphasis on ensuring that assessments are evidence-based, consider risk more comprehensively in all its contexts, and accountability" (Milner & O'Byrne, 2002, p. 1).

We noted earlier that social workers are involved in a very wide range of assessments, which can be thought of as a series of separate *protocols* governing how an assessment might be undertaken in a particular context. Some of these are mandatory, some advisory: You need to be very clear which is which!

Although you will learn about a wide range of assessments, it will not be possible or necessary to practice all of them to understand what assessment is about. As we have already emphasized, it is important that you learn how to help somebody to tell his or her story before you then learn how to squeeze it into an assessment framework.

Working in Partnership With People

An assessment can be transformed from a formalized checklist to a genuine partnership of enquiry by good communication skills, especially listening and interviewing skills (Trevithick, 2005, p. 53). This ability is especially important since, in reviewing the literature, Milner and O'Byrne (2002) were struck that there was "little evidence of the existence of well-developed skills in involving service users in the assessment process" (p. 3). The following quote from a social worker's portfolio reflects some of the confusion over the nature of assessment:

> Following a visit, my initial assessment was that she had let the tasks of the household get on top of her and she also appeared to be isolated.

This statement indicates that the everyday interpretation of the term *assessment* is that it is a judgment made by a relative expert about another's situation. Was the service user's assessment that she had let the tasks get on top of her and that she was isolated? We think not. Service users do not "make assessments."

Of course, practitioners and agencies have to make judgments about people's circumstances, and these will sometimes be quite different from those made by the people themselves. Let us, in that case, be honest and call them judgments, rather than hide behind the white-coat term *assessment*.

We have to exercise caution, too, in our use of the word *partnership*. It is an *apple pie* term and can be "used to describe anything from token consultation to a total devolution of power and control" (Braye & Preston-Shoot, 1995, p. 102). Genuine partnerships are not easily established, and the differences in power within the relationship between social workers and users and providers will always be a limit to the scope of the partnership.

Partnership involves an approach that is centered on the person rather than on the pro forma. For example, Kitwood and Bredin (1992) developed person-centered approaches in relation to work with people with dementia, looking at the care process and its effect on well-being. It highlights the service user's point of view and reminds us of the importance of considering strengths as well as problems.

Holistic Assessments

We have mentioned several conceptual and practical problems with "assessments." A further difficulty with highly structured assessment procedures is their tendency to blinker the person who is assessing, so that they only assess for narrow aspects of a person's life rather than allowing a fuller picture to emerge. The following quote from a social work postqualifying portfolio illustrates this:

> One of the difficulties of the assessment that Sure Start[2] completed was that it was about Ms X and the assessment was not a child-centered assessment. The difficulty was that Ms X was very needy herself and it is my belief that the Sure Start staff lost sight that the assessment was meant to be child-centered.

We cannot be confident that the social worker would have approached this from a holistic (all-encompassing) perspective either. Two assessments would emerge, the one parent centered and the other child centered. Which, if either, tells us the full story?

It is important not to confuse a holistic assessment (one that takes account of different dimensions in people's lives, including their strengths not just their problems) with a single assessment, which is one carried out by one professional rather than many. A single assessment is designed to prevent people having to endure multiple assessments from a number of different professionals, but it does not guarantee that the assessment process itself will take account of the service user as a person rather than as a "pain sufferer" or "an applicant for day care services."

Assessments and Interventions

Finding out is just one aspect of an assessment. Unlike journalists who do nothing more with their story than print it, social workers must use an assessment as a basis for further action or recommendation. Social work practice goes beyond assessments to interventions; indeed, assessment is one aspect of the social work intervention, although it may mark a definite stage (via a report, for example) before further work is or is not indicated.

---

[2]Sure Start is an organization working with families.

What follows an assessment will vary from one agency to another, but in social work practice, there are a number of models to guide the whole of your intervention, the best known of which is probably task-centered practice (P. Marsh & Doel, 2005). In this method of practice, the assessment stage is called "problem exploration." Task-centered work emphasizes people's strengths as well as their problems. It models making assessment in partnership, precisely because the social worker's expertise is not making judgments about the person's situation but engaging him or her in a new experience of building confidence, solving, or at least lessening problems and achieving goals.

Interventions vary from "short and fat" along a continuum to "long and thin" (Doel & Marsh, 1992, p. 90); in other words, your work may be characterized by relatively frequent contact over a short period of time or extended over a longer period with fewer contacts. It is important that your learning about assessments is linked to your wider learning of planning, completing, and evaluating interventions and that all of these processes are tied to an understanding of what partnership with people means in practice.

ASSESSING YOUR LEARNING

It is important not to lose sight of the "in partnership" in the title of this chapter. The temptation is to focus on the skills of making assessments for the agency in which you are placed, rather than focusing on learning about the assessment process as a whole and how it links to other aspects of your intervention with people. By all means use a particular assessment framework as an example, but keep in mind that it is just that, an example. The assessment of your abilities as a student in this area should focus on your capacity to enquire and to plan, complete, and evaluate your work together with all the people who have been involved.

FURTHER READING

Hepworth, D. H., Rooney, R. H., Dewberry Rooney, G., & Larsen, J. (2006). *Direct social work practice, theory and skills.* Belmont, CA: Brooks/Cole/ Thompson.

Milner, J., & O'Byrne, P. (2002). *Assessment in social work* (2nd ed.). New York, NY: Macmillan.

Parker, J., & Bradley, J. (2003). *Assessment, planning, intervention and review.* Exeter, UK: Learning Matters Ltd.

Sheafor, B., & Horejsi, C. (2008). *Techniques and guidelines for social work practice* (8th ed.). Needham Heights, MA: Allyn & Bacon.

CHAPTER 8

Working in and With Groups

No One Is an Island is designed to help students think about the kind of learning that can be achieved from involvement with groups. This activity builds on familiarity with the residents of Derby Street (Chapter 1, Activity 1, p. 29).

NOTES FOR INSTRUCTORS[1]

PURPOSE

Social workers are not independent clinicians. They must work closely with other people, both in formal teams and informal groupings. Service users and providers often live and work in groups; if they live alone, they may miss the company of others, too. This chapter helps to develop awareness of groups and the potential of group work, especially as a means for people to achieve collective control over their lives and a way of sharing power between workers, users, and providers. The chapter also makes links between groups and teams, as well as between sessions and meetings.

METHOD

Faculty instructors, supervisors, and students will need a copy of *Permission to Learn* (p. 29) to accompany *No One Is an Island*. Once the student has decided which of the four group scenarios to work with, the field instructor/faculty instructor might wish to provide further reading for the student to pursue.

---

[1]See the Introduction to the book for suggestions about how instructors and students can, separately and together, use the activities in this book.

Students will need time to prepare Parts 1 and 2 before discussion with the practice teacher/supervisor—perhaps the period between one practice supervision and the next.

NOTES FOR STUDENTS AND INSTRUCTORS

VARIATIONS

The field instructor can add to the four group scenarios in the activity to reflect the kind of group that is, or could be, characteristic of the agency setting. However, as we indicated in Chapter 1, it can be more instructive to use situations that are less rather than more familiar.

USE BY OTHER PROFESSIONS

Groups, teams, and networks lend themselves to multiprofessional involvement. Co-work with another professional in a group can help students to learn about both group work and multidisciplinary work. Three of the proposed groups in *No One Is an Island* involve a group leadership that is multidisciplinary, and it is illuminating to use the exercise with students from different professions if you have the opportunity.

EDUCATIONAL POLICY ACCREDITATION STANDARDS

The topics in this chapter relate to the following *Educational Policy and Accreditation Standards (EPAS)* 2008 Core Competencies (Council on Social Work Education, 2008):

1. Apply critical thinking to inform and communicate professional judgments.

2. Engage diversity and difference in practice.

3. (a)–(d) Engage, assesses, intervene, and evaluate with individuals, families, groups, organizations, and communities.

FOR STUDENTS AND INSTRUCTORS

ACTIVITY 8: *NO ONE IS AN ISLAND*

You will need a copy of Activity 1: *Permission to Learn* on hand (p. 29). We know from the information in Activity 1 that Avis Jenkins already attends a group called Memory Joggers to help her manage her failing memory, and the Kiyani brothers are members of a Kurdish support group. However, you are now aware that there are four other groups being planned in the community that might be of interest to some of the people living on Derby Street. The groups are briefly described below.

Parenting Skills Group

A group has been proposed by a social worker and a health visitor to help parents who are experiencing difficulties with their children's behavior. The group will meet once a week for a time-limited period; the co-leaders are planning 8 to 12 sessions of an hour and a half, with about eight group members. The group will use cognitive behavioral methods to help parents understand their children's behavior and also to rehearse different ways of responding.

You consider Zoë Benner a potential group member.

School Refusal Group

A group will be led by an education social worker and a teacher based at the school into which Kylie Benner's school feeds. At the moment they are thinking to recruit children ages between 11 and 14 years old whose problems are leading them to drop out of school. This would be a voluntary group, with no legal requirement, and parental permission will be needed for children to attend. It is proposed that the group will meet weekly for an hour to an hour and a half. It will be an ongoing group, with new members joining and existing members leaving as their attendance improves. The group will use activities, as well as discussion.

You consider Kylie Benner a potential group member.

A Volunteers Group

A local drop-in center, "The Hearth," opens its doors to homeless people and people with mental health and drug problems. The Hearth has very many volunteers who help out, some quite regularly and others on an occasional basis. A project worker at The Hearth is planning a group for local volunteers, not just for those based at the center. The main purpose will be to develop volunteers' skills and to share problems and experiences.

You consider Jason Dean a potential group member.

A Support Group

A community psychiatric nurse and a social worker are publicizing a new group that they want to start for people with depression. It will be community based, and their intention is to withdraw when the group can become self-help. They see the group as an opportunity for people to talk about their experiences and to offer mutual support, meeting once a week, but perhaps every 2 weeks when it has become established.

You consider Sam Weiner a potential group member.

Choose one of the groups above and consider the questions below.

Part 1: Offering the Group to a Potential Member

- What further details would you like to know from the group leaders before you discuss the group with the potential member?
- How might the potential group member benefit from this group?
- What reservations might the potential group member have about the group?

Part 2: Participating in the Group as a Co-Worker

If you were invited to be a co-facilitator in this group:

- What would you bring to the group leadership?
- What changes might you wish to suggest to the purpose, methods, or shape of the group as currently proposed and why?
- How would you find out whether the group had been successful?
- What would you hope to learn from involvement in the group?

Further Suggestions

If you have time, choose another of the groups and repeat this process with the new group and potential group member.

Later in your period of practice learning, return to the notes you kept from this activity and review them. What changes would you make in the light of your subsequent learning?

NOTES FOR INSTRUCTORS

TEACHING ABOUT WORKING IN AND WITH GROUPS

Opportunities for Working in and With Groups

It is not the purpose of this chapter to outline group work processes and purposes and so on. These can be found elsewhere (e.g., Doel, 2006; Kurland &

Salmon, 1998; Shulman, 2006; Wayne & Cohen, 2001). Our focus is the way in which students can learn about working in and with groups during their practice learning. To begin with, it is important to establish what knowledge of groups and group work the student brings. There is very little research in this area, but a study by Birnbaum and Wayne (2000) suggested that group work is poorly integrated into the social work curriculum in the United States. Indeed, in an earlier study by Birnbaum and Auerbach (1994), it was found that most social work schools offer group work only as an elective, and few students graduate with a course in this subject. Unfortunately, 18 years later, this continues to be the norm.

Whether there are plenty of opportunities to "do group work" or none at all, group processes are impossible to avoid. Your role as a practice teacher or work-based supervisor is to help students recognize these processes and to make best use of them.

Even if there are no existing groups with service users or providers in your agency, it is worth considering whether there are unmet needs that a group could satisfy. This brings us to a fundamental issue: the purposes of the practice learning. On one hand is the imperative to train the student to learn how to do various specified tasks; on the other is the student as an adult learner developing increasingly independent thinking and practice. This tension is reflected in the balance between the student observing and emulating "the expert practitioner" and the student creating and developing a new service.

Groups offer a real opportunity both for students to express their creative potential and for the agency to develop a service. However, this needs very careful consideration because the student will need much support (Cohen, 1995). In some circumstances, it may be necessary for both you and the student to consider strategies to influence agency policy. Again, this will be valuable learning for the student.

Balancing Various Needs

Clearly, a group cannot be created just for the sake of the student's experience or practice. There has to be an established need for a group and decisions taken about what impact the involvement of a student will have. Will this be single leadership, dual leadership, observer, user led, or what? Dilemmas in balancing student, user, and provider needs are not unique to group encounters, but they are more public in these settings, and the dynamics are more complex. The potential for group work to provide a vehicle for user participation is great (Ward, 2000). Expressing this in ways that fit with current concerns about social exclusion may be significant to attract the necessary funding to support a new group work initiative.

If you and the student are co-working a group, power issues in co-leadership are heightened, and you both need to consider how these will be addressed. Co-work in a group provides good opportunities for direct observation of the student's practice and for coaching. However, the student's need to develop more autonomous group leadership styles should be taken into consideration.

Fears About Group Work

It is important to acknowledge that group work is an area of practice learning that can generate much anxiety for students (Gitterman & Salmon, 2008; Knight, 1997; Shulman, 2006). Fears are often related to the semi-public nature of a group. Making mistakes or not being able to cope is more exposing in a group. Other apprehensions may arise from a worry that people will not attend, that there may be hostility, silence, or other difficult behaviors, or intimidation by the idea of the number and potential power of people in a group. Indeed, some of these fears might also be your own. It is important, therefore, to reflect on how *you* feel about supervising group work and whether you need support in this area. What is your own experience of groups, and what have been the positive and negative aspects of this?

Discuss possible fears about group work openly with the student as early as possible and clarify the expectations of the course in this area. The extent of students' knowledge and experience will determine whether it is appropriate for them to be a sole group worker.

Other Opportunities

There are other ways in which students can learn about group processes. One of these is participation in group supervision. In a study of the effects of reflective team supervision, Thomlison and Collins (1995, p. 234) found that students felt that they received more feedback than in one-to-one supervision; team and group supervision gave them information about how other students experienced them and how they came across to others. There were some concerns, too, about the need to adapt to different supervisors' styles and the anxiety of being observed. Used with care, group supervision can provide a more rounded experience for students and staff, as well as help bring different perspectives and a potential power shift into the supervision.

Bourne's study in Brown and Bourne (1996) perhaps explains why group supervision is not prevalent in social work. The group supervision in four out of the five teams that he studied folded shortly after the spotlight of his research terminated. He points to the public nature of group supervision (it takes a confident team leader to "perform" in front of the full team) and the difficulties arising from the different supervisory needs of the group members as key reasons for the relative absence of group work approaches to supervision. In addition, it is important for teams to be clear about the place of the group supervision sessions in relation to their other meetings; group supervision has to be qualitatively different from other forums; otherwise, it becomes yet another time-consuming meeting.

Conversely, group practice teaching might have more success because of the relatively common purposes and standing of students on placement. In many respects, the learning and support gained by students from one another balances the additional workload involved in supervising more than one student. Alternatively, if there are other students in your agency or vicinity, not necessarily social work students, you may wish to consider involving them in group supervision sessions, although you will need to make sure that lines of communication are well established with their individual supervisors.

If you intend to make use of the group of students *as a group* (i.e., consider the group dynamics of the student group), this must be made explicit from the start, with ground rules agreed so that the experience is one that is guided and constructive. You should exercise caution in using group supervision in an experiential way, especially if you have the power to assess the students' practice.

Students might also be learning from one another in the performance of group tasks or working on group assignments as part of their practice learning (Underhill, 2002). They need to have the chance to learn from this group experience, especially since an awareness of group processes is likely to improve their ability to work together and therefore to complete the task.

Teamwork

The creation of a new group with service users, or joining an existing group of service users, is not the only learning opportunity in this area. A much neglected group is the team; there are differences, it is true, from social group work, but teamwork has much in common. You need to give some thought to how you will help the student to understand the dynamics in the team or teams with which they will be involved and how they can begin to relate this to group work principles.

The following questions can be used as an observation checklist for the student to complete over time in preparation for discussion with you. However, given that you are probably also a member or possible leader of the team, it is crucial to agree how the student's observations may be used.

- What do you see as the team's purposes?

- How and why is the team structured as it is? Is it clear who is and who is not a team member?

- What kinds of roles do you see individuals playing in the team?

- Who holds what kind of power in the team?

- What rewards and sanctions are there in the team?

- What are the team's values? Are these widely shared in the team, or are there many differences? How are values demonstrated in practice?

- What happens to conflicts in the team?

- How are team processes recorded and reflected on?

- How does the team monitor its work?

- How do people outside the team view the team?

NOTES FOR STUDENTS

LEARNING ABOUT WORKING IN AND WITH GROUPS

Social Action

There are many models of group work, and those that are implied by the four proposed groups in *No One Is an Island* are worker initiated. In contrast, the social action model of group work hands over the agenda for action to the people themselves (Mullender & Ward, 1991). The four groups proposed in Activity 8 would imply different levels of partnership with the group members, different kinds of dialogue between group members, and different degrees of democracy and equality (Douglas, 1993). How might the proposals for each group be reframed in such a way that issues of social inclusion rather than social functioning are brought to the fore? How might group members be empowered to take collective control of these groups?

Links Between Groups and Teams

A careers choice survey[2] found quite a contrast between the views of students and those of employers with respect to the place of teamwork abilities. The survey of more than 1,000 students found only 25% of respondents thought it important to develop team working skills. In contrast, employers rated teamwork as their

---

[2]The survey was conducted by the Careers Research Advisory Committee and reported in *The Times Higher Education Supplement,* June 13, 2003.

number one priority. It is perhaps understandable that students are focusing on developing their own individual competence, but in the world of practice, it will be crucial that you have good abilities in teams and groups.

Teams vary considerably. Some consist of people doing much the same kind of work, in face-to-face contact (such as a team of workers in a residential unit) or independently (a team of field social workers). Others are composed of people with different but complementary skills, such as multidisciplinary mental health teams. Some teams are formalized as "Team X," with a life that transcends the membership of individuals, whereas others are time limited, formed around a particular task or person.

Groups, too, cover quite a range. Some are longstanding and open-ended, with a life that is independent of the individual membership; others are created for a specific purpose, with a definite beginning and ending. There are, therefore, a number of characteristics that link groups and teams, so that your learning from the one can be transferred to the other:

Groups and Teams:

a common sense of purpose

need to be fit for purpose (in terms of size, resources)

should consider process as well as outcome

influenced by their context

characterized by a range of leadership styles

members need both affirmation and challenge

clarity about roles, responsibilities, and expectations is important

What are some of the differences between groups and teams?

Meetings and Sessions

The focal point for teams and groups is the meeting or session, which can be actual or virtual. Although the work of teams and groups goes on outside meetings and sessions, it is at these times that they consolidate, refocus, consider progress, work on problems, negotiate present and future plans, review, reflect on past successes and failures, and celebrate individual and collective achievements.

The business of a meeting is often formalized around an agenda, while the degree of structure in individual sessions of groups varies considerably. Leadership is usually formalized in a meeting around the chairperson, whereas the styles of leadership in group sessions are, again, very varied indeed. Teams usually have just one chair, while groups commonly, although by no means always, have co-leaders (Doel & Sawdon, 1999; Shulman, 2006). The degree of democracy and partnership differs from group to group and team to team, although teams are more often characterized by a formal hierarchy, whereas the very reason for many groups is to empower the membership through collective action and experience. Individual meetings and group sessions are usually part of a larger pattern of meetings and sessions, although single sessions can also be appropriate (Ebenstein, 1999).

Learning From Groups and Teams

You will need to ask about the opportunities for working with and in groups in the preparation meeting prior to the beginning of your time in the agency. A realistic timescale will need to be agreed if you are to be involved in establishing a group, and in most cases, it is more likely that you will be joining an existing group or take part in plans that are already under way.

As well as these practical details, you need to be open about your feelings about groups. Do you feel comfortable in groups, or are there issues that concern you? Groups can be powerful, and this power can be used to various effects. Some well-known experiments have demonstrated this power, such as the Asch experiments (1952), which showed how people were influenced to agree with judgments they considered to be obviously wrong (the respective lengths of two lines, etc.) because the "plants" in the room all subscribed to them. Group pressure can work for good and ill.

Making the Work More Visible

The relative invisibility of the work done by social workers fails to promote social work in the wider community. Indeed, much of social work practice is invisible even to social work managers (Pithouse, 1998). Group work is one way in which social work processes can be made more public, especially if the group's purposes are outward directed, such as campaigning groups. Doel et al. (2002) have described how portfolios of group work practice at a postqualifying level have helped to document the impact of social work with individuals, making these accounts accessible to the agency and to other workers.

ASSESSING YOUR LEARNING

It is important to know what agency expectations there are for recording group work practice. With appropriate anonymity, it may be possible to make use of these records for your learning and assessment purposes. If you are co-working in a group, your co-workers may be able to play a role in giving evidence of your practice, and group members themselves have valuable perspectives on your work. As with any aspect of your assessment, it is crucial that everyone involved is clear about the expectations and that any potential conflicts in role are discussed. Group members need to be aware of how any feedback they give about your work will be used and reassurance that it will have no consequence on their position in the group.

FURTHER READING

Doel, M. (2006). *Using groupwork*. London: Routledge.

Gitterman, A., & Salmon, R. (Eds.). (2008). *Encyclopedia of social work with groups*. New York, NY: Haworth.

Wayne, J., & Cohen, C. (2001). *Group work education in the field*. Alexandra, VA: Council on Social Work Education.

PART III

Agency Practice

CONTEXT: CREATIVE PRACTICE AND PROCEDURAL REQUIREMENTS

Everybody at the Conference was asked to stand in a line. The line represented a continuum of how creative people felt they were able to be within their working lives. Sadly, the end of the continuum, which was marked 'not creative at all' was very much the most crowded place on the continuum. (Doel, 2002b)

One of the tensions in professional work is the potential for discomfort between individual practice and organizational performance expectations. In this chapter, we consider how discretion and creativity can be balanced with regulation and standardization.

PRINCIPLES UNDERPINNING PROCEDURES

Few people would disagree with the need to have procedures in place to ensure the quality and consistency of services available to the public. When decisions are to be made about whether to make resources available, it is important that there are agreed procedures to help regulate and distribute resources, and that these procedures should be fair and transparent. Similarly, procedures are needed that help to ensure standards of service and provide accountability to the community at large for the costs of these services. It is important that people in one state can expect as good a quality of service as those in another.

A procedure should build on what we already know is good practice, such that it provides guidance for practitioners, to help them to embed the required approach in their future practice. All of this is right and proper; indeed, much of it is enshrined in law, statutory guidance, and notions of "best practice" (see Chapter 14, this volume).

Students must learn about procedures for a number of reasons. They need to learn how to translate general notions of fairness and efficiency into actual practice, using the procedures that the agency has made available. This may be general guidance or, more commonly, a particular pro forma or set of pro formas designed to chart the practitioner's work with people. Students should also be helped to consider procedures critically. This does not mean moaning about them as a chore but a genuine critical analysis of their usefulness in achieving the principles of fairness, transparency, good standards, and efficiency. The fieldwork instructor should prepare examples of the use of procedures, illustrating aspects that are successful and others that are less successful in applying these principles. In this way, the student can begin to learn not just how to use a procedure but how to think about it critically about the specific procedure and the realities of day-to-day practice.

PROBLEMS WITH PROCEDURES

Procedures carry dangers, too. A procedure can too easily become a tool to aid the smooth running or self-protection of the agency rather than to promote the benefit of users. A procedure that is hastily designed in reaction to a single high-profile event can have unintended negative consequences on many more low-profile events. In other words, there is a tendency to follow any shock to the system with a set of procedures designed to prevent a recurrence of this shock. Unfortunately, the trauma from the shock means that a cool analysis of the potential secondary effects of the new procedure is absent. Although the procedure may be successful in preventing the highly unusual events that led to the initial shock, it may have unfortunate consequences on all the rest of the agency's less dramatic work. For example, is it likely that there will be an evaluation of the possible negative effects of the 26 recommendations referred to in the newspaper report that follows?[1]

> Social services and health managers in Cityville were this week criticized after two-year-old Andrew Coldwell died after drinking his drug addict mother's methadone. . . . They were "too tolerant" of Rebecca Hodgkins' drug habit and had not made a proper assessment of her parenting skills, an independent report said. . . . A total of twenty-six recommendations were made on how procedures should be tightened to avoid tragedies.

---

[1] Names have been changed.

The 2-year-old had drunk from a bottle of methadone that had been left with the top unscrewed. The same report also recorded that "there is no guarantee that a perfectly working child care protection system could have prevented his death." Would there have been the same action if a child had died because a parent left a bottle of bleach, rather than "a drug," with the top unscrewed? Would there be a reference to the "bleach-using parent" in the way Rebecca is called a "drug addict mother"? The report continued, "Each year more than 500 children in Cityville [pop 500,000] are taken to hospital because they have taken substances (medicines and alcohol) meant for their parents. Between 130 and 140 have to be admitted."

Procedures are an expression of power. Those who design a procedure have considerable power to shape future practice, yet they are often not the people who will have to implement the procedure directly. This can lead to procedures that are unwieldy and impractical. It can generate opposition, merely because those who must use the procedures do not feel any ownership of them. In these circumstances, the people who designed a procedure can view critical feedback from the people who are obliged to use it as obstructive rather than insightful. When procedures are developed and evaluated in your work setting, what opportunities exist for consultation or participation in these processes by practitioners and service users, and how can the student be involved in this?

Procedures can lead to lazy practices if they become a substitute for critical thinking and action, and a reliance on procedures can slip into routinized practice. Routines are essential to manage a heavy workload and are appreciated by users, if they guarantee a punctual and reliable service. However, if the routine fails to acknowledge important differences between one situation and another, it becomes dangerous practice, with automatic decision making replacing individual plans and interventions (O'Melia & Miley, 2002; Thompson, 2000b; Wayne & Cohen, 2001). Procedures can lead agency staff to believe that they have done all that is necessary; hence, it becomes difficult to change a procedure once it is in place, and the procedure comes to reflect a past reality rather than the current one. What opportunities for reviewing and changing procedures can the student learn about in your agency or work setting?

As a standardized process, a procedure does not lend itself easily to the highly individual nature of much professional practice and the complex circumstances of the people with whom these professionals work. Procedures can be by-passed or sabotaged, with the result that they become discredited. If the lines of communication in the agency are open, this will lead to a revision of the procedure, but where communication is poor, there will be a growing gap between what an agency thinks is practiced and the practice itself. The need for discretion should be openly discussed, so there is healthy debate about the limits of discretion and the kinds of circumstance where it can be applied. To close off this dialogue is to drive discretionary behavior underground and, therefore, to encourage dangerous practices.

One set of procedures can contradict another. Thus, for example, in a retirement community for older adults, procedures based on personalized care had allowed care staff to make individually tailored breakfasts for each resident, many of whom enjoyed the opportunity of choosing between eggs, sunny side up, over easy, soft boiled, hard boiled, scrambled, poached, or fried. A new director was appointed, and she was horrified that "procedures were not being followed." The procedures she invoked were health and safety, which she said required only catering staff to make breakfast (of whom there were insufficient numbers to make individualized breakfasts) and did not allow the cooking of a choice of types of eggs for residents "because of the risk of salmonella." Whose procedures should be followed? Did anyone ask the residents?

Perhaps the greatest challenge is how to achieve a balance between the need for procedures that can ensure quality, fairness, and accountability and at the same time allow for professional discretion to deliver an individualized and personal service—even one that may involve some degree of risk. In short, students need to learn how to use procedures in ways that are not procedurals and to develop routines that are not routinized. How can the student learn about the use of professional discretion in your agency, and are there open forums where these kinds of issues are discussed?

THE RETREAT FROM PROFESSIONALISM?

Human services are provided by five types of organizations: (1) public agencies, (2) private not-for-profit corporations, (3) private for-profit corporations, (4) self-help groups, and (5) religious organizations. Some services, such as day care, may be provided by any of these types of organizations. Other services, such as child and adult protection, are provided by public agencies or other designations (DiNitto, 2005). Consequently, many social services are provided by the private sector. For example, most child care centers are owned by private for-profit and private nonprofit organizations. Many of the intermediate residential care facilities that serve people with developmental disabilities are also privately operated. While for elders, many retirement communities that provide independent living, assisted living, and acute care are also privately operated and run for profit.

Over the past decade, managed care has played a more central role in the delivery of human services, but this form of practice is controversial because many for-profit organizations are more concerned about their shareholders' profits than about whether service users receive all the care required to an appropriate standard (Rubin & Babbie, 2008, p. 308). This "primacy of profits" puts social workers and other agency personnel in a very difficult position. To whom are they accountable to? The agency or the service user—or both?

Therefore, increasingly, the parameters of the social work profession may be determined by the managers of social work services rather than the practitioners or the users. With respect to community care, Lymbery (2000) notes that the central problem "has therefore been re-ordered—it is not the attempt to meet the needs of individuals and communities but is, rather, the management of budgets and resources" (p. 129).

This brief analysis concludes with the observation that one of the many consequences of the retreat from professionalism has been the increase in proceduralized practice, as evidenced in assessment procedures such as eligibility criteria to ration services, and the social work role reduced to a "technical operative" (Lymbery, 2000), with decreasing opportunities for practitioners to work in direct practice with service users (Jones, 2001; Reed, 2002).

Much of this analysis seems to lead away from the idea of "creative practice," to the extent that the reader may wonder, "Is there a positive way forward where creative practice can be the soul of social work?"

CREATIVE PRACTICE

It is no surprise that the social work literature is sharper in its analysis of the problem than it is in its presentation of examples of solutions. There is much analysis of the possible pathology of current practice, but what is urgently needed are specific examples of creative practice and opportunities to develop creativity through the practicum. In line with the moves toward positive psychology, the discipline of social work needs to focus less on what does not work and more on what does (Doel & Best, 2008).

One of the potential difficulties possibly lies in recognizing what creative practice might look like. Those conference participants that gathered around the "not creative at all" pole of the continuum (see the prelude to this chapter) might need some prompting to recognize some of their current practices as being creative. For example, one practitioner did some innovative work with a family, using flipchart sheets to help them represent their situation in graphic form and working in a way that was quite different and challenging for her, yet she did not see this as being creative, despite the novelty and the excellent evaluation from the users. Some people do not see themselves as creative, perhaps restricting the idea of being creative as something for the arts rather than a possibility for applied social science. "Creatives" are cast as artists, advertising executives, actors, and so on, with social work airbrushed out of the picture.

Is there an *art* of social work (Schubert, 2006)? What does creative practice look like? For some, it has to be something new and original, an innovative way of using existing resources, a special ability to be imaginative. In fact, creative practice is a way of looking at one's own practice rather than something that can be objectively defined. Let us remember that creativity is no less objectively defined in the world of art: Is an unmade bed a work of creative art?—one has been exhibited as such. Social workers who sees their work as creative would recognize that every time they meet with a service user, they create an atmosphere that they hope is conducive to the work, create space for the user to express himself or herself, create opportunities for the user to seek solutions, agree to plans, involve other people, and so on. And paradoxically, this social worker might experience all of this creativity quite routinely.

As an aside, we should also acknowledge the pejorative use of the word *creative*, meaning intentionally deceptive, as in "creative with the truth." We might worry if a colleague crowed about his or her "creative recordkeeping"!

There are many reasons why you should aim both to recast your existing work as creative and to seek new opportunities for creativity in your practice. Foremost is the question of job satisfaction. We are familiar with the impact of stress and burnout on social workers, but we know much less about those social workers who continue to enjoy their work. We have little evidence one way or the other, but it seems unlikely that the satisfied groups are any less busy or committed than the former burnt-out group, so what is it that makes the difference? Once again, we need to change the focus, to learn from those who are using successful strategies, rather than learn even more about those who do not. Job satisfaction is crucial if the students we are educating today will continue to be *creative* practitioners the day after tomorrow.

As well as a responsibility to yourself, you also have a responsibility to the people you work with. Creative practice is likely to be more engaging for service users, be more stimulating for the team and other professionals with whom you are involved, and lead to innovations in the ways in which services are provided. If one of a social worker's talents is to see situations from different perspectives, this is surely a key aspect of creative practice—reframing a situation so that it can be seen in a different light, triggering a fresh approach, and offering a new range of potential solutions or courses of action.

Some agencies may be suspicious of creative practice because it is likely to call into question existing practices. However, the "change agenda," as the jargon has it, has too long been driven by organizations and agencies themselves. The battery of changes imposed from outside the profession as part of the modernization ideology has tended to make people averse to the notion of change itself. This is understandable but mistaken. How much more powerful it would be if the direction and drive for change came directly from practitioners and service users. Creative practice would provide the evidence and the energy to promote changes (as opposed to "change") from bottom up rather than from top down.

PROCEDURAL AND CREATIVE PRACTICE

We have a great need, then, to consider how we can add the "c" of creativity to the other common "c"s of criteria, compliance, and competence (Phillipson, 2002).

Let us return to the idea of procedures. First, they are with us, like it or not. Second, the underpinning principles that we spelled out early in this chapter are important and necessary ones. Fairness, transparency, and good standards must be incorporated into all professional practice, and developing procedures is an important mechanism to promote these principles.

The dictionary has a definition of *procedure* as "established method": an established method or correct way of doing something. However, a second definition states, "*ANY method:* any means of doing or accomplishing something, [as in] an extremely unorthodox procedure" (Encarta, 1999).

This is a very helpful insight. Yes, its first meaning suggests there is only one correct way of doing things, but the second reminds us that procedures are just ways of doing something, and that these can be unorthodox as well as established. Basically, a procedure can be followed in a routinized or creative way; they can be highly formalized or any method used to accomplish something.

If we consider a method of working such as task-centered practice, we see that there are certain procedures associated with this method (Marsh & Doel, 2005). The various stages of the method have recognized procedures that help to guide the practitioner and the user. These procedures can be administered in a tick-box fashion, with outcomes implying that users seem to need or to want only the services that the agency can afford to provide, or they can be used to develop a spirit of partnership with service users, in which the users are, as far as possible, in the driving seat. Although some procedures are undeniably more helpful than others, it is not the procedures themselves that determine the nature of the experience for the service user; it is the way in which they are used, creatively or not, by the practitioner and the agency.

CHAPTER 9

Making Priorities

The activity *Home Truths* takes us back to the residents of Derby Street in the Green Hill housing development (Chapter 1, *Permission to Learn,* p. 29). Priority rehousing is possible for just one household, and the student is asked to consider the statements by each household before putting the applications into a rank order of priority. The learning from this activity comes from a consideration of the values that have underpinned the student's choices.

NOTES FOR INSTRUCTORS[1]

PURPOSE

The purpose of this activity is to encourage students to think about how they make decisions when there are conflicting priorities. Too often, these kinds of decisions are made without an awareness of the knowledge, values, and beliefs that underpin them. This activity makes these factors explicit and teaches students a framework, which will help them to continue to review the way they make decisions.

METHOD

The activity can be undertaken by two people (the supervisor and the student) or in the fieldwork seminar. A group of students in different settings can often provide contrasting perspectives.

---

[1]See the Introduction to the book for suggestions about how instructors and students can, separately and together, use the activities in this book.

1. Students should study *Home Truths* individually before the fieldwork seminar, making a brief note of their response to each household's statement and identify a list of their priorities (i.e., from the household they think should have highest priority for rehousing to the one they think has the least strong case).

2. The student's reasoning is discussed in the fieldwork seminar or supervision session, with an "objective" list of criteria by which cases for rehousing are then developed through this discussion.

3. The student and field instructor or supervisor together apply the "objective" criteria to see what differences (if any) this would make to the order of priorities.

NOTES FOR STUDENTS AND INSTRUCTORS

Variations

In "real life," there would be preexisting formal criteria and a prescribed set of procedures to decide how a resource such as new housing would be allocated (as well as the practical issue of a match between the size of the new accommodation and the applicants' needs). However, the ability to suspend these practical factors can lead students to greater "home truths" (i.e., deeper understandings about the way in which priorities are too often made, on the basis of "the deserving"—those who are most persistent, those who have good connections, etc.).

Once the *Home Truths* activity has been completed, you may like to draw up a set of competing priorities, which are more specifically tailored to the kind of situations found in your work setting. However, before setting the student down to the application of existing agency procedures, the *Home Truths* activity enables students to think critically about how criteria should be developed and to understand the link between procedures and the values, which those procedures seek to enforce.

Use by Other Professions

Whatever the professional group, some form of prioritization is needed to manage the gap between demand and resources. The *Home Truths* activity is applicable across a range of professions (indeed, social worker students have been using the activity to do what some would say is a housing worker's task). You may wish to revisit the exercise by tailoring it to the particular situations in your setting, pointing the student to literature in your professional area. For example, there are many examples of prioritization of services and treatment in health care professions; Harries and Harries (2001) explored how four occupational therapists managed and prioritized community mental health referrals using a form of "social judgment theory."

Where students work in a multiprofessional environment, they can be encouraged to explore the forms of prioritization used by other professionals.

EDUCATIONAL POLICY ACCREDITATION STANDARDS

The topics in this chapter relate to the following *Educational Policy and Accreditation Standards* (*EPAS*) 2008 Primary Core Competencies (Council on Social Work Education, 2008):

1. Apply critical thinking to inform and communicate professional judgments.

2. Engage in research-informed practice and practice-informed research.

3. Engage in policy practice to advance social and economic well-being and to deliver effective social work services.

4. Respond to contexts that shape practice.

FOR STUDENTS AND INSTRUCTORS

ACTIVITY 9: *HOME TRUTHS*

You should also refer to Activity 1, *Permission to Learn* (Chapter 1, p. 29) for more background detail on each household.

Read the statements for rehousing made by the various applicants. Make a brief note of your response to each household's statement and bring a list of your priorities—from the household you think should have highest priority for rehousing to the one you think should be lowest. Revisit these notes and make a list of the criteria that you have used to help you make your priorities.

Assume that the new accommodation is the appropriate size for each of the applicants (even though this could not be the case in reality).

Applicants' statements:

Zoë Benner

As a single parent with two teenagers and a baby daughter, I think I have a strong case for moving off this housing development. Jackson, my 14-year-old, has been getting in with a bad crowd and we need a fresh start, and our Kylie needs the opportunity of a fresh start at a new school. I would like to live nearer my daughter Tilly, who is currently living with foster parents, and this new accommodation would give me the opportunity of seeing much more of her. The chance of having our own garden at the new accommodation would improve our quality of life as a family, especially since my baby suffers a lot from asthma.

Jason Dean and Sam Weiner

We are very excited at the prospect that this new accommodation would give for us to move to more suitable accommodation. Although we are on the ground floor currently, the apartment is very unsuitable for Sam's disability; the prognosis suggests that Sam will need wheelchair access in one or two years, and this would make it impossible for him to use the bathroom in our current accommodation. Attached is a letter of support from our GP and the occupational therapist.

Avis Jenkins

I am writing this statement on behalf of my mother, who currently lives at 4 Derby St. I have recently divorced and I am planning on moving back to Cityville to be near my mother. However, because of the schooling situation for my son, for whom I have custody, I will be living across the city from Mrs. Jenkins's current address. The possibility of this new accommodation for my mother is ideal since it would be close to my new home, and I could give her the kind of support she clearly needs. I fear that without this support, she will not be able to maintain her independent living and that she is at risk of needing residential care. Also, she tells me that she is much disturbed by her current neighbors and is unhappy about the general quality of the area and the type of people who are moving in.

Loretta and Luke Carter

We see this as a great opportunity to better ourselves. It is very important for us, as we start to think about a family, to have a home with a garden where the children will be able to play. My husband's band is getting very successful, which means he needs to practice more frequently, and we are getting complaints from neighbors. He tells me that the new accommodation is close to some sound studios, which it would be possible to hire, so our new neighbors wouldn't be disturbed.

Jim Rafferty

I like this neighborhood, but I have to be honest with myself that, as a partially sighted person, I'm finding it increasingly difficult to find my way around and I now hardly go out. The local shop closed and I can't use the supermarket, which is across a very busy road with no nearby crossing, so I'm dependent on the kindness of others. Through the local residents association, we have tried very hard to lobby for improved street markings, but with no success. My sister took me to the new accommodation, and the surrounding area is very well marked for blind and partially sighted people—my independence and quality of life would be transformed, as well as escaping from the noise next door! I'm afraid that the prognosis for my sight is not good, and I enclose a letter of support from my rehabilitation worker and from the National Federation of the Blind.

Gregor and Stefan Kiyani

We hope to have successful application on account of very bad treatment we receive in our current home. People on our street are friendly, but there is a gang that continually threatens us from near here, and police seem not able to help us with this problem. We have many contributions to make to our new country but are frightened by possible violence where we live now. Also, the rooms are not good, with some wet on the walls, which has been told to Mr. James, but nothing is happening. We hope respectfully to have an opportunity for a better life that can be safe for us.

Shama and Gary Homes

This application is based on our role as provider and the possibility that the new accommodation (with more rooms) would give us to increase this role. We successfully care for a number of children with learning disabilities, giving them and their own carers a valuable break. We enjoy our work and treasure the many letters of thanks and appreciation we have received over the years. The new accommodation would enable us to expand our capacity and to give much-needed respite to even more children. Our own adult daughter has learning difficulties but is well established in an independent living foundation, and we now feel able to take on more responsibilities.

Ernie and Catherine Minkie

Catherine and I are very excited about the possibility of new accommodation. As Catherine's emphysema gets worse, she is going to require a nurse to come into the house twice a day to make sure she has taken the necessary medication and use her nebulizer. In addition, with my working schedule, she is also going to need one of the neighbors to stay with her a couple of times a week. With the location of the new housing, it will be much easier to get this person. Also, the apartment is closer to her doctor and nurse. Thanks for all your help.

NOTES FOR INSTRUCTORS

TEACHING ABOUT MAKING PRIORITIES

The value of *Home Truths* is that it gives students permission to reflect carefully on the reasons behind the decisions they make. In the safe environment of simulated practice, students can begin to question the reasons for their choices because there is time to reflect on them. This helps students to make better decisions at times of great pressure and gives a framework to evaluate the way they have made their priorities.

Good social work practice is self-aware and accountable. Students learn how to *give an account* of what they are doing and why they are doing it. Those students who can answer the question, "What am I doing and why am I doing it?" make their practice accessible, with every prospect of becoming accountable, through being explicit about their reasons for action. Students often learn to describe what they did and why they did it *after* the event, which only improves their skills in post hoc rationalization. As a supervisor or field instructor, you hope to improve the students' abilities to give an honest account of the choices that are available to them and to become aware of the criteria used to make these choices. This kind of activity can accelerate students' understanding (see, e.g., Barsky, 2006; Doel, 1988; Garthwait, 2008; Sheafor & Horejsi, 2008).

Below are a dozen criteria to test out during the discussion with the student. The situations in *Home Truths* are not especially urgent, so you may wish to inject some urgency into some of the situations to see how this might alter the student's rankings.

- How does the student think these criteria are ranked in practice?

- How does the student think these criteria *should* be ranked?

Ranking Criteria

1. *Consequences of delay and risk:* In these situations, the individual's life is at risk. What are the consequences of delay? How urgent is the immediate risk?

2. *Legal obligation:* What is the legal framework for the powers and responsibilities that govern this situation? What are the legal requirements on social work and other professionals in these situations?

3. *Agency expectations:* Does the agency have any policies that determine the priorities, and are these clear and accessible?

4. *Social pressures:* What are the broad influences on the worker's decisions? Is there such a thing as society's priorities and expectations? How do we determine what these priorities are and who defines them in the real world?

5. *Available resources:* To what extent do we make priorities to fit the available resources, so that resources define needs?

6. *Others' responsibilities and skills:* What other people could and should be helping? When would you expect other people, in your agency or other agencies, to be involved?

7. *Previous knowledge:* To what extent do previous assessments influence present attitudes?

8. *Degree of need and disadvantage:* Can one person be said to be needier than another, in a general sense and in this specific example, and how can these needs be measured and quantified? Are specific service user and provider groups particularly disadvantaged, and how should this influence the way we treat particular individuals?

9. *Likelihood of success:* Is it important to put energies into effective work, providing help to those who can use it? How is the chance of a successful outcome to be judged, and what do we do about those situations where failure is almost inevitable?

10. *Personal preferences:* How far does the acknowledgment of personal preferences for particular kinds of work clear or cloud the judgment (e.g., a preference for working with women)? Is this an honest self-assessment of personal skills and limitations or a rationalization of prejudice?

11. *Problem sensitization:* Are we more likely to respond quickly and favorable to problems that we can relate to, in connection with our own personal lives?

12. *Economic resources:* In view of current financial crisis and state budget shortfalls, is it economically prudent for a housing authority to build these larger apartments?

Opportunities for Making Priorities

If there are clear agency policies that define priorities, it is important to let the student know that you will be discussing these. However, agency priorities are not necessarily synonymous with professional ones, and to begin with, you will want students to express their own priorities. Make sure students do not try to avoid the issues by claiming they would never have to deal with all these things alone and that others would be involved. Of course, others would be involved, and students would not have to determine the priorities independently, but the point of the activity is to look at reasons for making choices and deciding priorities, not ways of avoiding them. To work effectively in a multiprofessional environment, students need to understand fully the reasons that underlie their own judgments.

You can ask students to reconsider their priorities from somebody else's point of view, such as the state legislator, the commissioner for the Department of Health and Human Services, the board of directors of your agency, the executive director of your agency, the director of a particular division of the agency, supervisors at the agency, social workers at the agency, and service users of the agency. All of the aforementioned have the well-being of the agency's service users at the forefront of their minds but are accountable to different constituents and have different priorities. Students should be encouraged to think about how they manage to deal with competing demands and to set priorities, both in the sense of making effective decisions and also in terms of managing any stress they may experience.

It is important to encourage students to consider how they might manage the priorities of their own day-to-day practice as well as the broader considerations about how the agency in which they are currently working approaches the problems associated with making priorities.

NOTES FOR STUDENTS

LEARNING ABOUT MAKING PRIORITIES

Decisions about priorities must be made by staff at federal, state, county, city, and individual levels. In a complex society, levels of expectations among the public about the availability of health and social goods are highly elastic. Decisions have to be made about not only those programs to be funded but also which service users and providers, at the individual level within a program, will receive priority over others and how much support they will receive. In Oregon, an experimental approach pioneered public choice in setting health and social care priorities by asking the electorate directly what level of taxation they would be willing to accept for a given level of services (Bodenheimer & Grumbach, 2002, pp. 154–155).

Deciding on priorities is not just a matter a matter of money; there are some hard moral choices to be made—sometimes as fundamental as whether to *live and let live.*

Live and Let Live

Consider the following vignettes:

Vignette 1: Better Use of Resources

Esmin Green was supposed to get help for her mental illness, but what she got was indifference and ineptitude from the very facility that was supposed to help her.

Green, 49, died on the floor of Kings County Hospital on June 19 after being left unattended in a chair for 24 hours and callously overlooked for an hour after she collapsed to the waiting room floor. Involuntarily admitted on June 18 for agitation and psychosis, Green spent her last day on earth sitting in a waiting room chair. Video footage from the facility shows several hospital staff walking around Green as she lay dying on the ground. A gurney and oxygen tanks finally arrived an hour after Green collapsed, but it was too late. Green was pronounced dead soon after efforts were initiated to save her. (*New York Times,* July 1, 2008)

Vignette 2: Don't Delay

Judi Campbell inches along at work with the help of a walker. Degenerative arthritis has ruined her hip and ravaged much of her body, so she takes prescription painkillers every four hours to cope.

"I cannot walk. I cannot live," she said. "I am in such pain. And I feel guilty about what I'm putting my husband through. If I have to get out of bed, I need his help."

Hip replacement surgery, however, will have to wait. Campbell, 62, already owes a Northampton hospital $1,000 for medical expenses not covered by her insurance—two $500 copayments for arthritis-related surgeries in 2007. She doesn't want to add to her debt, especially since the status of her secretarial job at a nonprofit organization is uncertain.

As the economic recession persists, people who are unemployed or worried about losing their jobs are putting off medical care and living with illnesses and conditions that aren't critical, but can be debilitating. Some are delaying having precancerous tumors removed; others are forgoing knee or shoulder surgery. While insurance often covers much of the costs associated with such procedures, there are usually deductibles and other out-of-pocket expenses that can add up to thousands of dollars. For those lacking insurance, the price of most elective procedures is beyond their reach. (*The Boston Globe,* May 4, 2009)

(Continued)

(Continued)

Vignette 3: The Value of Insurance

A higher percentage of the poor and uninsured—one in three—are being redirected from the University of Chicago Medical Center to Mercy Hospital and Medical Center than the typical rate of admission of such patients to hospitals in Illinois.

Nearly 7 percent of the patients cleared from the U. of C. emergency room and then transported and admitted to Mercy have no health insurance coverage, according to an eight-month period of data provided to the Tribune from U. of C., analyzing 396 patients. On top of that, 25 percent of patients transported by ambulance 5 miles north to Mercy were covered by the Medicaid health insurance program for the poor, which is known for paying hospitals low rates, particularly in Illinois.

At other Illinois hospitals, the number of uninsured and those covered by Medicaid is 26.4 percent, according to the most recent statistics from the state Department of Public Health. Of those, 3.7 percent are 'charity patients' with no insurance, and 3.2 percent are 'private pay,' who generally have no coverage or pay out of pocket. Medicaid covers 19.5 percent of admissions to Illinois hospitals, state figures show.

As part of its Urban Health Initiative, the U. of C. has been redirecting some patients to about two dozen health centers throughout the South Side. U. of C. defends the program as a way to get patients treatment at the appropriate location in a tough economy and to alleviate long waits in the emergency room. (*Chicago Tribune*, April 28, 2009)

The preceding vignettes and nature of the health care system raise issues for students to consider, such as the appropriateness of withholding potentially beneficial care to save, making access to health care dependent on one's ability to pay—a form or rationing, and the development of a two-tier health system.

Now that you have read the three vignettes, consider these questions:

1. Do you agree with the treatment decisions made in these cases?

2. What priority would you give to treating the people in the vignettes?

3. Is there any further information you would like to gather before taking action?

4. What criteria have you used to help you decide your position?

5. Can you envisage other situations that would have greater priority?

President Obama signed legislation on March 23, 2010, to overhaul the nation's health care system and guaranteed access to medical insurance for tens of millions of Americans. The landmark bill signed by Mr. Obama will provide coverage to an estimated 30 million people who currently lack it. The measure will require most Americans to have health insurance coverage; would add 16 million people to the Medicaid rolls; and would subsidize private coverage for low- and middle-income people. It will regulate private insurers more closely, banning practices such as denial of care for pre-existing conditions. (*New York Times,* March 26, 2010)

Rationing

Rationing has been more explicit in health care than in social work for some time. Unfortunately, that situation is changing rapidly in the United States. At the time of writing, we have witnessed states all over the country grappling with their budgets. Despite federal stimulus dollars, governors and legislators have been forced to make drastic cuts due to numerous programs.

There is much to learn by exploring issues in health care, not least because social workers are increasingly likely to be involved in situations where there is the following:

1. *Rationing of resources on the grounds of quality of life*—where individuals may be denied access to resources as these would not sufficiently improve their quality of life, or that their current quality of life does not justify the allocation of further scarce resources.

2. *Rationing of resources on the grounds of age*—the setting of priorities can be made on the grounds of age. With respect to health care, there is a well-established debate concerning the virtue of this form of rationing. In a debate format, A. Williams (1997) supports rationing health care on the grounds of age, advancing the argument that there is "no compelling argument to justify the view that the young should sacrifice large benefits so that the old can enjoy small ones" (i.e., quality of life of younger people is to be preferred against the quality of life of older people). Accordingly, those who are older have had life opportunities, and these should not be denied to those who are younger. Evans (1997) puts the case against age as grounds for rationing health

care because it is fundamentally unacceptable on ethical grounds to discriminate by age, given the equal moral worth of each individual.

3. *Rationing on other grounds*—other health priorities operate either explicitly or as an unintended consequence of the operation of particular systems. Rationing also occurs *on the grounds of choice of lifestyle*; for example, those who smoke are denied treatment for smoking-related illness unless they cease smoking. In such cases, they are treated as having made a lifestyle choice to smoke, rather than being treated as "nicotine addicts." There have also been reports of *rationing of resources on the grounds of moral worth*, such as the denial of treatment to vagrants for renal dialysis, when such treatment is being offered to others in similar need but with different lifestyles.

4. You might like to consider these various principles of rationing and think about whether you agree with any of them and, if so, why. Consider these two examples from health and social work:

• Example 1: Rationing is prevalent in the U.S. health care system by virtue of the number of individuals who are underinsured, lack coverage for catastrophic expenses, or are excluded from coverage for a having a preexisting illness (Bodenheimer & Grumbach, 2002, pp. 22–23).

• Example 2: Rationing and prioritizing has become a part of practice for some time and in some ways has been embraced by the social work profession. The use of professional skills may be effectively rationed to particular social groups. For example, according to Specht and Courtney (1995), many MSW students ultimately plan to have full-time private practice careers. Although these students express a desire to work with at least one of the disadvantaged groups traditionally associated with social work practice, these groups have less appeal than do service users with nonchronic psychological problems.

To what extent are there similar examples of the rationing of resources in social work more generally, and if so, what are the rationing mechanisms?

Are there examples known to you, in social work, where the setting of priorities is managed through moral worth rationing mechanisms, whether deliberately adopted or as the accidental consequence of policy decisions?

During World War I, the medical services were faced with the kinds of priorities we hope we will never have to make again. With scant resources, they had to make decisions that were, literally, life and death. They divided the casualties into three categories:

- Those whose injuries were such that they were likely to recover, even without treatment

- Those whose injuries were such that, without treatment, they were likely to die, but with treatment they were likely to survive

- Those whose injuries were such that they were likely to die, even with treatment

The medical services put all their energies into the middle category, leaving the first group to recover unaided and leaving the last group to die. This method of making priorities was called triage. Fortunately, the choices in social work are not so stark, but they are difficult nonetheless. The principle of putting your efforts where they are most likely to be effective is one you need to consider. As Gibbs and Gambrill (2002) comment,

> Evidence Based Practice is a process (not a collection of truths) in which the uncertainty in making decisions is highlighted, efforts to decrease it are made, and clients are involved as informed participants. An open environment in which critical appraisal flourishes will encourage ad rem (at the topic) arguments and discourage bogus objections that distract professionals from careful review of new ideas and methods as well as related evidence that may help us to help our clients. (p. 473)

The latter part of this assertion, concerning agencies, may or may not be the case in the agency where you are placed, but if you used the criterion of likely effectiveness as the main guideline for your work during the fieldwork placement, would there have been a difference in the kinds of priorities you have made? What do you think are the benefits and the limitations of using the effectiveness criterion in social work?

Extent of Rationing

The extent of rationing is a measure of the degree to which available resources are in balance with perceptions of need, whether professionally defined or service user and provider defined. As Bergmark (1996) notes, financial constraint due to cuts in public spending has increased the interest of Swedish municipalities in considering the way in which priorities are implemented. There is some evidence that decentralized decision-making processes lead to people in similar sets of circumstance being treated differently in different geographical areas.

In other words, the real world of social work practice is being radically and speedily reconstructed as the boundaries between health care and social care become more permeable and fluid as organizations merge, shift, and change. The picture presented so far is somewhat bleak; however, priorities for services are no longer a matter for one organization but have to be undertaken in partnership, especially at local and regional levels. Such partnerships are more likely to lead to open discussion about rationing and the setting of priorities. As Glendinning, Coleman, and Rummery (2002) suggest, three current policy initiatives influence priorities with respect to elders: "an emphasis on partnership; active demonstration of improved performance; and increasing involvement of frontline health professionals in decisions of services development" (p. 185). These factors shape the form, nature, and priority of services not only for older people but also for other groups.

ASSESSING YOUR LEARNING

To make a decision between competing priorities is not necessarily a particularly difficult task. We all have to make choices about all aspects of our lives, whether to have tea or coffee in the morning for breakfast, which job to apply for, with whom to develop relationships, and so on. What distinguishes each of these decisions is the extent and permanence of their impact on our lives, from the banal to the life defining. Some may matter a little, others greatly. What is truly important about making decisions is that you understand the reasoning that lies behind the decision; this is the case whether the decision concerns making a cup of tea or how to allocate resources between the competing needs of different service users and providers. It is with this reasoning that you make decisions about priorities that will be used to assess your abilities to make priorities.

FURTHER READING

Barsky, A. E. (2006). *Successful social work education: A student's guide*. Belmont, CA: Thomson Wadsworth.

Bodenheimer, T. S., & Grumbach, K. (2002). *Understanding health policy: A clinical approach* (3rd ed.). New York, NY: McGraw-Hill.

Garthwait, C. L. (2008). *The social work practicum: A guide and workbook for students* (4th ed.). Needham Heights, MA: Allyn & Bacon.

Sheafor, B., & Horejsi, C. (2008). *Techniques and guidelines for social work practice* (8th ed.). Needham Heights, MA: Allyn & Bacon.

CHAPTER 10

Managing Resources

ABOUT ACTIVITY 10: *TRAVEL AGENT*

Travel Agent invites students to consider buying one of a number of different vacations, the purchase of a vacation providing an analogy for the purchase of social services (case management). The student is asked to consider factors such as high, medium, or low season; the price of the vacation; and the remaining monies available for spending and so on.

NOTES FOR INSTRUCTORS[1]

PURPOSE

Travel Agent is designed to encourage students to consider some of the factors involved in making choices about services—in this case, a service they might wish to obtain for themselves. Thinking about the factors that are important in making decisions about a vacation helps us better understand the type of decisions that must be made in the provision and management of other *social* services. However, although it is possible to survive without a vacation, it may not be possible to continue living in the community without adequate social services.

METHOD

Travel Agent is best undertaken by a group of three or four students. It can also be undertaken by two people, such as the field instructor and student in a supervisory session. Students should read *Travel Agent* and, independently, consider the options for vacations. Ask the students to decide upon their first choice of

---

[1]See the Introduction to the book for suggestions about how instructors and students can, separately and together, use the activities in this book.

vacation. In making this selection, students may want to find out if others in the group are considering the same package. If two or more students take the same vacation package, the cost of the vacation is discounted (full details below).

Once students have decided on their vacation package, ask them to review the reasons for their selection and to consider the importance of the following list of factors (by no means exhaustive) that may influence decision making: type of vacation, overall cost, balance of costs (meals/accommodation, etc.), time of year, location and facilities offered, whether the holiday is "protected" and facilities inspected, available spending money, and other factors.

- Students should compare the relative importance of these different factors and any others that they may identify in making their preferences.

- In the fieldwork placement (supervision session), students should be encouraged to consider the differences and similarities between the purchase of a vacation and the purchase of services to help a person remain in the community.

NOTES FOR STUDENTS AND INSTRUCTORS

VARIATIONS

There is a variety of ways that this simulation can be modified to affect the issues considered by students. Different factors can be introduced into the vacation, such as the following:

- The safety or reliability of the travel agency (dice could help here to make some vacations riskier than others—students could lose part or all of the vacation for which they have booked).

- Service users and providers often have little real or effective choice, and students can experience this by having another student choose the vacation they think is best for them, without consultation.

- The student can be placed in a position, akin to that of a manager, with responsibility for purchasing "block services," such that the student is given the responsibility as a travel manager for buying vacations in bulk to then sell to others.

USE BY OTHER PROFESSIONS

Effective management of resources is central to all human service professions—the activity can easily be used by other professions that allocate resources. It is often assumed that early intervention and delivery of services will produce significant benefits. Does early intervention lead to significant change or resources being taken from other parts of an overstretched system? Pelosi and Birchwood (2003) attempted to answer this question regarding early intervention for psychosis. Therefore, by analogy, is it better to buy your vacation early and, if so, are you guaranteed that you would find the holiday of choice? On the other hand, if you buy the vacation later, do you get a bargain because the travel agent still has some left?

EDUCATIONAL POLICY ACCREDITATION STANDARDS

The topics in this chapter relate to the following *Educational Policy and Accreditation Standards (EPAS)* 2008 Primary Core Competencies (Council on Social Work Education, 2008):

1. Apply critical thinking to inform and communicate professional judgments.

2. Engage in policy practice to advance social and economic well-being and to deliver effective social work services.

3. Respond to contexts that shape practice.

4. Engage, assesses, intervene, and evaluate with individuals, families, groups, organizations, and communities.

FOR STUDENTS AND INSTRUCTORS

ACTIVITY 10: *TRAVEL AGENT*

Read the following extracts from vacation brochures and decide which vacation you would like to purchase, taking account of your income. Your choice will be influenced by a number of factors, such as the proportion of your budget you wish to spend on the vacation and the proportion this leaves you for spending money.

Discounts

Vacations are cheaper if you can share with another; if you want to negotiate with a fellow vacationer to share a vacation, you will both benefit from a 20% reduction (i.e., there will be a commensurate increase in your spending money—indicated in italics).

Note that Vacation G is a half-chance lottery: a 50% chance of your name coming up.

*A = Access for disabled people

*G = Guaranteed by the International League of Travel Agents

Vacation A: New York *A (4 days from $739)

Vacation features:

- Classic hotel or premium hotel
- Day 1: Arrive in New York; the remainder of day is at your leisure.
- Days 2 and 3: Two full days at your leisure to use your New York Pass. On one evening attend Broadway show.
- Day 4: Departure from New York
- Times Square, Greenwich Village, Wall Street, Empire State Building, cruise around Statue of Liberty and Central Park

Vacation B: The Best of Nova Scotia and New Brunswick Explorer *A (8 days/7 nights: Montreal, Halifax, Moncton)

Vacation features:

- 6 nights hotel accommodation
- 1 night onboard VIA Rail's Ocean in Easterly class from Montreal to Halifax; 1 breakfast and dinner
- VIA Rail in comfort class from Halifax-Moncton
- Tours of Halifax, Peggy's cove. Lunenburg and Le pays de la Sanguine lunch
- Three-day mid-size car rental with National historic sites pass
- Admissions to Kouchibouguac National Park, Hopewell Rocks, Fundy National Park, Fort Beasuejour, and Monument Lefebvre

Peak Season			
EuroPlan	Twin	Single	Triple
Deluxe	$1,465	$2,367	$1,277
Moderate	$1,325	$1,982	$989

Vacation C: Cross Canada *A (9 days/8 nights: Toronto, Edmonton, Jasper, Vancouver)

Vacation features:

- 5 nights hotel accommodation
- 3 nights on VIA rails Canadian in Silver and blue class between Toronto-Vancouver; all aboard meals
- Sightseeing excursions: Ice field Parkway, Edmonton City Tour
- Brewster Glacier Experience at the Columbia Ice field
- Admissions: CN tower, World Water Park, Galaxy Land, Jasper Sky tram

Priced from $1,800			
Spring Season			
EuroPlan	Twin	Single	Triple
Deluxe	$2,317	$2,976	$2,151
Moderate	$1,800	$2,229	$1,684
Summer Season			
EuroPlan	Twin	Single	Triple
Deluxe	$3,372	$4,287	$3,121
Moderate	$2,541	$3,074	$2,390
Autumn Season			
EuroPlan	Twin	Single	Triple
Deluxe	$3,116	$3,774	$2,950
Moderate	$2,436	$2,865	$2,320

Vacation D: Parks and Lodges of the Classic West (10 days from $2,339)

Vacation features:

- Day 1: Arrive in Rapid City
- Day 2: Rapid City, Badlands National Park, Custer State Park
- Day 3: Custer State Park
- Day 4: Custer State Park, Deadwood
- Day 5: Deadwood, U-Cross Ranch, Cody

- Day 6: Cody, Yellowstone National Park
- Day 7: Yellowstone National Park
- Day 8: Yellowstone National Park, Grand Teton National Park, Jackson
- Day 9: Jackson
- Day 10: Depart Jackson

Vacation E: Spectacular Alaska *A (10 days from $2,399)

Vacation features:

- Day 1: Anchorage
- Day 2: Anchorage, Valdez
- Day 3: Valdez, Cruise on Prince William Sound
- Day 4: Valdez, Delta Junction, Fairbanks
- Day 5: Fairbanks
- Day 6: Fairbanks, Denali National Park
- Day 7: Denali National Park
- Day 8: Denali National Park, Anchorage
- Day 9: Anchorage, cruise in Knai Fjords National Park
- Day 10: Anchorage

Vacation F: Treasures of the Yucatan (8 days from $1,729)

Vacation features:

- Day 1: Arrive Cancun, Mexico
- Day 2: Cancun, Tulum, Coba, Chichen Itza
- Day 3: Chichen Itza
- Day 4: Chichen Itza, Izamal, Uxmal
- Day 5: Uxmal, Kabah, Merida
- Day 6: Merida
- Day 7: Merida, Ek Balam, Valladolid, Cancun
- Day 8: Depart Cancun

Vacation G: Leisurely Ireland *A (9 days from $1,439)

Vacation features:

- Day 1: Overnight transatlantic flight
- Day 2: Shannon, Limerick
- Day 3: Limerick, Killarney
- Day 4: Killarney. Excursion to Garnish Ireland and Ring of Kerry
- Day 5: Killarney. Dingle Peninsula Excursion

- Day 6: Killarney, Dublin
- Day 7: Dublin
- Day 8: Dublin-Wicklow Excursion
- Day 9: Depart Dublin

Vacation H: Taste of Australia and New Zealand *A (18 days)

Vacation features:

- Day 1: Welcome to Australia
- Day 2: Melbourne city highlights
- Day 3: Phillip Island
- Day 4: Melbourne, Cairns/Palm Cove
- Day 5: Great Barrier Reef
- Day 6: Palm Cove
- Day 7: Cairns, Sydney
- Day 8: Sydney city sightseeing
- Day 9: Blue Mountains National Park
- Day 10: Sydney, Christchurch
- Day 11: Christchurch city highlights
- Day 12: Christchurch, Mount Cook, Queenstown
- Day 13: Queenstown
- Day 14: Milford Sound cruise
- Day 15: Queenstown, Rotorua
- Day 16: Rotorua sightseeing
- Day 17: Rotorua, Waitomo Caves, Auckland
- Day 18: Auckland city sights and departure

	Double	Single
Standard	$3,159	$4,349
First Class	$3,509	$5,189
Deluxe	$4,235	$6,639

NOTES FOR INSTRUCTORS

TEACHING ABOUT MANAGING RESOURCES

Complaints about the shortage of resources are commonly heard in social work agencies—indeed, across the social work profession generally. Students should be encouraged to hear these voices, whether they originate with other professionals, service users, local officials, or politicians. Although these complaints are frequently made, it is important for students to evaluate their validity. Are resources really insufficient? Could they be put to better use? In all agencies, the day-to-day business of providing social work will highlight many examples that illustrate how resources are prioritized. These can all be used to provide good opportunities for reflection and learning.

Travel Agent is an activity that simulates some aspects of choosing a vacation. At first sight, this seems far removed from social work practice; however, the factors that influence the selection of a vacation are similar to some aspects of choice available about services for those living in the community.

Key Influences on a Vacation Choice

No matter which route we take to choose a vacation, certain factors are likely to influence our final decision. The importance of each of these factors will vary from individual to individual and family to family. A disabled person might first look first at accessibility and then have to take his or her budget into consideration. A well-to-do family might look at available entertainment for the children, with less concern for price. Below are some of the factors that may apply when choosing a vacation; these should be discussed with the student during the fieldwork seminar or supervisory session.

- Access
- Availability
- Budget
- Climate
- Convenience
- Diet
- Entertainment
- Facilities
- Lifestyle
- Location
- Price
- Quality of service
- Time of year

Encourage students to think about the relative importance of these factors in making their decision about the vacation they have chosen. Broaden the discussion so that students consider the importance of vacations relative to a service that a person may be dependent upon for their well-being on a day-to-day basis, such as home care, meals at home, washing and bathing, respite, or permanent residential care.

Students should also consider the possible kinds of information they would expect to have available to guide their choice:

- Choice of travel agents for independent advice
- Information direct from travel agencies (the providers of vacations)
- Online information services to provide updated information about availability and price
- Ability to negotiate directly with the hotel or vacation resort
- Information available at no charge
- Detailed brochures available about a variety of vacations throughout the world
- Availability of many different types of vacation
- Varying levels and packages of insurance (concerning cancellation, theft, loss and medical costs, the company's liability, etc.)
- Procedures for complaints

Students can think about the similarities and differences inherent in the process of selecting a vacation and "choosing" a care package. People choosing vacations are able to decide independently, to book directly with the company, and to purchase the service they require; they are not obliged to consult a travel agent. Compare this with the process of gaining access to social work services when the person has to consult an "agent" (a social worker or particular agency).

How far are similar facilities and options open to the person who is making choices about care in the community?

NOTES FOR STUDENTS

Learning About Managing Resources

Case Management

According to Barker (2003, p. 58) case management is a procedure to plan, seek, and monitor services from a variety of agencies and staff on behalf of a client. Usually one agency takes primary responsibility for the client and assigns a case manager, who coordinates services, advocates for the client, and sometimes controls resources and purchases services for the client. As with our vacations and travel agencies, the emphasis is on the service users themselves, that indeed the responsibility of the professional is to work on behalf of the service user.

Similar themes are expressed in the 1975 United Nations (UN) Declaration of Rights for Disabled People, which emphasizes the importance of being self-reliant, to have choice over how to live, and to be able to participate in social, recreational, and creative opportunities of communities. However, the real question is not one of principle about desirability but how to achieve the UN Declaration of Rights or Barker's prescriptions in practice, within existing political and social structures.

Case management makes it possible for many social workers in the agency or different agencies to coordinate their efforts for a service user through professional teamwork, thus expanding the range of services offered. Indeed, the National Association of Social Workers (NASW, 1982, p. 17) has conceptualized social work practice as having four major goals:

1. Enhance the problem-solving, coping, and developmental capacities of people.

2. Link people with systems that provide them with resources, services, and opportunities.

3. Promote the effectiveness and humane operation of systems that provide people with resources and services.

4. Develop and improve social policy.

Realizing these goals relies, to a considerable extent, upon the adoption of a *strengths perspective.* Simply put, social workers help people solve problems. However, to do this effectively, the social worker must focus on the *strengths* of service users. According to Kirst-Ashman (2007, p. 58), focusing on the service user's strengths provides social workers with clues about how to proceed by building on these strengths. Strengths perspectives are closely related to a concept of empowerment, which has been defined by Barker (2003, p. 142) as the process of helping individuals, families, groups, and communities to increase their personal, interpersonal, socioeconomic, and political strength and to develop influence toward improving their circumstances. This is central to case management.

According to Rose (1992), there are five components associated with case management: needs assessment, service or treatment planning, linking or referring, monitoring, and advocacy. These are briefly reviewed.

Component 1: Needs Assessment

The purpose of needs assessment is to gain a broader picture of the problem or issue at hand. For example, if you were looking to provide services for elders in your community, at the core of the assessment would be a requirement to look beyond the individual and examine other impinging factors within the service user's environment. For example, how many elders live in the area, how many live on their own, how many live in retirement communities or nursing homes, and what are the services they require (e.g., additional medical services, transportation issues, day care centers, home care assistants, visiting nurses)? All of these components, and more, should be considered in an attempt to meet the needs of the service user *in the community*.

Component 2: Service or Treatment Planning

Service or treatment planning specifies what should be done. For example, the social worker and the service user should work together and prioritize the problems so that the most critical ones are addressed first. The social worker should help the service user evaluate the pros and cons of each course of action.

Component 3: Linking or Referring

Linking or referring is part of the process where the social worker makes referrals on behalf of their service user. For example, if a service user has a substance abuse problem, the social worker would refer the service user to an inpatient program or outpatient program. If a patient is being discharged from hospital, the social worker will attempt to ensure that all necessary services are available upon discharge.

Component 4: Monitoring

Monitoring is the process of determining whether a given change effort was worthwhile (Kirst-Ashman & Hull, 2001, p. 322). Social workers need to be accountable; that is, they must prove that their interventions have been effective. Each goal must be evaluated in terms of the extent to which it has been achieved.

Component 5: Advocacy

Ideally, services will be provided for service users when they are needed. At times, service users are placed on the agency's waiting list, or the agency's eligibility requirements are rigidly interpreted in a way that do not fit the uniqueness of a particular service user's situation. In these cases, the social worker may become an advocate for the service user and make appeals to an agency in order that the service user can obtain needed services.

Successful Organizations

In addition to the requirement that an individual social worker is competent, the social service organization also needs to be competent, efficient, and effective in order for the service user to receive necessary and appropriate services.

According to King, Fowler, and Zeithaml (2001, p. 106), there are five characteristics that successful social work agencies have:

1. They have a proven way of sharing work-related competencies with all workers so that high-level practice is sustained.

2. Worker competencies are retained during organizational and management changes.

3. Competencies are not lost when key workers or managers leave the organization.

4. Competencies are maintained and used when the nature of the service provided changes.

5. The values and mission of the organization are strengthened during periods of organizational change.

These characteristics contribute to the effective delivery of case management systems. Successful management needs to identify the competencies that lead to good practice and high organizational delivery of service, note those workers and supervisors who function competently, and move the organization in a direction that is defined by high-level practice for effective case management.

Resources and Change

WE TRAINED VERY HARD, BUT IT SEEMED THAT EVERY TIME WE WERE BEGINNING TO FORM INTO TEAMS WE WOULD BE REORGANIZED. I WAS TO LEARN LATER IN LIFE THAT WE TRIED TO MEET ANY NEW SITUATION BY REORGANIZING, AND A WONDERFUL METHOD IT WAS FOR CREATING THE ILLUSION OF PROGRESS WHILST PRODUCING CONFUSION, INEFFICIENCY AND DEMORALIZATION.

Petronius; 166 AD

The ground is continually shifting: Just when it seems as if we might have grasped the processes for managing resources, we find ourselves in a changed world. Moreover, the process of change is itself *changing*. Stanley (2002, p. 12) states that many management theorists believe that organizations that are underperforming need change that can be "wrenching, revolutionary and extremely painful." Rather, he believes that change should be pursued in a far more thoughtful and "plan-full" manner.

> Take the go-slow approach. They are steady, well-grounded and do not rush to embrace the latest fad. They change in order to bring about meaningful improvements that will increase productivity and profitability. Effective change is managed with attention toward making full use of all resources. When change is undertaken with an eye toward increased efficiency, it can be a gigantic motivating force. Architects of change bring down-to-earth decision making process to the multifaceted challenges that face every organization today. (Stanley, 2002, p. 12)

Many organizations embark upon unneeded change, when it takes place for the sake of change. This is not good practice and can result in a series of unintended consequences.

Managing Your Time

Your own time is one of the most important resources at your disposal. Yet the skills of managing time are not intuitive; they can be learned. A field placement can start to go wrong if field instructors make incorrect assumptions about students' basic abilities to organize their own time. Successful time management is the first step to managing the workload. It can seem pedantic to investigate how you remember the tasks you have set yourself or how you collect and store information for regular use. Perhaps this is one reason why these core abilities are often assumed to be present; they are the day-to-day backdrop to the "real work."

At the beginning of the fieldwork placement, you should share with your fieldwork supervisor a copy of your fieldwork manual. In the BSW or MSW fieldwork manual, direct your supervisor to the section that discusses some of the following:

- Journal writing
- Agency profile
- Learning agreement
- Personal reflections

- Mid-semester field experience check-in
- Community Resource Index
- Attendance sheet

This is not an exhaustive list, and perhaps your school or department uses different terminology. The purpose, though, is for you and your fieldwork supervisor to enter into a *joint conversation* about what are some of your expectations and those of the school, the fieldwork supervisor, the agency, and the clients. Indeed, some of these might be requirements of your fieldwork placement.

The following scenario, about Angelina and Carlos, is also a valuable learning tool that can be used by you and your fieldwork instructor:

Two students, Angelina and Carlos, were on placement in a small social work team. They met to discuss how they had arrived at their decisions about managing their own time. These principles came out of their discussion with the field instructor.

   1. Be clear about the status of each diary entry—is it tentative or definite?

"Can you tell at a glance what you're doing on Thursday at 2:30?" Angelina and Carlos confessed to making frequent scribbles and deletions; Angelina suggested using pencil until it was confirmed. "Some feasts are movable and some aren't."

   2. Prioritize diary entries according to urgency and others' expectations.

"Are you aware of the criteria you use to plan your diary time?" Angelina and Carlos had both used urgency as their main priority. Whose circumstances warranted contact early in the week and what promises, if any, had been made about contacting people? They had made very similar decisions about this and expressed pleasure at their like minds.

   3. Pace appointments economically.

"What about the space you've allowed between diary entries?" Angelina and Carlos were conscious of working in a neighborhood and were committed to the localization of services. They were careful to group their destinations to avoid either zipping back and forth across the map or twiddling their thumbs between appointments. They had taken account of their method of transport— car in Angelina's case, foot and public transportation in Carlos's.

4. Consider what times will accommodate other people involved in the work.

"Have you considered the use of other people's time?" Angelina and Carlos had thought about the circumstances of individuals and their families when planning appointments. Nine in the morning might be convenient to visit 83-year-old Mr. Cook but was not a time Mr. Cook would welcome. Planning a first visit to a family around school collection time or mealtimes was not wise either. Angelina liked Carlos's suggestion of an evening appointment to include a working parent, and both students had scheduled their diary to accommodate part-time and job share staff.

5. Anticipate the unanticipated by building dual-purpose times into the diary.

"How do you cope with unexpected work that disrupts your program?" Angelina and Carlos developed a metaphor that they had found useful in planning their diary time. A diary can be made of cast iron, netting, or elastic. A cast iron diary is unlikely to be able to respond to new demands; on the other hand, the holes in a diary made of netting are liable to see appointments falling through. Ideally, the elastic diary has a mix of firm appointments and dual-purpose times, which are scheduled for one purpose (e.g., reading a policy paper or making non-priority phone calls) but can stretch or contract for other purposes if necessary.

6. Anticipate the "imprint effect."

"What effect is the experience of one event likely to have on the next?" After the first few weeks of the placement, events in the working week are more familiar, so students can anticipate their aftertaste. For example, Angelina and Carlos could say whether the working party was likely to leave them feeling stimulated/bored, appreciated/isolated, or calm/angry. It is often possible to anticipate how you will feel visiting service users or providers that you already know. Using this information, it is possible to obtain the most "helpful mix" of diary entries—in theory!

7. Appointments with myself.

"What helps you to keep your batteries topped up?" The most difficult aspect of the diary for Angelina and Carlos was planning a regular hour's break each day and setting aside time for professional development when they could pursue their own research interests and keep abreast of developments in social work. These tended to be given the lowest priority and were readily swallowed up; yet, a midday swim and time for professional development were crucial to survival and avoiding burnout. They both agreed to pen, not pencil, "appointments with themselves."

If, as a student, you use these principles clearly, coherently, and consistently, you can feel confident that you are gaining command of your workload and you are helping to reduce the stresses of the job. It is much more important to *work smart, not hard.*

ASSESSING YOUR LEARNING

You need to be clear where the limits of your responsibility for managing resources lie and to reflect this in any assessment task for your portfolio of assessed work. Clearly, for most students, managing resources such as your own time is likely to be more of a priority than the management of high-profile agency resources. It is likely that you will have some responsibility for the management for some resources, such as your own time, from your earliest fieldwork opportunity. You will be expected to demonstrate your competence in using time constructively throughout the practice learning. In addition, you will be expected to demonstrate that you understand the difficulties of managing resources from the managers' perspectives and, most important, how the constraints that managers face affect the nature of choice for service users and providers. Acknowledging the worldview of the organization is not necessarily to accept it and certainly should not obscure the service users' views of the way in which resources are managed. You will be expected, therefore, to demonstrate that you understand the implications of resource management from a variety of perspectives.

FURTHER READING

Barker, R. L. (2003). *The social work dictionary* (5th ed.). Washington, DC: NASW.

Kirst-Ashman, K. K., & Hull, Jr. G. H. (2001). *Generalist practice with organizations and communities* (2nd ed.). Pacific Grove: CA: Brooks/Cole/ Thompson.

Rose, S. M. (1992). *Case management and social work practice.* New York, NY: Longman.

Stanley, T. L. (2002). Architects of change: A new role for managers. *Supervision,* 63(10), 10–14.

CHAPTER 11

Accountability

ABOUT ACTIVITY 11: *HELD TO ACCOUNT*

There are different mechanisms by which social workers can be held accountable to service users and providers, colleagues, and the wider society for their actions. This exercise focuses on exploring these mechanisms through which accountability can be made effective.

NOTES FOR INSTRUCTORS[1]

PURPOSE

This activity helps the student to think critically about the extent to which professionals can be held to account for their actions by their agencies, board of directors, grantees, supervisors, service users, and providers. In addition, students are encouraged to explore the mechanisms that are used to hold professionals to account and also how the ideal differs from the reality.

METHOD

This activity can be completed by a fieldwork supervisor and student jointly or by a field instructor/practice teacher and a group of students. A group of students who are placed in different kinds of settings produce a variety of perspectives.

Each person needs a copy of *Held to Account*. The activity can be used without prior preparation, or students can be given a copy of the activity in advance of the supervision session.

---

[1]See the Introduction to the book for suggestions about how instructors and students can, separately and together, use the activities in this book.

NOTES FOR STUDENTS AND INSTRUCTORS

VARIATIONS

Held to Account presents students with a series of examples where service users and providers might wish to find ways to hold social workers to account. Different scenarios can be developed and used in place of those suggested, for example, to explore the particular accountability issues in any given learning environment. You can also ask students to consider how other professionals are held to account (e.g., Dr. Thomas in one of the scenarios below).

USE BY OTHER PROFESSIONS

Increasing demands for greater professional accountability are not restricted to professionals working in the field of social work. For example, professional practitioners in education and health care have experienced similar pressures to be more accountable for their actions. An increasing emphasis on program evaluation in health and human service agencies is evident due to the impact of "managed care" (Rubin & Babbie, 2008). The term *managed care* has been defined in various ways and refers to a variety of arrangements that try to control the costs of health and human services. Care providers are willing to reduce the costs because the organizations pay for services for a great number of people. Providers are willing to meet the reduced cost demands of the large organizations so they will be eligible to have the cost of their services covered and thus get more referrals of clients covered under their managed care plans. Some common types of managed health care organizations are health maintenance organizations (HMOs), preferred provider organizations (PPOs), and employee assistance programs (EAPs).

Managed care is controversial. For-profit managed care organizations have been criticized for caring more about their shareholders' profits than about whether clients are really getting all the care they need (Levitt et al., 1999). Having insurance companies decide how much care is needed has resulted in a number of incidents where clients/patients are denied care for services that they deemed unnecessary but may well have been required. Over the past several years, these stories have become regular items on the evening news programs and in the daily newspapers. Nonetheless, it appears that *managed care programs* will be part of human services for the foreseeable future.

Managed care companies increasingly stipulate completion of standardized outcome instruments that have demonstrable reliability and validity (Mullen & Magnabosco, 1997). Even when standardized instruments are used, outcomes still tend to be measured in the context of simple pretest/posttest designs. Single-case evaluation designs have been proposed (Bloom, Fischer, & Orme, 2006; Corcoran & Gingerich, 1994; Johnson, Beckerman, & Auerbach, 2002) as one way to strengthen the assessment of client outcomes that fits well both with the expectations of managed care companies as well as the resource and time constraints of direct service practitioners and that, in addition, leads to the promotion of accountability.

Whatever designs direct service providers use to document their effectiveness to managed care companies, those program providers have a vested interest in reporting results that make their service look effective, as funding for their services is determined by demonstrable program effectiveness.

> *It would be prudent for students and fieldwork supervisors and fieldwork instructors to look at Part IV—the Social Worker as Researcher—in conjunction with this chapter.*

EDUCATIONAL POLICY ACCREDITATION STANDARDS

The topics in this chapter relate to the following *Educational Policy and Accreditation Standards (EPAS)* 2008 Primary Core Competencies (Council on Social Work Education, 2008):

1. Identify as a professional social worker and conduct oneself accordingly.

2. Apply social work ethical principles to guide professional practice.

3. Apply critical thinking to inform and communicate professional judgments.

4. Engage in research-informed practice and practice-informed research.

5. Engage, assesses, intervene, and evaluate with individuals, families, groups, organizations, and communities.

FOR STUDENTS AND INSTRUCTORS

ACTIVITY 11: *HELD TO ACCOUNT*

This activity draws on Chapter 1, Activity 1, *Permission to Learn* (p. 29). Three of the people who you met in the first chapter are service users in your placement, and the following issues present you with concerns that relate to accountability and access to information.

1. *Carefully consider the following additional information about three of the Greenhill apartment residents:*

Zoë Benner returns to her children's home 2 years after leaving and asks to see her records—having expressed some concerns about her treatment while living at the home. During the placement, you have read some past files, and these confirm your view that they contain very subjective, often destructive, opinions. Some of these workers are still employed in the home, but others have left. You are not sure about the department's policy on past files. At the staff meeting, Zoë's request is discussed. What's your view?

Sam Weiner is a regular visitor to the mental health day center where you are on placement. One morning he arrives very angry because he has caught sight of his notes at the local hospital (he opened the blue envelope carrying information about him from one department to another). He is being treated for a viral infection, and the notes from the consultant to the laboratory describe him as "a homosexual and a drug addict." Sam is openly gay but does not see this is relevant, and although he took an overdose in the past, he has not been dependent on drugs. Sam wants to know what he can do about this and what you can do to help.

Dr. Thomas, a psychiatrist at the local hospital that serves Greenhill apartments, writes a report to you about Avis Jenkins, who is about to be discharged following her admission 4 weeks ago, suffering from delusions that may or may not be a symptom of her physical health. Dr. Thomas states at the bottom of his letter that he does not wish Mrs. Jenkins to see the report because it might provoke a recurrence of her delusional state. What do you do?

---

2. *Prioritize these requests. In which order would you respond to these situations?*

Remember you will be held to account for your decisions, both by your managers and by service users and providers. You must be able to justify your decision, remembering that a personal preference for work with one kind of situation is not a justification (see Chapter 9—there is a considerable overlap between accountability and priorities).

3. *Consider how, in an ideal world, you would like to respond to these situations.*

Compare what you could actually do in your practice agency with what you would like to do by writing five key points that refer to each of these situations. Then, with your fieldwork supervisor or faculty instructor, explore the reasons for any differences between the ideal and reality.

The ideal	*The actual*
Zoë Benner	**Zoë Benner**
1	*1*
2	*2*
3	*3*
4	*4*
5	*5*
Sam Weiner	**Sam Weiner**
1	*1*
2	*2*
3	*3*
4	*4*
5	*5*
Avis Jenkins	**Avis Jenkins**
1	*1*
2	*2*
3	*3*
4	*4*
5	*5*

NOTES FOR INSTRUCTORS

TEACHING ABOUT ACCOUNTABILITY

Addressing issues of accountability at an early stage of the period of practice learning may seem premature, and you certainly need to avoid frightening the student unnecessarily. Nonetheless, students will want to advise people accurately about their rights in relation to the agency's responsibilities. There is a parallel with the preparations for the student's own fieldwork placement; is everybody clear about the procedures if there is disagreement or things go wrong? For example, if you have concerns about the student's competence or your student is dissatisfied with your availability to give supervision, is there a clear path to be followed? Similarly, students need to be able to advise service users and providers.

One way to encourage students to think about accountability is to encourage them to consider how they keep records—a very visible sign of being accountable. A good way for students to test whether they are making fair, accurate, and concise records of their work is to share these with service users and providers (Doel & Lawson, 1986). Through the dynamic use of records, students can demonstrate their accountability (except in a few of the most sensitive cases, usually concerning child protection investigations or mental health assessments for formal admission to hospital where agency policy may preclude the explicit sharing). The student receives immediate feedback from the service user and provider, both about the recording (use of language, etc.) and the work itself. The student and the service user or provider get to check out whether they are working along the same lines because it is hard to fudge the record. They are demonstrating mutual accountability.

OPPORTUNITIES FOR ACCOUNTABILITY

Initially, many students may think about "accountability" in terms of themselves (i.e., for what can they be held to account). To introduce students to the complex notion of accountability, it is helpful to take a real-world approach that can be used to illustrate the interaction between personal and institutional accountability. From the point of registration as a social work student to the point of qualification, issues of accountability arise through direct practice, the need to know about legislation, and professional requirements of state licensing boards, the National Association of Social Workers (NASW), the Council on Social Work Education (CSWE), and the International Federation of Social Workers (IFSW).

NOTES FOR STUDENTS

LEARNING ABOUT ACCOUNTABILITY

There is broad consensus about how to define and understand the notion of accountability. Clark (2000) states that

> accountability is an intrinsic part of collaboration. It refers first to the requirement upon a professional to perform her duties, in collaboration with colleagues, to the expected standard. Second it requires the professional to demonstrate the performance to the appropriate individuals, colleagues and authorities. (p. 60)

While DuBois and Miley (2005) assert that

> accountability means that social workers must be competent in their methods and techniques they employ in their professional practice. They need to take seriously their obligation to redress discriminatory and inhumane practices, act with unquestionable professional integrity, and implement sound practice and research methods. (p. 131)

Helpfully, Bamford (1982, p. 125) identifies five different forms of accountability in the context of social work:

- Personal accountability
- Accountability to the employer
- Accountability to other agencies
- Public accountability
- Accountability to the client [i.e., *service user and provider*][2]

To these, one might add the notions of "professional accountability" and "legal accountability." We will use these different forms of accountability as a framework to explore the notion further.

Personal Accountability

We are accountable to ourselves and to others for the way that we conduct our affairs: This accountability may be expressed in various ways such as through religious commitment to a moral code or through a secular commitment to treat others as they would wish to be treated themselves, perhaps most famously expressed in the categorical imperative (Kant, 1785). Alternatively,

---

[2]Italics added.

our behavior may also depend on the outcomes (as in utilitarianism) rather than motive or adherence to a moral code.

Accountability to the Employer

Employees are accountable to their employers for work undertaken as part of their role and duties. It is for the employee to adhere to any codes of conduct that the employer may require. A range of employment legislation, different in all countries, exists to protect employers from abusing the position that they hold. Employers may not require or expect that employees be asked to perform illegal or immoral acts as part of their employment. When joining an organization, as student, for a period of practice learning, it is essential to keep to the rules and requirements expected of employees. Accountability to the employer is perhaps the most visible form of accountability.

Accountability to Other Agencies

The existence of the mixed economy of welfare has had many consequences for practitioners, service users, and providers alike. One of the most clearly evident has been the fragmentation of service delivery. There are now many more service providers than previously, both in the not-for-profit and the private sectors. At an institutional or governmental level, the fragmented character of service delivery, whatever the desired ideological characteristics, is problematic in the context of ensuring that service providers are publicly accountable for the quality of service they provide. Sullivan (2003) has suggested that it is necessary to move away from traditional notions of public accountability where one central body (i.e., government) holds others to account—so-called vertical accountability. Instead, it is important to adopt "horizontal" accountability mechanisms, whereby locally based organizations join in mutually interactive accountability structures—something that, nonetheless, requires local government to adopt a strong coordination role. An example of how to develop a "horizontal" approach to neighborhood-based governance through the relationships and participatory mechanisms evident in various community organizations in three cities was examined by Chaskin (2003). You might like to consider the extent to which local organizations are part of horizontal systems of accountability. To what extent are the organizations able to hold each other to account?

Public Accountability

Increasingly, federal and state governmental units and private funding sources are requiring that the effectiveness of service programs be measured. Programs found to be ineffective are being phased out. The profession has an obligation to those that provide funding to provide the highest quality of services. Hence, social workers need to become skilled at evaluating their effectiveness in providing services. A wide variety of evaluation techniques are now available to assess the effectiveness of current services and to identify unmet needs and service gaps (Zastrow, 2008).

One approach to ensure accountability is management by objectives (MBO). This technique involves identifying objectives for each program, specifying in measurable terms how and when these objectives are met. Many agencies are now requiring each of their workers, with the involvement of their clients, to (a) identify and specify what the goals will be for each client, (b) have the client and the worker write down in detail what each will do to accomplish the goals, and (c) assess the extent to which the goals have been achieved when the intervention is terminated (Zastrow, 2008). The achievement or not of these program goals can be an important mechanism to demonstrate accountability.

Accountability to Service Users and Providers

High-quality social work practice is founded on the notion that the social worker is accountable to service users and providers for the work done with them or on their behalf. In many professions, this accountability is direct, immediate, and individualized through the payment of fees. If the service users or providers are not satisfied with the service they receive, then they may go elsewhere. For example, in the United States, where there is a significant volume of private social work practice[3] (unlike many countries where service users and providers do not pay social workers), the service user has the option of terminating services with the social worker—an arrangement that is similar to which private physicians provide services to patients. Irrespective of whether accountability to service users and providers is mediated by money, it is essential that the social worker *feels* and *is* accountable to the service user or provider for the work done.

The mechanisms to provide for accountability to service users and providers are as follows:

- appeal mechanisms (i.e., to be able to appeal against a decision that has been made—for example, not to be awarded a place in a home for older people);
- complaints procedures (i.e., to be able to complain against the maladministration or delivery of services—for example, if a social worker repeatedly fails to make visits);

---

[3]Also called psychotherapy and group therapy on a fee basis.

- the provision of high-quality information (i.e., if service users and providers receive full and detailed information about what is done on their behalf and records are truly open, they are enabled to challenge the social worker and hold the social worker to account);
- statutory review mechanisms enacted through, for example, a children's rights commissioner (often termed an ombudsman) who will investigate complaints if these cannot be resolved at lower organizational levels;
- each state, the District of Columbia, Puerto Rico, the Virgin Islands, and every Canadian province have laws that define and regulate social work practice, involving some form of licensure or certification. A major purpose of licensing is to protect clients from unqualified service provides and maintain the legitimacy of the profession (Ginsberg, 2001).

We should be cautious in assuming that these mechanisms deliver anything but a flawed accountability to service users and providers. For example, Preston-Shoot (2001) has criticized the impact of complaints procedures under the title "A Triumph of Hope Over Experience?" The availability of such mechanisms does not in itself entail that they are accessible or can be used by service users and providers—it is incumbent upon social work agencies to develop approaches that enable service users and providers to make use of these mechanisms.

Me Holding Others to Account. To get a *feel* of the service user or provider perspective, you might like to consider how it feels to have records made about you. Your service users and providers are the subjects of the records that you write. You are the subject of many records, too. Make a note of all the different agencies that you know will have some form of written record about you (your doctor, your bank, etc.). Are there any agencies, which you suspect, will have some record but which about you are not sure? How could you find out what is written about you in these files? How could you hold these agencies to account?

Professional Accountability

Professional codes of ethics have been adopted by many national professional social work associations—for example, NASW (1999) and CSWE (2008) and, at an international level, the IFSW (2003). Such codes present, to the external world, a consensus about how the membership of an organization defines the nature and purpose of social work and the professional obligation to the broader society. Moreover, such codes indicate desired behavior by professional social workers and specify prohibited behavior. As such, they provide a form of accountability on a geographically bounded context, as these codes vary from country to country (for a comparison of the United States and England, see Reamer & Shardlow, 2009).

Legal Accountability

In the United States, there is considerable concern in professional circles about the extent to which social workers may be held legally liable. The NASW website (www.naswassurance.org/social_worker_professional_liability.php?page_id=11) advertises professional liability insurance that covers the following eventualities:

- Treatment without proper consent
- Incorrect treatment/improper diagnosis
- Failure to consult with or refer a client to a specialist
- Failure to prevent a client's suicide
- Causing a client's suicide
- Failure to protect third parties from harm
- Inappropriate release/detainment of a client in a hospital, confinement
- Sexual involvement with clients or other sexual misconduct (subject to reduced limits)
- Breach of confidentiality
- Defamation
- False imprisonment
- Failure to provide adequate care for clients in residential settings
- Failure to be available when needed
- Termination of treatment
- Improper child placement

In other countries, social workers may be less likely to be held legally liable and to be sued at law for professional actions that are taken in the course of their work. However, it behooves all practitioners to consider carefully the nature of the society in which they practice and the extent of liability that they face.

ASSESSING YOUR LEARNING

Accountability is about a commitment to connectedness with others and also a demonstration of the extent and nature of that commitment through a range of formal mechanisms.

If, as a student, you believe that you can "go it alone" or that you don't need much help from others, then you may be in danger of thinking that you are only accountable to yourself—to your own well-developed moral conscience. If you tend toward these feelings, you need to consider very carefully your commitment to being fully accountable to others.

Accountability is about engagement with others and your willingness to explain to others what you are doing and why you are doing it. This may be demonstrated through examples of your practice where you have made service users and providers fully aware of their rights—for example, by providing information about how decisions made by your organization may be legitimately reviewed.

Remember that in terms of your practice as a student, your fieldwork supervisor may very well be legally liable and accountable for the actions that you perform in your direct work with service users or providers (Gelman, Pollack, & Auerbach, 1996; Gelman & Wardell, 1988; Reamer, 1994; Shardlow, 2000)—not a matter to be taken lightly.

FURTHER READING

Bloom, M., Fischer, J., & Orme, J. G. (2006). *Evaluating practice: Guidelines for the accountable professional* (5th ed.). Boston, MA: Allyn & Bacon.

Rubin, A., & Babbie, E. (2008). *Research methods for social work* (6th ed.). Belmont, CA: Brooks/Cole/ Thompson.

Zastrow, C. (2008). *Introduction to social work and social welfare* (9th ed.). Belmont, CA: Brooks/Cole/ Thompson.

CHAPTER 12

Challenging Situations and Resolving Conflicts

Dial "D" for Danger consists of six different scenarios, which students rank according to the perceived level of difficulty and risk for the service user or others. By taking account of this ranking of levels and types of difficulty and risk, students can explore their propensity to intervene in given types of professional situation.

NOTES FOR INSTRUCTORS[1]

PURPOSE

Dial "D" for Danger is intended to help students explore the complex issues involved where social work practice is at the crossroads of caring for people and seeking to control some aspects of their lives.

METHOD

Before undertaking this activity, you will need to copy the dials on page 189. This consists of six dials of dangerousness and six dials of intervention.

---

[1]See the Introduction to the book for suggestions about how instructors and students can, separately and together, use the activities in this book.

Dial "D" for Danger is best completed by a group of students and the fieldwork instructor working together, although it can be used by a supervisor-student pair. Give the students the list of case scenarios (p. 29), and ask them to rank these vignettes according to the dial of dangerousness (about 10 minutes). Then, ask the students to indicate their propensity to intervene (a further 10 minutes).

If you are working with a group of students, you can encourage them to discuss why they have made their particular risk-ranking decisions and to explore the reasons for their propensity to intervene in any given situation.

NOTES FOR STUDENTS AND INSTRUCTORS

VARIATIONS

You may find it is better to devise your own distinctive scenarios to fit with the nature of practice in your own fieldwork agency; for example, if the student is placed in a children and family setting/team, you may wish to create vignettes that relate only to these kinds of situations. Alternatively, you could use the scenarios derived from the information about the residents of Derby Street (Chapter 1, p. 29). However, as we have stated before, the value of situations that differ from the placement setting cannot be overemphasized.

Dial "D" for Danger can be completed independently by students and used as an exercise for discussion in your fieldwork seminar or in supervision.

USE BY OTHER PROFESSIONS

All professionals have to engage with risk: The airline pilot must decide whether the plane is safe to fly; the midwife must assess the level of risk involved in a particular birth plan chosen by an expectant mother. The nature and extent of risk encountered by each profession is different. Similarly, new developments in technological achievement, government policy, or social expectations change our conceptions of risk. For example, the federal government's response to the events in the global financial markets in 2008–2009 was to provide loans to major financial institutions. In this case, the risk taken by individual financial institutions has been effectively unwritten by government to avoid the collapse of the banking system due to excessive risk taking by some agents within the system such as market traders. For some, this intervention is justified; for others not. In either case, risk has been spread from individual institution to the state and taxpayer. Similarly, in health care, where there is a much debate about a major overhaul in the health care system in the United States, this turns on whether the individual should have to carry the risk paying for treatment for illness or whether the risks should be shared across a larger community. These developments have the potential to change societal views about the nature and desirability of risk taking (Institute of Medicine, 2001).

EDUCATIONAL POLICY ACCREDITATION STANDARDS

The topics in this chapter relate to the following *Educational Policy and Accreditation Standards (EPAS)* 2008 Primary Core Competencies (Council on Social Work Education, 2008):

1. Identify as a professional social worker and conduct oneself accordingly.
2. Apply social work ethical principles to guide professional practice.
3. Apply critical thinking to inform and communicate professional judgments.
4. Engage diversity and difference in practice.
5. Engage in research-informed practice and practice-informed research.
6. Apply knowledge of human behavior and the social environment.
7. Engage in policy practice to advance social and economic well-being and to deliver effective social work services.
8. Respond to contexts that shape practice.

FOR STUDENTS AND INSTRUCTORS

ACTIVITY 12: *DIAL "D" FOR DANGER*

Degree of Risk

Think about the following six vignettes and consider the following:

1. How challenging the situation is for the service user or for others
2. Your own willingness to intervene in each case

Propensity to Intervene

Taking account of your perception of the degree of risk in the situation, grade your willingness to intervene by rating from 1 (no inclination to intervene) to 12 (no option but to intervene).

Scenario 1

Gillandi is a 49-year-old woman who is a chronic alcoholic (and has been so for at least 10 years). She has a husband who is self-employed as a painter-decorator and two children, both young women ages 17 and 19. Recently, she has been drinking particularly heavily. There have been a series of incidents where she has almost injured herself or others. A week ago, she was almost run over by a car; 2 weeks ago, she allowed food to burn on the stove in the kitchen, causing a small fire in the kitchen.

Scenario 2

Winston, an African American man age 19, has been found guilty of several different crimes (including burglary and taking and driving cars) by the courts. He has been sentenced to 6 months' home-based curfew between the hours of 8 p.m. and 8 a.m. for 6 nights per week. During the first 3 months, he does not seek to break the curfew and spends the one night that his curfew is not in force working at a youth project for offenders. He is very well liked by all at the youth project. In the second part of the sentence, Winston continues with the work at the youth project and maintains his curfew except for one night each week. He is evasive and will not tell you what he is doing during that time. In all other respects, Winston is conforming to all of the court's expectations.

Scenario 3

Ruben is a well-educated White man in his 30s. About 2 years ago, he lost his job—one carrying considerable responsibilities with a large commercial enterprise. Since then, he has experienced financial difficulties, leading to the breakup of his marriage and loss of family home. He now lives on benefit in social housing. He is adamant that he can care for the two children, a boy age 6 and a girl age 8. The school has expressed some concerns about the children not being fed properly and arriving at school hungry.

Scenario 4

In the area served by your office, there is a large block of apartments managed by the housing authority. These apartments are in a poor state of repair and decoration. Many of the apartments are damp. No facilities exist for children to play, and there have been many muggings and attacks on local residents in the elevators and communal areas. There are several residents who wish to take action to improve the state of the apartments. One of the residents asks you to organize a public meeting to bring people together to take action about the condition of the apartments, but some of the other residents are not enthusiastic about involving social services.

Scenario 5

Patrick is a White 85-year-old, living on his own in a small apartment provided by the housing authority. For the past year, he has encountered difficulties in living on his own. Neighbors have complained to the local authority that his apartment is smelly and that there is trash accumulating inside and outside the apartment. On a visit to his apartment, he allows you to see the inside; it is in a chaotic condition. Patrick is obviously not eating properly, and the state of the kitchen is filthy. His clothes are dirty and smell. In conversation, his memory appears to you to be failing, yet he says he is content.

Scenario 6

Robert and Sally have moderate learning difficulties. They are both in their 20s and have married and set up home together in a local housing apartment. They are determined to be as independent as possible. They decide to have a baby and, just before the baby is due to be born, state to their social worker that they do not need the help of social services any longer now that they are to become parents themselves.

Dials of Dangerousness

Without consulting with anyone else, complete the following rankings for each of the vignettes listed in *Dial "D" for Danger*.

Figure 12.1	*Dial "D" for Danger*

The more dangerous you consider the example, the higher the ranking on the dial of dangerousness (minimal risk = 1; mild risk = 2/3; moderate risk = 5/6; considerable risk = 9/10; maximum risk = 12). The numbers in the center of the dials refer to the vignettes in the previous pages.

Dials of intervention

Taking account of your perception of the degree of risk in the situation, you should now grade your willingness to intervene by rating from 1 (no inclination to intervene) to 12 (no option but to intervene).

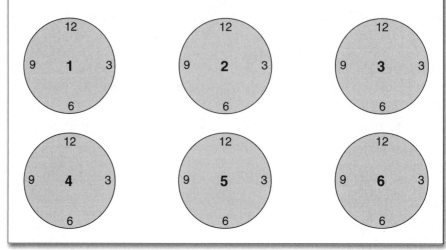

NOTES FOR INSTRUCTORS

TEACHING ABOUT CHALLENGING SITUATIONS

Dial "D" for Danger presents students with an apparently simple task—to categorize their propensity to intervene according to their perception of the degree of danger in a range of situations involving service users and carers. The degree of dangerousness and the propensity to intervene encourage students to compare two different dimensions of response to these situations. It might be assumed that a high degree of danger would have a correlation with a high propensity to intervene and therefore lead to intervention. However, we know that this is not the case (e.g., many women are in situations of extreme danger in domestic disputes, but this does not necessarily lead to a police presence); there is a wide range of factors that come into play. Encourage students to explore the reasons for their responses, using the following prompts if needed:

- Attitudes to taking control
- Cultural views about acceptable behavior
- Fears of making mistakes
- Fears about own safety
- Beliefs about the role of the social worker
- Confidence about professional judgment
- Knowledge of the legal context of social work practice

Ascertaining levels of risk is always a complex issue (Adams, 1995; Klassen & O'Connor, 1994; Newhill, 2003; Singleton & Holden, 1994). Students may identify that a situation has a high level of risk for one or more individuals but may be unsure of the grounds upon which they might intervene. Usually, powers of intervention will be defined by statute (see Chapter 14, this volume). Students can be encouraged to think about whether intervention in these situations is likely to be perceived by others as a demonstration of care or the imposition of control over the way that individuals conduct their lives—or a combination of both.

Example

Sue Shuk Wan had achieved a high level of competence in her first placement with children and families. Her second placement in an adult's team was proving a little more difficult. Sue's Chinese parents had moved to the United States when she was only 2. Brenda, her fieldwork supervisor, noticed that Sue found great difficulty in deciding when to intervene in the lives of older people. When Sue completed *Dial "D" for Danger,* she gave a very high dangerousness ranking to

Scenario 5, yet demonstrated a very low propensity to intervene. In discussion, she was reluctant to discuss her reasons, but it was clear to Brenda that Sue had difficulty with this scenario. No more was said at this point. A few weeks later, Brenda asked Sue to repeat the exercise with some specially created vignettes, all about older people. One of these concerned the situation of an older Chinese woman living alone, which mirrored Sue's grandmother's situation. Using this example, she found it possible to discuss her own attitudes about old age and intervening in the lives of older people, which were located in her own personal and cultural identity.

Intervening in the lives of other people may curtail their rights to live independently and may challenge a central notion of social work practice—the commitment to promoting empowerment. Students should be encouraged to reflect upon the tensions between intervention and the promotion of empowerment.

OPPORTUNITIES FOR CHALLENGING SITUATIONS

There may be a tendency to try to protect students from exposure to risk. Unnecessary risks can be minimized, yet risk is inherent in all forms of social work. We serve students best, and the people they will work with, if we honestly acknowledge levels of risk and enable students to work with those risks and to manage them effectively.

NOTES FOR STUDENTS

LEARNING ABOUT CHALLENGING SITUATIONS

It is sometimes suggested that we live in a society in which levels of perceived risk are increasing (Beck, 1990). Risk is a complicated notion. It is not, for example, a legally defined concept (so we cannot base our professional practice upon the law and legal precedent). However, "risk" is now a central concept in professional practice and is the subject of considerable interest (Stalker, 2003). We need to explore ways to deploy effectively the concept of risk in practice.

Risk Assessment

According to Manthorpe (2000), *risk assessment* is the "process of identifying hazards which may cause accident, disaster or harm" (p. 298). As Newhill (2003) asserts,

> An effective comprehensive risk assessment involves clinically examining a number of overlapping areas. These include demographic risk factors,

personality risk factors, psychiatric disorder, psychiatric symptoms, biological risk factors, historical risk factors, and environmental and situational factors. (pp. 122–123)

Predicting risk is inherently problematic as it involves making a judgment about likely future outcomes. There is always uncertainty about whether a particular event will occur, and chance plays a part in the outcome of any course of actions or events. There are two broad approaches to the assessment of risk:

1. Clinical (i.e., where a clinician or practitioner in a given field estimates the likelihood of a particular occurrence—for example, a depressed person committing a serious act of self-harm)

2. Actuarial (i.e., where statistical methods are used to identify risk to general situations or groups—for example, we can predict with some certainty the proportion of smokers within a given population who will have died from smoking-related illness by a certain age but not necessarily which individuals in particular)

If it is possible to estimate the level of risk with some degree of accuracy, then a professionally balanced decision about whether it is necessary to intervene is also possible. The estimation of level of risk is dependent on detailed knowledge about the potential causes of risk and how to apply that knowledge to a particular situation. Reviewing the available evidence at the time, Kemshall (1996, p. 136) suggests that clinical prediction of risk has "a poor record of accuracy" with respect to mental health, while Corby (1996) notes that in the field of child protection, there has been considerable growth in the number of risk assessment instruments, which is especially evident in the United States.[2]

Assessing risk is very difficult when people have a number of different risk factors in their lives; the identification of risk that a child might be abused by his or her parents requires different knowledge from the estimation of risk that people with mental illness will harm themselves or others; different again are the risks associated for some people with physical disabilities in performing certain tasks. Kemshall and Pritchard (1996) have collected details of how to assess risk for particular types of service users. However, in each case, there are common questions to be considered when making a judgment:

- What is the nature of the risk—is it life threatening or a minor inconvenience? For example, there is some risk attached to crossing the road, yet

---

[2]One of the most widely used is Milner's Child Abuse Potential Inventory (Milner, 1986) for which a very high success rate is claimed.

for many people, it is a risk taken every day because the incidence of accidents is low relative to the number of people crossing roads.

- Is there a risk to a minor or a vulnerable person? For example, is it a risk to people who are able to judge the level of risk for themselves, or are they prevented or unable to do so, for whatever reason?

- Is this a subjective or an objective definition of risk? Is there agreement among those involved about the determination of the risk?

- What protection can people take themselves against the risk?

- Are there risks if you do intervene, and how are these weighed against nonintervention?

The answers to such questions have been collected into a matrix model proposed by O'Sullivan (1999). This matrix graphically makes visible the strengths and weaknesses of a particular course of action—in this case, whether to allow a child to remain in a foster home. The strengths and weaknesses might be identified as follows in Table 12.1.

| Table 12.1 | A Strengths/Hazards Analysis of the "Staying in Foster Home" Option |

Present	Future
Hazards Difficulties in relationship between foster parents Zena's history of running away	*Danger* Foster home will suddenly break down
Strengths Experienced foster family Foster family from same ethnic background	*Benefit* A caring and stable base to work towards Zena's reconciliation with her family

SOURCE: O'Sullivan (1999, p. 141).

Such a diagrammatic approach can be used in other situations to aid decision making.

Typology of Risks

When making an assessment of risk, it can be helpful to think about different types of risk (Manthorpe, 2000; Newhill, 2003). Stevenson and Parsloe (1993) identify three categories where intervention may be required:

- Physical risk: Circumstances where individuals may harm themselves or cause harm to others; in these cases, social workers may have to decide, either alone or in conjunction with others, on the extent of that risk, as in the case of somebody who is mentally ill and threatening harm to himself or herself or others.

- Social risk: Individuals whose behavior isolates and alienates them from others should be encouraged to behave in a more socially acceptable fashion; in addition, neighbors and family can also be encouraged to understand and manage these behaviors.

- Emotional risk: Where the physical health or emotional well-being of people is put at risk by the role that they occupy; for example, where a person has the sole care of another highly dependent person.

It is worth remembering that all human action carries some risk. Try doing a risk assessment on yourself for the day, then making recommendations about how your life should be limited to lessen all these risks. Helpful? Probably not (see "soft-boiled egg syndrome" in Part III, this volume). de Bono (2000, p. 83) calls risk assessment "black hat thinking," with statements that are often preceded by "I see a danger of. . . ." A focus on degrees of risk has potential for disempowerment.

Risk Management

Risk management is the tension between individuals' autonomy and protecting them from themselves or ensuring the protection of others. A difficulty for social work has always been to determine when to intervene, even if there are legal grounds for so doing; in other words, what standards of risk are acceptable, and what risks prompt social workers to intervene? As Newhill (2003) comments,

Effective comprehensive risk assessment involves clinically examining a number of overlapping areas. Some of these areas should be addressed, if possible, prior to interviewing the client; some are relevant to the interviewing process itself; and some involve people, places, and events that make up the client's environment and the context of the client's current situation. (pp. 122–123)

Newhill's advice is sound, but it does not deal with the problem of determining socially acceptable standards for intervention; these remain a complex issue for society in general and social work practice in particular. Stalker (2003) suggests that,

> risk management moves along a continuum between control, legitimate authority and empowerment. Between the controlling ends of the continuum lie models of risk management which seek to reduce harms and maximize benefits. (p. 218)

A problem may arise when social workers have almost complete control over the lives of vulnerable individuals, as in group care, and there have been several well-reported examples where that power has been abused (Clough, 1996). There is no reason to suppose that autonomy and protection cannot be balanced. Being a parent involves both caring for a child and controlling the child's behavior, and successful parents are able to demonstrate both love and control—if not without tensions! As a Scottish respondent in a research study about parenting commented,

> It seems as if there's no happy medium. You either let them out and you're careless, or you keep them in and you're over protective, and your lad's gonnae have an accident because you cannae teach it to be street wise if you've got him in the house. (H. Roberts, Smith, & Bryce, 1995, p. 66, from a study by Brown and Harris)

This parent well expresses some of the dilemmas implicit in both caring for somebody and also seeking to put limits on his or her behavior. People may value their autonomy more highly than they value being protected from harm and that they are happy to accept the risks of everyday life. Where a sharp distinction has to be made is where there is a risk to others. In such cases, action must be taken to minimize the risk of harm to others, where potential harm is significant and the "other" is a person in a vulnerable situation. Professional codes of practice for social workers may be of some help in providing guidance about such matters (National Association of Social Workers [NASW], 1999).

A range of different tools to identify the nature and extent of risk is used. Table 12.2 gives details of a young man with Asperger syndrome. Using the format, it is possible to both identify potential risks and also specify how these are managed. It is not necessary to have a narrative to describe the situation—the relevant professional information can be gleaned from the schedule.

Table 12.2 An Example of a Risk Assessment Harm-Benefit Analysis

	Harms	Benefits
FINANCIAL: Potential for abuse?	Increased cost of care package. Is vulnerable to exploitation due to Asberger's syndrome and his inability to understand financial matters.	Enabling to remain in his home environment. Chandler's parents collect his benefits and manage finances. He always has enough money to purchase items.
SOCIAL: Who the person lives with/lives alone The ability/inability of people to continue caring The presence/lack of home/social support Ability/inability to cope alone in own home	Lives with mother and father in family in home. There are tensions between parents, which increase Chandler's anxieties and lead to behavioral outbursts. Chandler's mother struggles to cope with aggressive behaviors. She provides most of the care for Chandler. She has little support from her husband or extended family. Risk of carer breakdown and consequential need for 24-hour residential care.	Is very close to family. This is a familiar environment where he feels comfortable. Does not respond well to change and needs predictability in his life. Has regular respite care at a local not-for-profit facility, which gives parents frequent breaks from caring.
ENVIRONMENTAL: Home conditions (e.g., gas, fires, obstacles, neighbors, friends, support/lack of) The threat of removal of care networks The nature and extent of hospitalizations	Dislikes large, crowded, and noisy environments that heighten his anxiety and result in behavioral outbursts. Places heavy demands on his carers, who are frequently the subject of physical assaults. Requires support from staff who are experienced in meeting the needs of individuals with severe challenging behaviors.	Has many friends/ acquaintances at his day service. Chandler receives regular respite to maintain the family situation. Has a number of staff who support him with day services and are experienced in meeting his needs.

(Continued)

Table 12.2	(Continued)

	Harms	Benefits
PSYCHOLOGICAL: The anxieties of significant others. Significant cognitive impairment. Mental health issues? Threats to safety of self/others	Becomes anxious when he experiences unplanned change, busy environments, or people invading his space. Has Asberger's syndrome and severe challenging behavior. Behaviors include repetitive speech, verbal threats, and physical assaults on staff/service users.	Has his day presented to him in picture format so that his day is as structured and predictable as possible.
FAMILIAL: The impact of the risk on carers/family members The lack of home/social support The anxieties of significant others High levels of conflict with relatives	Chandler's family is at risk of physical injury. Risk of carer breakdown.	With a high degree of structure and routine in his day. Regular respite to facilitate breaks from caring.
PHYSICAL: High levels of disability Older age General health	Risk of physical injury to self and others.	Least restrictive alternative is always employed when supporting through behavioral difficulties.
OTHER:	Risk of physical injury to support staff and other service users at the day service. Risk of physical injury to staff/service users on transport. Risk of injury to Chandler's sister who transports him.	Chandler's s sister transports him in her car without any incidents yet reported.

NOTE: This assessment is a live example used by one local authority in the United Kingdom. It is important to make explicit an estimate of the scale of the harm, the potential for future harm, the strengths of a situation, and the manageability of the risks.

You can encourage your student to produce a similar schedule with respect to one service user or provider. Alternatively, invite the student to construct a similar schedule with respect to one of the Derby Street residents.

Risk Avoidance

Risk avoidance may either lead to desirable professional behavior through enabling service people to avoid behavior that carries a high level of detrimental risk[3] or result in overcautious professional practice that places people in more danger. For example, it would be unthinkable to allow children in group care to behave as they pleased, yet there must be acceptable limits to the ways in which behavior is controlled. The protection of one individual, whether child or adult, may entail a restriction on his or her rights to behave as he or she chooses, or it may restrict others. In such situations, social workers are placed in an invidious position in having to meet two contradictory imperatives. This is exemplified by the cartoon below. The social worker is placed in a difficult position and seems to be in a lose-lose situation.

Figure 12.2	"The Social Worker Cannot Win?" by Kevin Kallaugher

SOURCE: Reproduced from *Modern Social Work Practice* by Mark Doel and Steven M. Shardlow, Ashgate, Aldershot, 2005.

---

[3]It should not be forgotten that some individuals enjoy a "high-risk" lifestyle—for example, mountaineers.

The microscope of potential public scrutiny can be a very effective inhibitor to appropriate professional risk taking. There is a very real danger that the avoidance of risk becomes the primary determinant of the social worker's actions. It may be that the overwhelming sense of risk perceived by the social worker is not the risk to the child, service user, or provider but the risk to the practitioner. This sense of risk can then tip the balance in favor of a professional practice that is designed first and foremost to protect the individual practitioner—a defensive practice (Thompson, 2000a, 2000b).

Social workers can be subject to a range of risks through engaging in professional practice: for example, in some contexts, the risk of contracting highly infectious and potentially life-threatening illness, as well as the potential risk of violence from some service users and providers (see Astor, Behre, Wallace, & Fravil, 1998; Beaver, 1999; Jayaratne, Vinkur-Kaplan, Nagda, & Chess, 1996; Lyter & Martin, 2000; Mace, 1989; Newhill & Wexler, 1997; Rey, 1996; Skolnick-Acker, Atkinson, Frost, Kaplan, & Pelavin, 1993).

In 1995, Newhill documented that physical and emotional violence by clients toward workers was increasing in all settings. It would appear that the trend toward violence against human service workers has not abated (Spencer & Munich, 2003). According to Shields and Kiser (2003),

Social workers were subject to physical assault, and all workers were routinely subjected to psychological aggression, such as outbursts of anger, profanity and intimidation. (p. 13)

This begs the following question: What can social workers do in the context of violence? Dewees (2006, p. 305) suggests the following possibilities:

1. Always inform your service user of the time you expect to make a home visit.

2. When you leave the office, always inform someone of your schedule.

3. Pay attention to your surroundings.

4. Don't put yourself physically in a position to be trapped in a potentially violent service user's home.

5. Don't challenge an angry service user with rebuttals or consequences.

6. Report incidents of any kind to your supervisor, or use an agency-designated process if there is one.

In conclusion, you should always identify these risks with your seminar instructor or fieldwork instructor and determine strategies to minimize and manage the level of risk.

ASSESSING YOUR LEARNING

When working in challenging situations that involve levels of risk, you may tend to respond *as a novice practitioner,* either by being overcautious—leading to unnecessary and unjustified intervention—or by being overtolerant of risk, such that intervention is not made when required. Of course, there is no absolute measure of the extent of risk, and judgments about the nature of risk will vary between individuals. The extent of that variance and the reasons for such judgments are central to determining whether you have fully understood the notion of working with risk. This is an ability that you need to be able to demonstrate in your assignments and through your practice. The process of professional socialization will enable you to develop more commonly held *professional* norms about working with risk. If your view is significantly at variance from other professionals, you need to consider carefully why this may be the case and to be able to produce a convincing and persuasive reason. Variance does not automatically mean that your views are incorrect. This is one area of practice where simulation can provide excellent opportunities for assessment as it does not place you in a vulnerable position where you have to make actual decisions, which could be prejudicial to the safety of the service user or provider. Simulations enable you to experience the potential gravity of some situations without the danger. You may want to discuss possible simulation options, which assess risk, with your seminar instructor or fieldwork supervisor.

FURTHER READING

Lyter, S. C., & Martin, M. (2000, March). *Playing it safe: A survey addressing dangers in the field.* Paper presented at the annual program meeting of the Council on Social Work Education, New York, NY.

Newhill, C. E. (2003). *Client violence in social work practice: Prevention, intervention, and research.* New York, NY: Guilford.

Stalker, K. (2003). Managing risk and uncertainty in social work. *Journal of Social Work, 3*(3), 211–233.

PART IV

Themes of Practice

The purpose of the social work profession is to promote human and community well-being. Guided by a person and environment construct, a global perspective, a respect for human diversity, and knowledge based on scientific inquiry, social works purpose is actualized through its quest for social and economic justice, the prevention of conditions that limit human rights, the elimination of poverty, and the enhancement of quality of life for all persons. (Council on Social Work Education [CSWE], 2008, Preamble)

Unfortunately, there is a widespread assumption that graduates of social work programs rarely use research findings in their practice and even less that they conduct research in their practice. In 1991, the Task Force on Social Work Research, chaired by David Austin, concluded that insufficient effort was given to research efforts to build the knowledge base of professional practice. Since publication of that report, there has been tremendous progress in building the profession's research infrastructure. Nonetheless, for many social work students, the research process remains shrouded in mystery and inspires fear and dread (Alexander & Solomon, 2006, p. xxi). Many are under the impression that research is "all about statistics." For those social work students whose attraction to liberal arts courses was in part to get away from math and science, the idea that research can be both fun and useful is unlikely to be part of their lexicon (Alexander & Solomon, 2006, p. xxi). Epstein's (1987) observation that "no other part of the social work curriculum has been so consistently received by students with as much groaning, moaning, eye-rolling, bad-mouthing, hyperventilation, and waiver-strategizing as the research course" (p. 71) is probably as true now as it was in 1987. Briar (1980) noted a widespread belief among social workers that the same person cannot be both a good researcher and a good practitioner. He asserted,

> The personal qualities believed to make good researchers are seen as handicaps for a practitioner, and the reverse also has been said to be true. The stereotypes are familiar. Researchers are supposedly intellectual, rational, unfeeling creatures who lack the sensitivity to understand the subtle nuances that are of primary concern to practitioners. Practitioners are purported to be intuitive, sensitive, creative persons more akin to artists than scientists; they emphasize the importance of seeing clients as whole persons who should not be subjected to the categorization and atomization that research allegedly requires. (p. 31)

It is perhaps not surprising if many social work students enter the research class with some fears. One of the challenges facing those who teach this course is to attempt to demonstrate that what students are practicing in their fieldwork placements *is* research, but this requires a whole change in perception about the subject so that it can become real, manageable, and perhaps even enjoyable. There are numerous and compelling reasons why social work students and social workers should be familiar with research, not least that it is essential that social work students, social workers, and their supervisors become actively engaged in research. Rather than being an abstract concept, research should inform practice—and practice should inform research.

HISTORY OF SOCIAL WORKER AS PRACTITIONER-RESEARCHER

Social work has long had an ambivalent relation to research. Writing in the early 1950s, Margaret Blenkner, a leading social work researcher, apparently believed that caseworkers and researchers (whom she referred to as "scientific workers") were endowed with different personality traits:

> Probably two of the most important characteristics of the good caseworker are intuitive, imaginative and a capacity for deep identification with other of the sort Murray [Henry A. Murray] terms "critical empathy," coupled with a strong drive to succor the person in distress. . . . The good scientific worker, on the other hand, must have traits of a different order: a conceptual, analytical approach to phenomena and drive at conclusion through rational induction or objective deduction from explicit principles. . . . While the traits of the good caseworker and the good scientific workers are not

mutually exclusive, to find them in good measures in one and of the same person is rare and may indeed be a source of blocking and confusion their otherwise fortunate possessor. (Blenkner, 1950, pp. 55–56)

Social work educators of that period also seemed to share this point of view. For example, Menscher (1959), author of *Research Methods in Social Work Education* part of the CSWE Curriculum Study, writes, "The approach of this study has been that the master's curriculum for the practitioner of service methods does not present a realistic opportunity for preparing practitioners to undertake research independently and that the inclusion of this objective tends to confuse curriculum planning" (p. 5).

Throughout the history of social work research in the United States, there has been an ongoing interest in practitioners conducting research on their own practice. Mary Richmond (1917), regarded by many as the founder of social work in the United States, wrote, "The practitioner of an art must discover the heart of the whole matter for himself" (p. 103). One of the major recommendations of the Milford conference of 1929 was the "urgent call for increased research activity, especially, the creation of a cadre of practitioner-researchers who understand both practice and research" (Briar, 1974, p. 12). Cabot, the first president of the National Association of Social Workers (NASW), made this evaluation the subject of his inaugural address in 1931:

I appeal to you, measure, evaluate, estimate, appraise your results in some form, in any terms that rest on anything beyond faith, assertion, and the "illustrative case." Let us do this for ourselves before some less knowledgeable and gentle body takes us by the shoulders and pushes us into the street. (Cabot, 1931, p. 6)

Fritz Redl (1957), a leading social work researcher in the 1950s, wrote, "The practitioner has an odd complaint. He politely admits that the research expert produces a lot that is important. His complaint is that the research expert does not answer the questions he asks" (p. 16). The first major social work research text written by social workers was published in 1960. One of the authors offered the following observation:

The [social work] profession is a mystery, not only to those who seek help, but to those who give it. The practitioner claims to know the answers but in fact knows few of them; and he shrouds himself in his rites to protect his professional status. (Wolins, 1960, p. 247)

During the 1970s, three major works by Mullen and Dumpson (1972), Fischer (1973), and Jayaratne and Levy (1979) were published that addressed the need for what would now be termed *evidence-based practice* but in the terminology of the time called for social work to be able to establish its effectiveness.

Mullen and Dumpson's (1972) classic book, *Evaluation of Social Intervention,* examined 16 field experiments that tested the effects of social work interventions, including casework, social group work, and community organization. The volume included the entire body of known field experiments conducted through 1971 that had examined social work interventions. Fifteen internationally recognized social work experts critically assessed these findings and discussed the implications for social work practice and education. Contributing editors included Boehm, Borgatta, Breedlove, Feldstein, Geismar, Jones, Lewis, Meyer, Harris Pearlman, Slavin, Turner, Walker, and Webb. The editors convened a national conference to discuss the studies and the book chapters. The conference was attended by 125 representatives of most of the U.S. graduate schools of social work and was held at Fordham University in 1971. This was the first major call for a move toward evidence-based practice in social work (A. L. Roberts & Yeager 2006).

In his classic article, "Is Casework Effective? A Review," Joel Fischer (1973) underscored the importance of carefully conducted research in order to determine whether casework was effective. His book led to a strident debate on the role of research in social work practice. This debate continues today, and the profession still struggles with the importance of research in measuring treatment effectiveness.

Jayaratne and Levy (1979) asserted these three critical concepts regarding practice:

1. The clinician-researcher must have a thorough understanding of the treatment methods being employed (p. 9).

2. The clinician-researcher must have an empirical orientation toward the process of intervention (p. 10).

3. The clinician-researcher must have the ability to functionally use empirical feedback that is obtained during intervention (p. 12)

In the 1980s, the term *evidence-based medicine* was coined to describe a process in which a medical professional could use the best evidence available in making clinical decisions about the medical care of individual patients (Rosenthal, 2006). Gray (2001) stated that the call for evidence-based practice arose in relation to the medical profession for the following reasons: differences between the intervention suggested by research findings and actual interventions, variations in clinical practice, economic pressure, and the impact of the information revolution. In the most widely used definition, Sackett, Straus, Richardson, Rosenberg, and Haynes (2000) defined evidence-based medicine as "the integration of best research evidence with clinical expertise and patients' values" (p. 1). The notion of evidence-based medicine laid the groundwork to apply similar principles to other helping professions.

With respect to social work, Gambrill (2006) suggests that evidence-based practice "is a new educational and practice paradigm for closing the gaps between research and practice to maximize opportunities to help clients and avoid harm" (p. 339). How might a social worker use evidence-based practice? Research knowledge, clinical expertise, and clients' opinions are all integrated in evidence-based practice, which, according to Sackett and colleagues (2000), requires the adherence to the following five steps:

1. Convert information needs into answerable questions. Such questions are stated specifically enough to guide a computer search, concern the person's welfare, relate to a problem that has some chance of a solution, and, ideally, are formed in collaboration with the client. A well-formed question describes the client, course of action, alternate course(s) of action, and intended result.

2. Track down with maximum efficiency the best evidence with which to answer the question. (This requires electronic access to bibliographic databases and skill in searching them efficiently and quickly enough to guide practice.)

3. Critically appraise the evidence for its validly and usefulness. (This entails applying a hierarchy relevant to several question/evidence types.)

4. Apply the results of this appraisal to policy/practice decisions. This requires deciding whether the evidence applies to the decision at hand based on whether a client is similar enough to those studied, access to interventions described in the literature, weighing anticipated outcomes relative to concerns such as number needed to treat, practical matters, and clients' preferences.

5. Evaluate outcome. This may entail recordkeeping, including single-case designs (as described in Sackett, Richardson, Rosenberg, & Haynes, 1997, p. 3, and reported by Gibbs & Gambrill, 2002, pp. 453–454).

The premise that social work practice must be based on empirically tested and verified knowledge is now widely accepted and endorsed by leaders and social work organizations. Concern still exists, however, that research evidence is not easily accessed by practitioners and is not readily translated into practice (Gambrill, 2000; Howard, McMillen, & Pollio, 2003). It is the scope of social work practice that has led to difficulties in defining contemporary evidence-based treatment in social work. However, we have a responsibility and duty to help those who are referred to us. Unless we are willing to evaluate our own practice, how can we assert that we are effectively serving our consumers?

NEED TO EVALUATE INTERVENTION OUTCOMES

The context of social work practice increasingly requires that social workers be proficient in evaluating intervention outcomes. The essence of successful practice is to help resolve people's problems and to help them attain their objectives, without creating problems for others. Probably the most clear and socially accountable way of determining whether our practice is successful is through systematized, objective evaluation methods that can be replicated (repeated) by others.

Hence, the *social worker as researcher* needs to combine the following elements in his or her practice:

1. Use the results of research and evaluation to the extent possible to select intervention techniques and other procedures that have proven effectiveness.

2. Systematically monitor and evaluate one's practice.

3. Keep searching for new and more effective ways to serve consumers.

4. Conduct practice as a problem-solving process, where the core task of the practitioner is investigation and discovery.

5. Maintain a commitment in words and deeds to the values of the helping professions, a sensitivity, care, and concern for the well-being, rights, and dignity of service users.

The continued growth and acceptance of social work knowledge depends on social workers' appreciation and support of research as well as their competence in engaging in research efforts and using others' research findings. This assumes that social workers develop an early appreciation of the need and place for scientific inquiry for the resolution of social problems.

The application of the phrase *social work researcher* to professional social workers is becoming increasingly common as new challenges arise and old problems continue unresolved. Although the phrase may sound somewhat awkward, it does express a profound perception about the nature, process, and function of modern social work. The social worker as a "practitioner-researcher" continuously and consciously expands his or her professional base and repertoire of skills through self-initiated research and evaluation projects and through the published findings of others. This expansion into new knowledge and new skills is a lifelong process that begins in an undergraduate program, continues through a master's program, and will grow and flourish throughout each stage of a professional career as caregiver, advocate, change agent, and so on.

Being a *social worker/researcher* is to be able to make use of basic research methods and to integrate research knowledge with professional social work practice, alongside an awareness of both qualitative and quantitative research designs and strategies. Indeed, the entire social work research curriculum should prepare students for the pursuit, production, and discriminating use of knowledge for social work practice. Upon completion of the research sequence, students will be able to judge the effectiveness of research studies, adapt relevant research findings to practice, and appraise the success of practice interventions. The following student vignette illustrates the making of the connection between research and practice:

> An understanding of how research and social work go hand in hand also helped me to achieve my goals. I began reading research articles and literature on older adults with dementia. Reminiscence therapy was a psychosocial intervention I was already familiar with from prior class work. In conducting further research, I discovered evidence of reminiscence interventions' effectiveness in practice with older adults. I then decided to use reminiscence therapy in my field work with the residents. (Rosa, a master's student)

The following table demonstrates the similarity between the social work process and the research process. It is imperative that the similarity is harnessed for the development of research within social work; for example, practitioners can use skills developed through practice to engage in research and vice versa. Help and guidance exists for the practitioner who wants an understanding of research (Mark, 1996). In addition, there are many good examples of practitioner research from which to draw (see, e.g., Courtney, Piliavin, Grogan-Kaylor, & Nesmith, 2001; Haber & Toro, 2004; J. C. Marsh, D'Aunno, & Smith, 2000; Smith, 2003).

Social Work Processes	Research Processes
1. Social worker/project worker is presented with a problem.	1. Researcher is presented with a problem or question.
2. Social worker collects facts that illuminate the nature and purpose of the problem.	2. Researcher searches the literature on the problem or question.
3. Social worker makes a plan of action.	3. Researcher designs a study.
4. Social worker attempts to carry out action plan, noting progress.	4. Researcher collects material and collates it.
5. Social worker reviews work and may make new plans.	5. Researcher analyzes material and produces conclusions and possibly recommendations for future action.

SOURCE: Whitaker and Archer (1989).

RESEARCH METHODOLOGIES

> Professional knowledge does not emerge automatically from the hectic activities of practitioners. . . . Only through the use of systematic and rigorous methods of critical inquiry—that is research—can theoretical or practice knowledge be developed. . . . Professions cannot succeed by faith and practice ideology alone. (Kirk, 1991, p. 4)

This view leads us to ask, "What types of research can the practitioner undertake so as to fully incorporate research knowledge into his or her practice and, therefore, provide high-quality services?" First, before undertaking research, it is important to remember the requirement to seek review from the university Institutional Review Board (IRB), which is responsible for determining the ethics and governance issues in the proposed research. The following are five possible research methodologies, among many others, that could form the basis for professional and scientific enquiry.

EXPLORATORY

This type of design is used with topics about which very little is known or little information is available—for example, the first studies on the psychosocial impact of AIDS on the lives of gay men; the de-institution movement in the 1960s, spurred on by additional pharmacological discoveries; litigation that protected patients' civil rights against involuntary commitment and institutionalization; and emerging community mental health programs. The findings of these studies are not conclusive or definitive, and they are more likely to generate research questions and hypotheses for additional investigation.

DESCRIPTIVE

Many social work studies seek to describe situations or events. Descriptive studies are larger scale efforts that attempt to characterize a population group in a definitive way. The U.S. census is an excellent example of a descriptive social scientific research project with an aim to describe accurately and precisely a wide variety of characteristics of the U.S. population, as well as the populations of smaller areas such as states and counties. The studies can provide precise information, for instance, on what proportion of the homeless are single women, women with children, young men, middle-aged men, persons of color, and so on.

EXPLANATORY

The aim in this approach is to provide the "why" for phenomena—for example, to identify why some states have higher child abuse rates than others. It is common with an explanatory study to develop a hypothesis in which certain theories are tested and a control or comparison group is used. A study may seek to test the hypothesis that female adolescents who are sexually abused are more likely to run away than female adolescents who have not been sexually abused; we could consider any differences between an experimental group and a control group. If we discovered that adolescents who had been sexually abused were more likely to run away, we would also need to consider other variables that might also associated with this finding. If we wished to make any broader generalizations, we would need to apply statistical tests for significance.

PROGRAM EVALUATION

It is important to know if our programs and intervention strategies are effective. Do we know if we are doing what we purport to be doing? Many agencies publish brochures listing the programs they provide. These state the goals of the agency, identify different populations they serve, and promote their intervention programs. Are these programs successful and, if so, to what extent? Evaluative research seeks to find this out. With increasing reliance on grants, state, and federal funding and internal accountability to board members, there is a greater need for this continuous evaluation.

SINGLE-SUBJECT RESEARCH DESIGN

Of all the possible approaches, single-subject research design (SSD) is particularly applicable to social work as it provides social workers with the knowledge, skills, and procedures to evaluate their own practice, so the researcher and the social worker are likely to be the same person. Single-subject research design has a number of advantages. First, social workers are learning how to study their own practice and to learn from this direct experience. Second, the language of SSD is not abstract but an accessible description of specific interventions used by social workers as they emerge in their own practice, so it is a practice-based evaluation methodology. Third, by using SSD, social workers can demonstrate the effectiveness of their interventions. Increasingly, the social work profession is being asked to demonstrate its effectiveness and to be highly accountable.

LOOKING FORWARD

Whatever type of research strategy is incorporated, the issue of accountability and responsibility of the practitioner to the service user, the group, the agency, and the public is paramount. It is imperative not just to embrace these strategies but to know how to use them effectively in order to represent both our own profession and the people we work with as effectively as possible.

In this final part of the book, we consider four *dimensions* of practice: multicultural practice, law-informed practice, generalist and specialist practice, and comparative practice. All these themes of practice require practitioner-researchers to be reflective and to evaluate their own practice systematically, if the practice is to be successful. This also complies with Educational Policy 2.16—Engage in Research-Informed Research:

Social workers use practice experience to inform research, employ evidence-based interventions, evaluate their own practice, and use research findings to improve practice, policy, and social service delivery.

Social workers comprehend quantitative and qualitative research and understand scientific and ethical approaches to building knowledge. Social workers:

- use practice experience to inform scientific inquiry and
- use research evidence to inform practice.

About 60 years ago, William Gordon (1950) defined social work research as

the spirit of searching or seeking, the spirit of carrying through until something is found, and the sense of accountability or responsibility for the reliability of the findings. These are the essential elements in the research process in any setting. (p. 111)

We need to capture that spirit through meaningful practice-based research done by social workers.

CHAPTER 13

Multicultural Practice

The Drawbridge is taken from Judy Katz's (1978) book, *White Awareness: Handbook for Anti-Racist Training*, although its use has been adapted for our current purposes. It asks the student to make fine-tuned moral judgments about responsibility. Out of their response to this story, the students can learn more about where they are located in terms of their understanding of power, oppression, and social structures.

NOTES FOR INSTRUCTORS[1]

PURPOSE

A relatively neutral device can be very effective in exploring loaded subjects. An apparent distance in place and time can free people to consider issues of power and oppression much closer to home. *The Drawbridge* helps students to consider how service users and other colleagues may have very different perspectives and the impact this can have on the work.

METHOD

- *The Drawbridge* is best done without preparation since discussing the exercise beforehand defeats some of its purpose. Everybody involved should have a copy of the exercise, and it is most effective if it is read

---

[1]See the Introduction to the book for suggestions about how instructors and students can, separately and together, use the activities in this book.

out loud. Once the story has been concluded, all participants should spend 3 to 5 minutes rating each of the six characters according to how responsible they think each is for the death of the Baroness. It is important to emphasize that there are no specifically "right" or "wrong" ratings for responsibility. This will prevent students from second-guessing what they think you want to hear.

- Subsequent discussion is centered on why the participants have made the decisions they have made. Further discussion should be guided by the notes in the "Teaching About Multicultural Practice" section that follows, although it is better for students not to consult that part of the chapter until after their own discussion.

NOTES FOR STUDENTS AND INSTRUCTORS

VARIATIONS

The Drawbridge is suited to small groups, where there is a better chance of a variety of opinions arising. The activity gains from dissent rather than consensus, itself illustrating the value of diversity. It can be used with groups of service users, as well as students and colleagues.

USE BY OTHER PROFESSIONS

The activity can readily be used by different professional groups. It would be interesting to compare the range of opinions across disciplines. As you can see from the chart on page 227, social work students reflect great differences in their views.

EDUCATIONAL POLICY ACCREDITATION STANDARDS

The topics in this chapter relate to the following *Educational Policy and Accreditation Standards* (*EPAS*) 2008 Primary Core Competencies (Council on Social Work Education [CSWE], 2008):

1. Apply social work ethical principles to guide professional practice.

2. Apply critical thinking to inform and communicate professional judgments.

3. Engage diversity and difference in practice.

4. Advance human rights and social and economic justice.

5. Apply knowledge of human behavior and the social environment.

FOR STUDENTS AND INSTRUCTORS

ACTIVITY 13: *THE DRAWBRIDGE*

As he left for a visit to his outlying districts, the jealous Baron warned his pretty wife, "Do not leave the castle while I am gone, or I will punish you severely when I return!"

But as the hours passed, the young Baroness grew lonely; despite her husband's warning she decided to visit her lover, who lived in the countryside nearby.

The castle was situated on an island in a wide, fast-flowing river. A drawbridge linked the island to the mainland at the narrowest point in the river.

"Surely my husband will not return before dawn," she thought and ordered her servants to lower the drawbridge and leave it down until she returned.

After spending several pleasant hours with her lover, the Baroness returned to the drawbridge, only to find it blocked by a Gateman wildly waving a long, cruel knife.

"Do not attempt to cross this bridge, Baroness, or I will have to kill you," cried the Gateman. "The Baron ordered me to do so."

Fearing for her life, the Baroness returned to her Lover and asked for help. "Our relationship is only a romantic one," the Lover said. "I will not help."

The Baroness then sought out a Boatman on the river, explaining her plight to him, and asked him to take her across the river in his boat. "I will do it, but only if you can pay my fee of five marks." "But I have no money with me," the Baroness protested. "That is too bad. No money, no ride," the Boatman said flatly.

Her fear growing, the Baroness ran crying to a Friend's home and, after explaining her desperate situation, begged for enough money to pay the boatman his fee.

"If you had not disobeyed your husband, this would not have happened," the Friend said. "I will give you no money."

With dawn approaching and her last resource exhausted, the Baroness returned to the bridge in desperation, attempted to cross to the castle, and was slain by the Gateman.

In order of priorities, who is most responsible for the death of the Baroness? Use the boxes below to rank the six characters: 6 for most responsible, 5 for next most responsible, and down to 1 for least responsible ranking.

Baron	
Baroness	
Gateman	
Lover	
Boatman	
Friend	

SOURCE: Katz (1978, pp. 70–71).

NOTES FOR INSTRUCTORS

TEACHING ABOUT MULTICULTURAL PRACTICE

You should familiarize yourself with the material in this section before you embark on *The Drawbridge* with students. What follows will assist you in helping the students to relate their particular responses to a wider canvas. The section on "Learning About Multicultural Practice" (p. 226) introduces the student to some of the central issues in multicultural practice.

Helping the Student to Learn From *The Drawbridge*

There can be no clear right or wrong in the moral debate about responsibility in the story of *The Drawbridge* because it depends on what system of beliefs are used to measure and weigh responsibility. Although students may feel that the idea of theory is something rather distant and obscure, in fact they draw on their own personal theories to explain this story. They may not formalize this into a fully coherent theory; nevertheless, they use a conceptual framework, a *paradigm,* to begin to make sense and meaning of the world.

There are many paradigms, and individual students using the same paradigm may yet come to different conclusions about responsibility. The examples below are collected from numerous occasions when *The Drawbridge* has been used with new social work students in their very first week of training. All the quotes are taken from students' own statements.

Psychological Paradigm. "I think the Baroness has poor self-esteem"; "the Friend was too frightened to help"; "the Baron has a power complex"; "the Baron is really very insecure"; "the Baroness didn't think he really meant it."

These statements are characteristic of a set of explanations that seek to explain the behaviors of the players in motivational terms and look for psychological causes for their actions.

Legal Paradigm. "Although he was acting under duress, the Gatekeeper actually murdered her, so it's obvious that he was most responsible"; "there was an employment contract between the Gatekeeper and the Baron."

For some people, it is the legal framework that is the ultimate arbiter. When applying levels of responsibility, the current laws are used as the yardstick.

Cultural Relativism Paradigm. "In those days that was how things were done and the Baron was only doing what he did because that's all he knew"; "if it was now, I'd think differently."

Using this paradigm, what is of most significance are the indications that the events are somehow not of this time or place, so it is considered right to apply a different set of moral standards that takes these spatial and temporal contexts into account.

Individualism Paradigm. "Everybody is responsible for their own actions, and the Baroness knew what the consequences would be"; "he may have been acting under duress, but the Gatekeeper is responsible for his own actions"; "the Lover chose not to help."

Western philosophy lays great emphasis on our rights, duties, and obligations as autonomous individuals. We are considered to be moral agents with free will and the ability to exercise choice, and this is seen as overriding collective responsibility or social determinants. This philosophy was expressed in its extreme by Margaret Thatcher's declaration that there was no such thing as society.

Class Paradigm. "Why should the Boatman give her a free ride? That's his livelihood and who's she to be going around with no money?"; "the Gateman will be scapegoated because he's just one of the workers."

As a worker, the Boatman is near the bottom of the social order, and the Baroness is a member of the oppressive ruling class, so why should he not rejoice at her downfall? The Gateman, too, is a member of the oppressed lower class, even if he is its unwitting agent.

Feminism Paradigm. "The Baroness was the victim of a patriarchal society"; "she was subject to male abuse"; "the men let her down at every turn."

All of the players are male (except the Lover, whose gender is not determined). The woman is killed by a man on the orders of a man, and no man comes to her aid. However, there is an alternative feminist paradigm that would claim that it is patronizing to see the Baroness as a victim and that their feminism leads them to conclude that she was the author of her own downfall.

Fundamentalist Paradigm. "The Baroness broke her wedding vows"; "no matter what the reason, she has sinned against the promises sanctioned by marriage in the eyes of God."

There are many different religious paradigms, but a conservative one would measure responsibility against their church's teachings, in which adultery is a sin.

Power Paradigm. "The Baron had the power of life and death and, in using that power, he is the most responsible"; "no one else had that kind of power."

Using a paradigm of power, the Baron is seen as an instrument of an oppressive society in which power is unequally distributed and cruelly enforced, with others in relatively powerless positions coerced into obedience.

Relating the students' ratings for *The Drawbridge* to broader paradigms is important in three ways. First, it begins to demystify the idea of theory. The notion of paradigm is more readily grasped, and students can begin to see how what they have often viewed as unassembled or disconnected ideas are, in fact, part of a more coherent belief and value system. Second, it becomes apparent that other people *really* do see the world in very different ways, especially if the student has the opportunity to discuss *The Drawbridge* with a significant number of other people. Students can appreciate how easy it would be to become stuck or oppositional with colleagues and service users who may be observing and explaining the world from very different paradigms.

Finally, in addition to learning to value the difference and diversity that is apparent from the responses to *The Drawbridge,* students also begin to paint these personal beliefs on a broader canvas. The bigger picture is one where not all paradigms are considered equal. Some paradigms are seen as "normal," and those who hold different paradigms are marginalized, pathologized, or trivialized. This first level of awareness is essential to multicultural practice.

OPPORTUNITIES FOR MULTICULTURAL PRACTICE

We live in a pluralist society—multiethnic, multiracial, multiclass, and multi-faith. Much has been written about multicultural practice in social work and the need for competence in working with people from whom one differs in regard to these and other aspects (Fong, 2004; Fong & Furito, 2001; Green, 1999; Lum, 1999, 2004; Protocky-Tripodi, 2002). As social workers, we should be able work with people from wide and different communities. Schools of social work attempt to prepare students for practice in a culturally diverse world (Goldberg, 2000). In contemporary social work practice, this is referred to as being "culturally competent" or "multiculturally competent."

Many helpful definitions of these core concepts are available. For example, the NASW (2001) defines cultural competency as being able to respond

> respectfully and effectively to people of all cultures, languages, classes, races, ethnic backgrounds, religions, and other diversity factors in a manner that recognizes, affirms, and values the worth of individuals, families and communities and protects and preserves the dignity of each.

Green (1999, p. 87) states that ethnic competence involves several related but distinct areas: awareness of one's own cultural limitations; openness to cultural differences; a client-oriented, systematic learning style; the appropriate use of cultural resources; and the acknowledgment of the integrity of culture.

Webster's New World Dictionary of American English (1990) refers to culture as "ideas, customs, skills, arts, etc of people or group, that are transferred, communicated, or passed along . . . to succeeding generations" (p. 337), and to Becker (1986, p. 12), culture is "concerted activity" based on shared ideas and understanding. Although culture is a fundamental component of human existence, it has been described as a complex and elusive concept (O'Hagan, 2001). Cultures comprise subtleties and peculiarities that are often taken for granted by members of cultural groups and may not be understood by those outside the group. Understanding the meaning of culture, to ourselves and others and our own cultural limitations, is critical to the development of culturally responsive social work. Whenever a practitioner is working with diversity—ethnicity, gender, sexuality, faith, disability, age, or across class—an appreciation of the dynamics of culture will foster greater recognition and responsiveness to elements of prejudice, discrimination, and oppression in practice. However, the ability to be culturally responsive in practice goes beyond skill proficiency and sensitivity to cultural diversity alone (Yee Lee, 2003).

Multicultural Practice Teaching

Three key areas need to be addressed to implement responsive practice: practitioner attitude, practitioner knowledge, and practitioner skills (Diller, 2004; Ka Tat Tsang & George, 1998; Lum, 2003). These are all considered below.

Practitioner Attitude. It is fundamental to culturally responsive practice that practitioners have a sufficient depth of understanding about their own cultural identity and attitude to diversity. Developing this awareness, both conscious and below the level of conscious thought, requires reflection. This is a process that Weedon (1987) identifies as "subjectivity": an awareness of your sense of self and how you understand your relationship to the world. An examination of your personal subjectivity necessitates an understanding of the values and norms that inform your worldview, including the sociopolitical history that supports that worldview. These processes of self-examination can be challenging and may require some students to reorientate their worldview.

Practitioner Knowledge. Much of the recent literature has focused on acquiring knowledge for the range of skills required for cultural encounters. This approach has been conceptualized as the cultural literacy approach (Dyche & Zayas, 1995). Despite the dominance that this approach has attained, it has a number of limitations. First, it is impossible for all social workers to have an in-depth knowledge about all the cultures they come into contact with. Second, the approach has a tendency to create overgeneralizations of cultural groups. Third, this approach could place the practitioner in a position of seeming an "expert" despite the likelihood of him or her being in a position of relative cultural ignorance.

Practitioner Skills. Practitioner attitudes and knowledge require active translation into a repertoire of professional skills for culturally responsive practice (Ka Tat Tsang & George, 1998; Lum, 2003). Lum (2003) categorizes three types of skills: process skills, conceptualization skills, and personalization skills. Process skills relate to the business of doing social work as an integrative activity with people and include the ability to engage with clients, develop rapport, and conclude client-practitioner relationships using a range of micro skills. Conceptualization skills comprise core analytical skills that enable workers to analyze a case, uncover themes in verbal and nonverbal messages, and plan effective assessment and intervention strategies. Finally, personalization skills require the ability to demonstrate empathy with the client and to be open and respectful of challenges made by service users without taking a defensive stance.

These three components—*practitioner attitude, knowledge,* and *skills*—should be viewed as mutually interdependent. This interwoven fabric takes time to develop and is based on a desire and commitment to learn.

The first step toward achieving cultural competence is understanding and accepting the reality that openness to long-term, ongoing, and persistent development is required. As in all professional development there is no ideal completion . . . any serious initiative to work effectively with diverse client populations begins with this premise. (McPhatter, 1997, p. 260)

In contemporary social work practice, culturally competent practitioners need to have the knowledge to understand and interact with people from diverse backgrounds that include but are not limited to culture, ethnicity, class, gender, generation, sexual orientation, disability, religion, and national origin. The practitioner needs to have an awareness of historical and cultural experiences shaping people's lives; in addition is an understanding of the dynamics and consequences of social and economic injustice as expressed through processes of oppression and discrimination.

Twofold efforts are required to produce culturally competent social workers. First, social work students need to be educated to become self-aware and have an appreciation of their own value systems. Second, they need to be immersed in cultural experiences where they observe the uniqueness of every individual. Diversity education can be regarded as both a belief and an area of ethical practice rather than a specific knowledge area. Self-awareness and positive attitudes enable social work students to become more skilled in working in diverse settings.

Looking for opportunities for the student to learn about *multicultural practice* is like looking for opportunities to breathe, yet if it is not labeled "opportunity for multicultural practice," then, like breathing, students tend to be unaware.

Starting with your own relationship with the student, as supervisor, in what ways do your biographies differ and in what ways are they similar? Discussing the potential impact of difference and similarity in this core relationship is a first step to students considering difference and similarity between themselves and the various people with whom they work. What is your mutual commitment to promoting equality as an ethical stance (Loewenburg & Dolgoff, 2000)? Consider your own commitment to modeling multicultural practice.

As well as teaching about multicultural practice, it is important to demonstrate multicultural practice teaching. Lefevre (1998) focuses on the importance of recognizing and addressing imbalances of power between practice teacher and student to achieve a partnership approach to practice learning that exemplifies antidiscriminatory practice. The complex relationship between teacher and learner, assessor and student, mirrors the complexities at large. A simple analysis would suggest that the supervisor is more powerful than the student, and in some important dimensions, this is true; however, in addition to the possible complexities of race, gender, and so on (an African American female field instructor with a White male student?), good field supervision requires a willingness to expose one's work to a scrutiny that other practitioners do not experience. When it works well, the relationship between student and supervisor is a powerful one for all concerned, demonstrating the fact that power need not be a question of "if you have more, I have less."

NOTES FOR STUDENTS

LEARNING ABOUT MULTICULTURAL PRACTICE

Language

It is important to remember that multicultural practice equates with the fundamentals of good social work practice: the pursuit of equality and social justice. Multicultural practice requires an understanding of social structures and their impact on individuals and communities; in addition, it requires a commitment to ethical principles that value difference and diversity and to a form of practice that is both *self*-aware and *others*-aware.

Anxiety about language is sometimes a barrier to learning, especially the fear that you have to learn what it is "right" to say or believe. Often this is related to a belief that multicultural practice is about knowing the right terminology (Chand, Doel, & Yee, 1999). This is often referred to as "political correctness," which is an insidious attempt to trivialize important issues and too often has been successful in diverting attention from the serious issues that lie behind the use of language. We should not produce a list of taboo words but develop "a sensitivity to the complex role of language" (Thompson, 2002, p. 52).

It is the issues that lie behind the use of language that are important, not learning by rote a supposed list of right and wrong terms. Addressing these potential concerns very early in your studies with your practice teacher is the best way to free up discussion; this is not to give the green light to insensitive language but to open the door to a genuine dialogue about the impact and sensitivity of language. For a very clear explanation of terms such as *diversity, difference, discrimination,* and *oppression,* see Kirst-Ashman (2007).

Using Your Learning From *The Drawbridge*

We hope you have had the chance to work on *The Drawbridge* with others and to experience a wide range of opinion. We have used the exercise with many different groups, including social work students at the beginning of their training, and the results of the group of social work students (see Table 13.1) is typical of the diversity of the responses. What is your response to this?

Table 13.1	Student Responses at the Start of Their Social Work Training $(n = 25)$: Numbers of Rankings by Character					
	Ranking					
	6	5	4	3	2	1
Baron	10	7	5	0	0	3
Baroness	10	8	2	2	0	3
Gatekeeper	4	6	6	4	3	2
Lover	1	3	12	8	1	0
Boatman	0	0	0	4	12	9
Friend	0	1	0	7	9	8

NOTE: 6 = most responsible for the Baroness's death; 1 = least responsible.

The issue of responsibility is important. For instance, one of the most powerful weapons that insider groups use against outsider groups is guilt and blame. To the practical burden of poverty add the moral burden of guilt for not being able to find work or support a family adequately. It is important for social work to help people to untangle responsibilities and to challenge ideas of blame that the in-groups (in work, in money, in luck) attribute to the out-groups.

One of the most virulent examples of blaming out-groups is that attributed to people with positive HIV/AIDS status. Blaming somebody for catching a disease through sexual contact is as ridiculous as castigating a cholera victim for drinking contaminated water. With more knowledge of risks, of course individuals have increasing responsibility for their own behavior (witness the prosecution of individuals who knowingly infect others), but the attribution of blame to those with the virus is a typical example of the insider-outsider phenomenon.

The notion of insider-outsider groups reflects the general subtleties of multicultural practice. Within insider and outsider groups, there are yet more insider and outsider groups, sometimes called subcultures. For example, elders are often regarded or perceived as an out-group. We may hold many stereotypes about elders and see them as being a homogeneous group—yet they may belong to very different age cohorts. Indeed, some younger people hold the view that elderly people are inadequate, of lesser or little value, and unworthy of notice. These views and opinions are discriminatory and fail to uphold human dignity and appreciation of human diversity. Yet, lesbian, gay, and bisexual (LGB) people experience an additional dimension of discrimination. Tully (2000, p. 197) suggests that "gaying" (gay aging) results in additional stresses and scenarios not experienced by older heterosexuals; for example, health insurance policies often do not include nonheterosexual partners. Hospitals, nursing homes, and other health facilities may not acknowledge LGB relationships.

Social work is perhaps unique among professions in that it works largely with people who, in some way or another, are outsiders. Often, it is their very status as an outsider that brings them into contact with social work. In his historical analysis, *The Reluctant Welfare State,* Jansson (2005) provides insightful examples that demonstrate how, historically, many of the groups that social workers come into contact with have been regarded as out-groups.

- Immigrants: diversity; adjustment issues; language; mental trauma
- Women: feminization of poverty; lack of family leave; lack of child care; cuts in federal funding to programs for counseling about abortion
- Children: poverty; homicide; overcrowded schools; numbers of children in foster care
- Elderly: catastrophic health conditions; Alzheimer's—fourth greatest killer of elders; lack of day treatment programs
- Gay men and lesbians: AIDS epidemic; job discrimination; housing discrimination; access to Social Security
- People with disabilities: poverty; access to technology; closing of large institutions; lack of support in community

Undoubtedly, outsider groups often develop the strongest sense of identity. We hear little about "a White perspective" or "the heterosexual community." It can be illuminating to reverse the situation and subject insider groups to the scrutiny that outsider groups experience:

- What do you think is the cause of your heterosexuality?

- When did you first realize you might be heterosexual?

- Have you told your parents? What do they think?

- Would you say that you had an inadequate mother or father figure?

- Don't you think your heterosexuality might be a phase you are going through?

- Isn't it possible that what you need is a good gay partner?

- More than 90% of child molesters are heterosexuals. Would you feel comfortable about entrusting your children's education to heterosexual teachers?

SOURCE: "Do You Need Treatment?" (1989)

People who resist or change their identification arouse strong feelings in some others. This is especially true regarding gender and sexuality, as witnessed by the heated controversy over "outing" homosexuals, the ridicule that transsexuals experience, and the public fascination for transvestism as an entertainment. The strength that both in-groups and out-groups derive from identifying themselves in relation to each other (i.e., heterosexual as "not gay," homosexual as "not straight") is shown by the particular hostility reserved for groups that challenge this polarization, such as bisexual people and people of dual heritage.

Power and Empowerment

One especially important social work value is empowerment—the "process of increasing personal, interpersonal, or political power so that individuals can take action to improve their life situations" (Gutierrez, 2001, p. 210). Not all population groups enjoy equal opportunities for accessing environmental opportunities. Oppression, discrimination, dehumanization, and victimization prevent full participation in society. The conditions that cause people to seek help from social workers and social services are invariably consequences of oppression and injustice (Gil, 1994, p. 257).

A growing literature examines social work practice using a paradigm of power. O'Melia and Miley (2002) consider how people acquire and maintain power, with a number of contributors presenting their reflections and practice examples to represent work in a multiplicity of settings and with diverse populations. Thompson (2003, pp. 13–20) analyzes the way inequalities of power and opportunity operate at three levels—personal, cultural, and societal. The personal includes individual practice and personal prejudice; the cultural relates to commonalities, consensus, and conformity; and the structural refers to social divisions and oppression at a sociopolitical and institutional level (e.g., the fact that women are more likely to be imprisoned for a first offense).

At all three levels, it is necessary to consider how issues of social justice and equality can be advanced. As a student, and subsequently as a qualified social worker, you are likely to have most opportunity to promote equality at the personal level, some opportunity at the cultural level, and less at the structural level. However, your impact on the day-to-day experience of many individuals, families, and their communities is considerable, and you have regular opportunities to confront injustice and to increase people's sense of power. These opportunities are almost always dilemmas, too. How far to confront agency policies that disempower? How to sensitize an individual to his or her own sense of internalized oppression while not adding to that oppression? How to recognize and use your own power in ways that empower others? This is a lifelong quest.

Diversity and Difference

The commitment to promote social justice and equality is not new, and multicultural practice, therefore, has historical roots. There is not space to explore this here (see Fong, 2004; Fong & Furito, 2001). However, it should be remembered that the notion of diversity and difference is a current manifestation and that it, too, will evolve. Unfortunately, differences more often lead to discrimination than to celebration, and as a social work student, you need to work with this. Indeed, social work is itself an out-group. It will always make itself unpopular by its constant reminder of the out-groups' existence and disadvantage. It will not receive thanks or recognition (and, of course, it is but one small player in these changes), and there is still huge inequality and discrimination. Nevertheless, it is important not to internalize feelings of powerlessness as a profession and to celebrate those things that make our profession different and of value.

In the United States, the commitment of the social work profession to social justice and equality expresses itself through notions such as ethnic-sensitive and culturally competent practice. Unfortunately, discrimination and oppression often result from an acceptance of stereotypes—fixed mental images of members belonging to a group based on assumed attributes that reflect an overly simplified opinion about that group. However, one of the great strengths and beauties of the United States is not only its geographical diversity but also its human diversity. This vast range of differences among groups includes those related to "age, class, color, culture, disability, ethnicity, gender, gender identity and expression, immigration status, political ideology, race, religion, sex, and sexual orientation" (CSWE, 2008, Education Policy 2.1.4).

Despite the social work profession's commitment to social justice and the celebration of diversity, many people are extremely prejudiced toward those who are regarded or perceived as different, and there is, therefore, much work for social workers and others to do.

It is important to be aware of the dangers of internalized stereotyping. For example, a Jewish hospital social worker doubted that the doctors' concern that an infected rash on the leg of a Jewish child was exacerbated by dirt; as an insider, she knew that "Jewish mothers fuss and bathe their children a lot." However, in this case, it turned out that the child's rash was, indeed, worsened by lack of hygiene. The worker's insider knowledge of "proper Jewish behavior" misled her, and she subsequently described herself as feeling insulted by this mother's behavior. Her assumptions as an insider slowed the process of helping the mother come to grips with the problem (Devore & Schlesinger, 1999, p. 191). It is an interesting example of how easy it is to internalize stereotypes from *within* an outsider group, as well as the potential for discriminative oppressive practice. Notions of ethnic-sensitive and culturally competent practice are valuable, but they can neglect the structural levels of power and oppression.

ASSESSING YOUR LEARNING

The opportunities to assess multicultural practice are as ubiquitous as those to learn about it. A key hurdle to overcome is the idea that it is something special and discrete, which might occur on Tuesdays. Every encounter offers opportunities to promote equality and to work with diversity.

General statements of good intent are especially common in the area of multicultural practice, so avoid statements such as, "I worked with Jean Smith in a multicultural way." It is much more illuminating for yourself as well as for any assessor to be specific about how you promoted equality or, indeed, to be upfront about the dilemmas you have faced in terms of power, discrimination, diversity, and difference. As we have already noted, it is not a question of being able to write the "right phrases," whatever these might be, but to exemplify your own small part in the uneven struggle toward social justice and equality.

FURTHER READING

Diller, J. V. (2004). *Cultural diversity: A primer for the human services.* Belmont, CA: Brooks/Cole Wadsworth.

Devore, W., & Schlesinger, E. G. (1999). *Ethnic-sensitive social work practice* (5th ed.). Boston, MA: Allyn & Bacon.

Fong, R. (2004). *Culturally competent practice with immigrant and refugee children and families.* New York, NY: Guilford.

Lum, D. (Ed.). (2003). *Culturally competent practice: A framework for understanding diverse groups and justice issues* (2nd ed.). Pacific Grove, CA: Brooks/Cole/Thompson.

CHAPTER 14

Law-Informed Practice

A–Z of the Law consists of 24 situations in which there is a possibility that a law has been broken. Students are not being tested on their knowledge of the law but are asked to judge how *confident* they are that a law has been broken or not and to consider their own attitudes to the law.

NOTES FOR INSTRUCTORS[1]

PURPOSE

This chapter is designed to help students to understand the legal context and framework of law that governs their practice. In speaking of "law-informed practice," the activity recognizes that it is not possible for social workers to have detailed knowledge of all the laws that are significant to social work practice and that students need to be as aware of what they don't know as what they do. The activity aims to start a process that demystifies the law and legal processes.

METHOD

A–Z of the Law can be undertaken either by the field instructor and student together or in the fieldwork seminar. Make the exercise available beforehand, so that answers to the questions on the sheet can be prepared. Students should indicate against each item those situations where they are confident that a law has been broken, those where they are confident that it has not, and those where they are uncertain.

---

[1]See the Introduction to the book for suggestions about how instructors and students can, separately and together, use the activities in this book.

Discuss each item in turn; looking at the further question, if a law has been broken, should it be invoked? Follow the student's own interest in pursuing two or three of the situations further. Ask the student to do some follow-up work in relation to a couple of the scenarios that relate to the kind of work done during the placement.

NOTES FOR STUDENTS AND INSTRUCTORS

VARIATIONS

Once you, the student, are sensitized by this activity to the importance of law-informed practice, it is helpful for the instructor to provide case material tailored to the placement setting as examples of the ways specific laws can influence, guide, or determine practice. A case example that is set at different stages in its development helps students to look at the legal options at various steps in the "career" of the case and the consequences of choosing or not choosing particular paths.

USE BY OTHER PROFESSIONS

Other professional groups are likely to operate within different legal contexts depending on the nature of their role and function. The scope of the questions can be adapted to fit with those responsibilities—for example, the administration of drugs, housing law, and obtaining consent to a particular procedure.

EDUCATIONAL POLICY ACCREDITATION STANDARDS

The topics in this chapter relate to the following *Educational Policy and Accreditation Standards* (*EPAS*) 2008 Primary Core Competencies (Council on Social Work Education, 2008):

1. Apply social work ethical principles to guide professional practice.

2. Apply critical thinking to inform and communicate professional judgments.

3. Engage diversity and difference in practice.

4. Respond to contexts that shape practice.

FOR STUDENTS AND INSTRUCTORS

ACTIVITY 14: *A–Z OF THE LAW: SPIRIT AND LETTER*

Has a law been broken?	Yes	No	Unsure
Sixteen-year-old Arnie has been sniffing glue in the bathrooms at school.	▪	▪	▪
The Benner family has their electricity disconnected because of nonpayment of bills.	▪	▪	▪
The Creswells have parked their van in a disabled-only car parking space. They do not have a disabled badge.	▪	▪	▪
Jason Dean does not declare his volunteer work to the unemployment benefits office.	▪	▪	▪
Social worker Eve claims 50 extra miles on her car allowance to subsidize a trip for the members of her substance abuse group.	▪	▪	▪
Landlord Mr. Friesen has locked a tenant out of the apartment, complaining of "filth and squalor."	▪	▪	▪
The housing authority has failed to provide a stair-lift to Ms. Goodman, who suffers from multiple sclerosis and lives in her own two-story house.	▪	▪	▪
Eighteen-year-old Howard, who is severely disabled, requests his key worker to masturbate him. His key worker Ian agrees to do this.	▪	▪	▪
Jackson reveals he had sexual intercourse with a 14-year-old girl 3 years ago.	▪	▪	▪
There is no leaflet available in Kurdish for Stefan Kiyani to read about social services in his area.	▪	▪	▪
Mrs. Lehry is not registered as a child minder, but she minds two children after school twice a week.	▪	▪	▪

Michael tells a group for young offenders that
his parents grow marijuana on their allotment.

Mrs. Nyczeski was not informed when
her granddaughter was fostered.

Probation officer Pat is told that the Pilzs
have reconnected their electricity.

The Quereshis are denied attendance at the case
review of their daughter who is in residential care
with the Department of Health and Human Services.

Fearing for Jim Rafferty's safety, his home care
attendant Rose breaks a kitchen window
in order to gain entry.

Ten-year-old Sam has stolen a chocolate bar
from the sweet shop.

Seven-year-old Tilly Benner has been smacked
in a public place by her foster parent.

Social worker Una makes an emergency call on
her mobile phone, while driving to inform the home
for older people that she is bringing Mrs. Unwin
to stay in an emergency.

Twelve-year-old Vinnie has been left unattended
at home for an hour in the evening.

Care worker Wendy has locked a door to stop
Mrs. Williams (who is demented)
from leaving the center.

A note signed "Mr. X" is dropped through
the Kiyani brothers' mailbox telling them to go
back to where they came from.

On the way to an urgent call, corrections officer
Yvonne drives at 37 mph in a 30-mph zone.

Zoë Benner is denied access to her case file
by her social worker.

If a law has been broken, should it be invoked?
If so, what steps would you take to invoke it?

NOTES FOR INSTRUCTORS

TEACHING ABOUT LAW-INFORMED PRACTICE

The *A–Z* activity has two main purposes. The first is to sensitize the student to the importance of the legal context of social work practice, and the second is to dispel some of the mystique about the law, offering clear, hard, and fast rules. These two purposes may seem paradoxical—the one elevating the profile of law and the other diminishing it. In fact, the activity is an opportunity for the student to develop law-informed practice, tuning into the connections between social work and a legal framework. According to Stein (2004, p. 4), for a variety of reasons, knowledge of the law is essential to effective social work practice, as the law determines

1. which programs will be established,

2. the level of funding that will be provided,

3. which services will be available,

4. which populations will be served,

5. the rules social workers must follow when they provide services.

Students need to be honest with themselves about their attitude toward the law. For example, where would the student rate the following statements on a scale of 1 to 10 (strongly disagree to strongly agree)?

The law is

- A weapon the powerful use to keep the powerless in their place
- A safeguard for the individual against the state
- Relatively arbitrary in the way it is applied
- A reflection of social tensions and dilemmas
- Something that can only be created by a religious body
- An intrusion into the lives of individuals
- Slow to catch up with social changes
- White, male, and middle class
- An ass
- A mechanism to regulate social exchange
- Something that should never be broken

Linking Social Work and the Law

Helping students to understand the relationship of social work and the law can be aided by encouraging them to discuss three distinctions, which help to expose different aspects of law and its relationship to social work:

Distinction 1: The Relationship of Law and Social Work. Braye and Preston-Shoot (2002, p. 62) characterize the complex relationship between social work and the law in three different ways:

1. Law provides the "defining mandate" for practice (i.e., it provides a specification of what must be done).

2. Law describes a generalized "ethical duty of care," which determines the responsibilities of the social worker.

3. Both of these polarities (1 and 2) are key determinants of social work, and it is for practitioners and managers to determine the balance to be struck in any given situation.

Ask the student to consider the implications of each of these characteristics.

Distinction 2: Domains of Law. Braye and Preston-Shoot (2002) also helpfully draw a distinction between the different domains of *social work law* and *social welfare law*:

social work law, which includes powers and duties that expressly mandate social work activity, and *social welfare law,* comprising statues with which social workers must be familiar if they are to respond appropriately to service users' needs but which do not permit or require specific actions by them. (p. 63)

Ask the students to relate the notion of domains to a situation with which they have been working.

Distinction 3: Types of Legal Instrument. Various types of legal requirement derive from different forms of legal instrument:

1. **Federal and State Constitutional Law:** The U.S. Constitution[2] is the supreme law of the land.

---

[2]Available at *www.archives.gov/exhibits/charters/constitution_transcript.html*

This entails that laws are made to carry out the purposes expressed in the U.S. Constitution, for example, to protect the right to free speech or to ensure that due process under the law is the supreme law of the land. In addition to the U.S. Constitution and the Bill of Rights, each of the 50 states has its own constitution, and many have its own bill of rights.

2. **Statutory Law:** Congress and the legislators of each state make statutory law. The majority of social welfare programs are created because a legislative body passed a law to channel public funds to programs that assist people in need.

3. **Executive Branch of Government:** At both federal and state levels, the executive branches of government participate in lawmaking in three ways:

    a. Bill of interest to the president or governor is introduced by a member of the executive's political party.

    b. The president or governor engages directly in lawmaking by issuing executive orders.

    c. Administrative agencies that are part of Health and Human Services or the U.S. Department of Education guide those who are responsible for implementing legislation. Administrative law is of central importance to human service providers because the rules govern the day-to-day operation of social welfare programs.

4. **Common Law:** commonly accepted laws, which are interpreted by the judiciary, based upon precedent; the common law is modified by judicial judgments and forms a body of case law.

5. **Judicial Review:** refers to the power of the courts to review other branches of government, to overturn those that violate the U.S. Constitution or the constitution of a state, or, in the case of administrative law, to rule that regulations are not supported by the statute that they seek to clarify.

6. **Quasi-legal Statements:** documents produced by various nongovernmental bodies that provide for the setting of standards and regulations. The Council on Social Work Education (*EPAS* standards) and National Association of Social Workers (*Code of Ethics*) are examples.

Ask students to consider an aspect of practice and to identify the various forms of legal instrument that govern their practice in this field.

When organizing learning opportunities for students, it is helpful to encourage them to be clear about the way in which they conceptualize the relationship of social work to the law in these and other ways. At present, the Council on Social Work Education does not require students either at the undergraduate or graduate level to take law as part of a professional social work program. This is very troubling when we consider the numerous areas of practice where knowledge of the law is central to good professional practice (see "Learning About Law-Informed Practice").

While there are some dual degrees being offered (MSW/JDs), it is to be hoped that the CSWE may in the future incorporate law into its educational policy and accreditation standards. Increasingly, social work professionals and attorneys are working together to promote the well-being of their clients, and there is a great deal of intersection between legal and social work concerns. Hence, law must be a central part of social work teaching and pivotal to professional practice (i.e., that law is the "defining mandate" of social work).

There are also critics of the prescriptive approach to teaching law. Braye and Preston-Shoot (1990, 1992) stated that teaching law and its subsequent application "must be considered in a conceptual frame of practice dilemmas which confront every practitioner and create role conflict, uncertainty, ambiguity, and insecurity." These dilemmas, "posed by taking account both of the law and the ethical duty of care in professional practice, can lead social workers into the eye of the storm." There are several tensions, such as rights versus risk, care versus control, needs versus resources, duty versus power, and legalism versus professionalism. They suggest that it is not just knowledge of the law that must be conveyed "but the problems and the dilemmas in applying it." It is interesting, then, to note that in the United Kingdom, where law is taught, the teaching of law for social workers has come under considerable and sustained criticism because social workers in the United Kingdom in the past have been seen as neither knowledgeable about nor able to make effective use of the law (Ball, Harris, Roberts, & Vernon, 1988).

Opportunities for Law-Informed Practice

Of particular interest to field instructors are Braye and Preston-Shoot's (1992) findings about ways to help students learn, retain, and apply law teaching. The group of students with whom they worked had reservations about the lack of practice opportunities, feeling that it is difficult to retain knowledge of the law without putting it to use. Practice-led methods of learning were preferred by two thirds of the student group, where a case example was used to trigger discussion and subsequent teaching inputs linked directly to concerns arising from the discussion. It is interesting that Braye and Preston-Shoot (1992) saw evidence of "an unsettling effect" as some of the students moved from a state of blissful ignorance to a realization of what they did not know.

Approaches to teaching law have been developed in a range of ways: For example, Duncan, Piper, and Warren-Adamson (2003) describe how an eco-logical approach to practice can be used to develop an understanding of the ever-widening circles of law that may be relevant. While Braye and a group of students comment on the benefit of using enquiry action methods for learning about the law (Braye, Lebacq, Mann, and Midwinter, 2003), and Broadbent and White (2003) explore how "decision-making" techniques can be used to promote students' appreciation of the law.

Seeking Legal Expertise

Writing some time ago, Stevenson (1988) doubted whether it is desirable or feasible to acquire factual legal knowledge during basic professional education and questioned the reliability of such knowledge. Inaccurate legal advice given to a service user or provider is worse than no advice at all—but the function of a social worker is not to provide definitive legal advice. Even so, students do need to recognize that social work sits within a legal framework, and they should know how that framework constructs their work. It is important that students cultivate an understanding of what they don't know and the skills to know when and how to seek additional expertise. Increasingly, there is an expectation that at the point of qualification, students will have more than a generalized familiarity with the way in which social work is constructed by the law—that they will have a working knowledge of some aspects relevant to par-ticular areas of practice.

Initially, students need to develop a clear picture of the practice goals in a particular piece of work, with the people involved and *within a legal framework*. Once they have this picture, they should know how and where to seek the advice that will help them to achieve those practice goals; detailed legal advice will, in turn, reshape some aspects of those practice goals, but it is a myth to believe that "application of the law" will by itself bring clarity to the picture. The law is not cut-and-dried; it seldom offers concrete conclusions because—like social work practice—it, too, reflects the dilemmas in society. Braye and Preston-Shoot (1997) expose other myths about the law: that it is helpful and neutral, confers substantial powers, and provides good and right solutions.

In conclusion, knowledge probably sticks when it is related to specific prac-tice examples and when the student has used it personally. It needs consistent reenforcement. Students need some detailed legal knowledge within the context of developing law-informed practice, so that they know which questions to ask and where and how to seek appropriate legal expertise to provide the detail.

NOTES FOR STUDENTS

LEARNING ABOUT LAW-INFORMED PRACTICE

> Social workers have been criticized for being over-zealous in their use of the law and for failing to use available legal powers. (Preston-Shoot, 1993, p. 65)

This quotation neatly encapsulates the *actual* response of social work to the law. It is extremely difficult to achieve a balance in the way that the law is deployed in social work on account of the complex situations with which social workers have to deal.

Opportunities

Most placements will provide you with some opportunities to develop law-informed practice, if not a detailed knowledge of the law.

1. *Families and the law:* Social workers play a key role in providing services to families, and you might have a placement in a family services agency, child welfare agency, hospital, or school. Here, you are likely to encounter family law that is concerned with marriage and divorce, family violence, child custody, visitation and support, adoption, ownership of property, and inheritance rights.

2. *Care and protection of children:* Parents have a right to the care, custody, and control of their children, as well as a duty to protect them from harm. If parents fail to meet their responsibilities, the state—under the doctrine of *parens patriae,* meaning the state as parent or protector—has the authority to intervene in family life to protect children from harm. In addition, states are funded for their child protection work with two federal statutes: the Child Abuse Prevention and Treatment Act of 1974 (CAPTA) and the Adoption Assistance and Child Welfare Act of 1980 (AACWA).

3. *Adoption:* Social workers are significant actors in all phases of the adoption process, which provides a family for children whose parents have died, voluntarily relinquished their rights, or had their rights terminated. First, it would be the social worker who would initially meet with the individual or couple who wish to adopt. Second, the social worker comes into contact with the child in need of permanency planning. Third, a social worker is asked by the court, an attorney, or social service agency to prepare a preadoption home study, consult on any matters that arise in a pending adoption, or testify on matters before the court.

4. *Domestic violence:* Usually this term refers to a dispute between two adults in an intimate relationship; indeed, this definition is used by the U.S.

Department of Justice, which defines domestic violence as criminal acts occurring between individuals with an existing or formerly close relationship. However, in some states, the term *family violence* has replaced *domestic violence,* and this term embraces child abuse and elder abuse as well. The earliest federal response to domestic violence occurred in the 1980s when Congress enacted the Family Violence Prevention and Services Act and the Victim Compensation and Assistance Fund. In 1994, Congress passed the Violence Against Women Act (VAWA). In some states, the courts take into account domestic violence when deciding child custody.

5. *Elder abuse:* This phenomenon came to attention in the late 1970s, following public awareness of and statutory reform that addressed child abuse and domestic violence between adults in intimate relationships. State laws governing adult protective services (APS) define vulnerable adults age 60 or 65 and, in some states, anyone older than 18 who is vulnerable because a disability prevents the individual from acting on his or her own behalf. Abuse of a vulnerable adult may be prosecuted as a civil or criminal matter.

6. *Legal issues in health care:* The work of social workers is affected by publicly funded programs, such as Medicare, Medicaid, the State Children's Health Insurance Program, and programs operated by the Indian Health Service and the Veterans Administration, as well as by private insurance. Social workers play a significant role in the health care field by

   a. Providing direct services to patients and their families

   b. Planning for patients' aftercare needs

   c. Helping patients understand their rights

   d. Participating in the evaluation of adults whose competency to make medical decisions is challenged

   e. Advocating for the patient

7. *Mental health and the law:* Social work practice is influenced by publicly funded programs such as Medicare and Medicaid; by the Mental Health Block Grant, which provides funds to support community-based treatment services; and by programs operated by the Indian Health Service and the Veterans Administration, as well as by private insurance schemes. Social workers also play a significant role in the field of mental health by

   a. Providing direct services

   b. Evaluating individuals and families

   c. Preparing reports and treatment plans

   d. Interpreting reports for nonprofessionals

   e. Initiating commitment proceedings

   f. Advocating for the rights of people mentally ill

Legal Consequences of Professional Actions

In addition to a knowledge of the legal framework, it is also important for you to be aware of your own feelings about how the law should be invoked. This involves careful consideration of the legal consequences of professional actions as well as understanding what is legally permissible. In some countries, the individual practitioner can be legally held to account for actions taken. For example, in the United States, there is a growing interest in liability issues in relation to social work practice (Houston-Vega, Neuhring, & Daguio, 1996).

According to Stein (2004, p. 151), there are a variety of conditions that render social workers, their supervisors, and/or the agencies that employ them vulnerable to suit, including the following:

1. An increase in the number of states that license social workers and the provisions in licensing law for disciplining those whose practices do not conform to statutory mandates

2. Ethical codes and standards of practice that provide yardsticks against which behavior can be measured and judged as suitable or lacking

3. Laws that mandate reporting of child abuse and neglect and that provide penalties for failure to report

4. Laws that require a professional to warn a third party whose health or safety is threatened by a client and provide a basis for suits that allege a "failure to warn"

5. An increase in the number of states that have waived their sovereignty immunity, thereby eliminating a shield that barred suits against state employees

6. The litigious nature of our society and the conviction of some that a legal remedy exists for all injuries, also with an increase in the number of social workers going into private practice, which increases the visibility of the social work profession

7. The growing trend to provide internet-based services, which raises new issues with regard to maintaining confidentiality and ensuring that those who seek help reside in the state in which the social worker is licensed to practice

It should be borne in mind that the law does not provide definitive answers for practice:

The law cannot tell social workers what to do in every circumstance: it can only set out a framework. The law cannot resolve the everyday tensions and dilemmas of social work practice, since there is no ready prescription for resolving the complex problems that sometimes confront social workers. Above all the law cannot substitute for sound professional practice. (Johns, 2003, p. 7)

Approval-Disapproval Continuum

Return to the scenarios in *A–Z*. Your response to the law in different situations is an important influence on your actions. How strongly do you feel about each of them? Take your three lists (one where you think a law has been broken, one where you think it has not, and one where you are uncertain) and draw a *continuum line* for each list. Using one end for strongly approve of the action taken (1) and one end for strongly disapprove (10), place each scenario on its continuum:

A LAW HAS BEEN BROKEN

strongly approve	neutral response	strongly disapprove
(1)	(5)	(10)

A LAW HAS NOT BEEN BROKEN

strongly approve	neutral response	strongly disapprove
(1)	(5)	(10)

UNCERTAIN WHETHER A LAW HAS BEEN BROKEN

strongly approve	neutral response	strongly disapprove
(1)	(5)	(10)

Are there situations where you are confident that a law has been broken but where you feel less disapproval than situations where a law has not been broken?

Ball et al. (1988) describe these categories of legal activity:

- Enforcing the rights of service users and carers
- Protecting the vulnerable
- Protecting society
- Enforcing compliance

Which category do you think each of the situations in *A–Z* might fall into?

ASSESSING YOUR LEARNING

The assessment of law-informed practice can focus on two broad areas:

1. The extent to which you understand the relationship of social work practice to the law—in other words, the context and importance of law in a particular site for social work practice

2. Legal knowledge and the ability to apply elements of the law in practice (e.g., in the contexts described earlier: families and the law, care and protection of children, adoption, domestic violence, legal issues in heath care, mental health)

You need to be very clear which is required. Other professions engage in rote learning of law pertinent to their practice. Social work has resisted this, but the increased importance given to this aspect of practice suggests that there should be a stronger emphasis on assessing your abilities to work effectively with the law in day-to-day practice.

FURTHER READING

Brayne, H., & Carr, H. (2003). *Law for social workers* (8th ed.). Oxford, UK: Oxford University Press.

Cull, L.-A., & Roche, J. (2001). *The law and social work: Contemporary issues for practice*. New York, NY: Palgrave.

Johns, R. (2003). *Using the law in social work*. Exeter, UK: Learning Matters.

Stein, T. J. (2004). *The role of law in social work practice and administration*. New York, NY: Columbia University Press.

CHAPTER **15**

Generalist and Specialist Practice

ABOUT ACTIVITY 15: *ESSENCE OF SOCIAL WORK*

Essence of Social Work is designed to trigger a consideration of what is different about, and what is common to, the various manifestations of social work. In this chapter, students are encouraged to look for the "core" of social work practice.

NOTES FOR INSTRUCTORS[1]

PURPOSE

One of the major continuing shifts in the construction of social work practice is the emphasis given to generalist and specialist practice. This activity is designed to explore some of the differences between these different kinds of practice, and the chapter will help to clarify some of the confusion in understanding these terms.

METHOD

- Read the advertisements in the *Essence* activity. They are all taken from the website of Job Search Monster.com. The names of employing agencies have been changed, contacts and addresses have been omitted, but in all other respects, the advertisements are unaltered.

---

[1]See the Introduction to the book for suggestions about how instructors and students can, separately and together, use the activities in this book.

247

NOTES FOR STUDENTS AND INSTRUCTORS

VARIATIONS

Five or six detailed job descriptions from your own agency might draw out the commonalities and differences even more clearly. Try comparing these with adverts from other non–social work journals for related posts (e.g., nurses, psychologists, or teachers)—how different and how similar are they?

In the United States, for a variety of reasons that will be discussed in more detail later, members of the social work profession see themselves as the providers of specialist practice or, at the very least, as specializing in specific fields. To begin to understand the great diversity in the way specialisms are represented, students can be asked to make a note of all different types of specialist social work practice of which they are aware. A harder task may be to identify the "social work" function in these different forms of practice.

USE BY OTHER PROFESSIONS

The nature and desirability of specialist practice is a matter of debate within many professional disciplines. Specialists are well developed in medical practice. In addition to the "territorial" approach or functional approach to medical specialists, there are other kinds of demarcation. Acupuncturists, chiropractors, and homeopaths specialize in alternative *methods* of practice. By contrast, social work does not have a strong base in practice methodology. It seems that everyone either is eclectic (code for agnostic) or claims to practice in a task-centered way, despite the absence of all the formal elements of the task-centered model. Indeed, agencies would tend to be suspicious of practitioners declaring that they are method specialists; seeking a position as a "Brief Solution Specialist" or a "Cognitive Behaviorist Specialist" would be unlikely to carry much weight.

EDUCATIONAL POLICY ACCREDITATION STANDARDS

The topics in this chapter relate to the following *Educational Policy and Accreditation Standards* (EPAS) 2008 Primary Core Competencies (Council on Social Work Education [CSWE], 2008):

1. Apply critical thinking to inform and communicate professional judgments.

2. Engage in research-informed practice and practice-informed research.

3. Engage in policy practice to advance social and economic well-being and to deliver effective social work services.

4. Respond to contexts that shape practice.

ACTIVITY 15: *ESSENCE OF SOCIAL WORK*

Social Work Supervisor

About the Job

Description:

Child welfare agency New Options for Children, Inc. (NOC) is an innovative child welfare agency located in Manhattan, which provides services to medically fragile children and their families. NOC is currently seeking applicants for a Social Work Supervisor.

Responsibilities:

1. Reports to the Assistant Director/Director of Foster Care and Adoption, and supervises four (4) MSW level foster care and adoption social workers.

2. Ensures that social workers are conducting permanency planning activities in an appropriate and timely manner, that workers are identifying the needs of each case, and are either providing directly or are accessing the entire range of clinical and concrete services that the case requires.

3. Assists supervisees in prioritizing workloads.

4. Ensures that social workers are meeting all ACS and NAC mandates and paperwork requirements.

5. Attends Family Team Conferences, Service Plan Reviews, and Case Reviews.

6. Prepares social workers for court proceedings, and be willing to testify.

7. Works collaboratively with colleagues in an interdisciplinary team model.

8. Ensures supervisees' adherence to all agency personnel policies and procedures.

9. Has responsibility on a rotating basis for 24 hour on-call duty and Saturday office administrative coverage.

Additional Qualifications:

1. MSW with a minimum of 5 years post graduate experience.

2. Prior experience in child welfare, supervisory experience preferred.

3. Knowledge of health-related factors in working with physically disabled and/or chronically ill children, as well as experience in the area of child development.

4. LCSW.

Hospice Social Work Manager

About the Job: The staff and volunteers of the Hospice Care Program combine sensitivity and compassion with knowledge and skill. Our goal is to promote comfort and quality of life for terminally ill patients by providing the best medical, emotional and spiritual care at home. Join us in making a critical difference at a difficult time in the lives of our patients and their families.

In this role, you will be responsible for developing, coordinating, implementing and evaluating direct social work services to patients and families in Hospice Program. You will function as a co-manager with the Hospice Team Manager for the Social Work staff.

Licensure: License and current registration to practice as a Licensed Social Worker in California required. Valid driver's license may be required, as determined by operational/regional needs.

Education: Master's Degree in Social Work from an accredited school of social work required.

Experience: Minimum five-years of experience as MSW in a health care setting required, preferably in a Hospice setting. Minimum of one-year experience in supervision of Certified Social Workers or graduate Social Work Students required. Experience dealing with terminally ill patients and families required. Effective oral and interpersonal communication skills required.

Social Worker

Hazelnut Creek, CA 94595

HCR Manor Care provides a range of services including skilled nursing care assisted living post-acute medical and rehabilitation care hospice care home health care and rehabilitation therapy.

Responsible to provide medically related social work services so that each resident may attain or maintain the highest practicable level of physical mental and psychosocial well-being.

In return for your expertise you'll enjoy excellent training industry-leading benefits and unlimited opportunities to learn and grow. Be a part of the team leading the nation in healthcare.

Two years of social work supervised experience working directly with geriatric clients in a health care setting desirable.

EDUCATION:

Bachelor's degree in Social Work or similar professional qualifications.

Social Work Manager—Health Outreach Program

Making it Possible: Arkansas Hospital

Behind every patient success story—before every clinical breakthrough—stands the unparalleled team of professionals at Arkansas Hospital.

With leading specialists in every field of medicine, the advances pioneered at Arkansas Hospital have improved the lives of people everywhere. We deliver the highest level of inpatient, ambulatory and preventative care. Be one of the people who make it possible. Social Work Manager—Health Outreach Program

Among the oldest Social Work Departments in the country, Arkansas Hospital continues a long-standing emphasis on clinical expertise within our five centers of excellence. As a leader in social work practice, education and research, we are proud that 99% of our staff is Master's-prepared, demonstrating our commitment to a highest level of performance. Our mission is focused on improving the quality of life and advocating for patients and their families; maintaining and enhancing professional social work standards; and providing education and training to the greater community at large.

In this role, you will oversee Health Outreach, an older adults community-based outreach program. This program includes a caregiver's service and a personal emergency response system (PERS). The Social Work Manager is responsible for providing leadership, supervising and managing the programs. You will also be responsible for program and staff development, marketing, and producing newsletters. This position requires a high degree of creativity, flexibility, and ability to network and market programs to professionals and clients.

Arkansas State Licensure as a LCSW and a minimum of three years supervisory experience working in a geriatric or health care setting.

Experience working with older adults, caregivers, health education, budgetary experience a plus.

Child Study Center

Is currently seeking a highly motivated individual to join our dynamic team!
   This is for a full-time Social Worker position!
   This position will coordinate and facilitate the administrative aspects of the Autism Services Department.
   Key areas of responsibility:

1. Educating families on services available,

2. Assessing family and patients' current social situation,

(Continued)

(Continued)

3. Coordinating all administrative activities,

4. Coordinating interdisciplinary staffing for children served in the Autism Services Department,

5. Serving as clinical care manager for selected patients,

6. Establishing referral patterns and coordinating and facilitating referrals,

7. Monitoring compliance with funding sources,

8. Evaluating and updating patient reading materials,

9. Coordinating educational opportunities for families.

The successful candidate will possess a Master's Degree in Social Work, current license as a Social Worker (LSW) in the State of Texas and two (2) to five (5) years of experience working with children with Autism Spectrum Disorders required. Exceptional communication, problem solving and organizational skills required. Must be able to relate well to the public, demonstrate good communication skills, knowledge of community resources and ability to establish and maintain good working relationships with staff and community agencies.

Child Study Center offers a comprehensive benefits package, which includes: Medical, Dental, Vision, Paid Time Off, 401k, Life and Disability insurance.

Social Work Supervisor—Foster Boarding Home

About the Job

Making a difference since 1942, Cardinal O'Brien Services (COS), is a well respected not-for-profit human service agency providing abused and neglected children, at risk families and developmentally disabled adults with the hope for a brighter future by providing countless hours of service each year to more than 3,100 and 2,000 families. COS provides care daily to more than 1,500 children and their families and nearly 100 adults and teens with mental retardation, helping to enhance the quality of their lives and support the sanctity of family.

COS is recruiting for the position of Supervisor in our foster and therapeutic foster boarding departments in Florida. The supervisor is an integral member of the Foster Boarding Service management team, ensuring all casework units are meeting agency mandates, policies and procedures. The supervisor assumes a teaching role as to the purpose, structure, and function of the Agency, together with on-going and new methods of sound Social Work practices. Good practice involves a readiness to listen and an ability to apply the benefits of prior experience to new situations and strives to encourage all supervisors to develop a sense of awareness of their own responsibility to share in the making of such decisions.

Successful candidates will be able to:

- Provide, thorough regular weekly Supervisory Conferences, on-going direction, training, and guidance to Case Workers in fulfilling their responsibilities.
- Monitor and ensure that a permanency goal has been established for each and every child and to monitor progress in the achievement of that goal.
- Orient new Case Workers to the Agency and their responsibilities.
- Ensure the timely implementation of clinical, academic, and other recommendations.
- Maintain supervisory log of weekly supervisions and case reviews.
- Provide emergency and overnight cell phone coverage.
- To ensure Case Workers' delivery of service in accord with the standards promulgated by NYC Child Services and NYSDSS.
- To ensure the Agency's accountability as related to the above via Progress Notes, FASP, Permanency Hearings, etc.
- To participate in Service Plan Reviews.
- To participate in Transfer Conferences.
- To formally review the plan for each child via the Service Plan Review Update on a semi-annual basis.
- To ensure supervisory entry and review of all data into CONNECTIONS.
- To participate in In-Service Training.
- To participate in Monthly Supervisor's Team Sessions and Staff Meetings.
- To evaluate the performance of each Case Worker in the unit, sharing significant information with that worker and with the Director when indicated.
- To provide supervisory case coverage in the absence of the Case Worker.
- To approve both the accumulation and expenditure of overtime.

POSITION REQUIRES A MASTER OF SOCIAL WORK DEGREE. APPLICANTS WITH DEGREES OTHER THAN MSW WILL NOT BE CONSIDERED. Two to five years supervisory experiences required. Must be computer literate, versed in the Connections applications.

- What do you consider are the main similarities and what are the main differences in the work that these job advertisements reveal? Compare the idea of "social work" found in each of them.

- What do you think the job adverts tell you about current social work practice? Try asking five people who are not connected with social work (friends and relatives, for instance) what social work is.

NOTES FOR INSTRUCTORS

TEACHING ABOUT GENERALIST AND SPECIALIST PRACTICE

What Is Generalist Practice?

Social work practitioners regard the profession as "generalist": As such, members of the profession are encouraged to take a broad look at the human condition when working with people, not to specialize simply in one aspect of practice. A belief in the interdependency of individual and social issues lies at the heart of the profession's core principles. When helping someone who is physically dependent on alcohol, for instance, the social worker does not merely help the individual but also considers working with his or her family, neighbors, peers, co-workers, and the broader social context to effect change.

Generalist social work practice can involve a wide range of situations: a homeless family, a child unable to get along with peers, a pregnant teenager, a sick elderly person unable to care for himself or herself, an alcoholic parent, a community that is trying to address its drug abuse problem, or a public assistance agency struggling to amend its policies to conform to new federal regulations. Therefore, generalist practitioners must be prepared to address many kinds of difficult situations.

Generalist practice involves working effectively at many different levels. It requires the assumption of a wide range of professional roles and involves the application of critical thinking skills to the planned-change process. It emphasizes client empowerment within the broader context of his or her environment.

The social work profession has struggled with the concept of generalist practice for many years. In the past, new practitioners were educated in only one skill area (such as work with individuals, groups, or communities) or one area of practice (such as children and families or policy and administration). Although many social workers contend that the generalist approach has been central to social work practice since its inception, only recently has there been analysis and exposition of this practice approach. With the new *EPAS* standards of 2008, Educational Policy 2.0 asserts that the BSW curriculum prepares its graduates for generalist practice through mastery of the core competencies. The MSW curriculum prepares its graduates for advanced practice through mastery of the core competencies augmented by knowledge and practice behaviors specific to a concentration (CSWE, 2008, p. 3).

Definition of Generalist Practice

The Social Work Continuum Committee of the Association of Baccalaureate Program Directors (2009) defines "generalist social work practice" as follows:

Generalist social work practitioners work with individuals, families, groups, communities and organizations in a variety of social work and host settings. Generalist practitioners view clients and client systems from a strength's perspective in order to recognize, support, and build upon the innate capabilities of all human beings. They use a professional problem solving process to engage, assess, broker services, advocate, counsel, educate, and organize with and on behalf of client and client systems. In addition, generalist practitioners engage in community and organizational development. Finally, generalist practitioners evaluate service outcomes in order to continually improve the provision and quality of services most appropriate to client needs.

Generalist social work practice is guided by the NASW Code of Ethics and is committed to improving the well being of individuals, families, groups, communities and organizations and furthering the goals of social justice. (www.bpd.online.org)

The Derby Street community (see Chapter 1, *Permission to Learn*, p. 29) illustrates the need for a variety of situations that call on generalist social work practice. Many of the issues are complex and require the social worker to look at a complete picture of the individual and their networks. A useful supplementary activity is to ask students to consider which workers from their own agency and from other agencies might be involved with the different residents and what opportunities there are for interprofessional working. Evidently, there is a social work *role* to be played in each and every household and also with the neighborhood as a whole.

Significance of the Generalist-Specialist Debate

Students may consider the issue of generalist and specialist social work to be of historical rather than current interest. Why might it be important, then, for them to consider these issues?

Definition of Specialist Practice/Advanced Practice

According to the Council on Social Work Education (2008, *EPAS* standards, Educational Policy M 2.2),

> Advanced practitioners refine and advance the quality of social work practice and that of the larger social work profession. They synthesize and apply a broad range of interdisciplinary and multidisciplinary knowledge and skills. In areas of specialization, advanced practitioners assess, intervene and evaluate to promote human and social well-being. To do so they suit each action to the circumstances at hand, using the discrimination learned through experience and self improvement. Advanced practitioners incorporate all of the core competencies augmented by knowledge and practice behaviors specific to a concentration. (p. 8)

It is important to help students see the continuing significance of these issues, as part of their enquiry into how social work is conceptualized. The heart searching about "what is social work?" and repeated concerns about the survival of the profession point to at least two major issues:

- First, practitioners are uncertain about conceptualizations of social work. This chapter may assist students and practitioners alike to set their own practice in a wider, intellectual context.

- Second, even when a conceptual map for social work has been agreed and understood, the nature of a generic core is by no means a given. There will still be debate about what is it that is common to all forms of practice, which we call social work.

OPPORTUNITIES FOR GENERALIST AND SPECIALIST PRACTICE

One of the challenges facing students and qualified social workers in the United States is that many agencies that offer internships have historically been associated with a specific population, or sectarian group (e.g., Jewish Child Care Association, Young Adult Institute, Catholic Charities, Salvation Army, United Cerebral Palsy, the Alzheimer's Association, Hebrew Home for the Aged, Veterans Administration). Historically, these agencies have viewed their function as serving a particular demographic group or subsection of the population, and many students when they enter schools of social work assert that they wish to work or specialize with a particular population.

LEARNING ABOUT GENERALIST AND SPECIALIST PRACTICE

The note on the flysheet of Zofia Butrym's book, *The Nature of Social Work,* was written in 1976 but remains apt today:

> This book argues that the present lack of consensus about the nature and the functions of social work constitute a serious problem which, if allowed to continue, will result in loss of purpose and usefulness by social workers. It therefore attempts to answer the question: *What is social work?*

Twenty years on, the title of Malcolm Payne's book asks, *What Is Professional Social Work?* His narrative, which runs through the book, "implies that being involved in education and management, being in the voluntary and statutory sectors and doing community, policy and development work can all be regarded as social work" (Payne, 1996, pp. 9–10).

If experienced social workers in educational and practice settings are *still* asking "What is social work?" you can be forgiven for pondering the same question. In this chapter, we have taken one abiding tension in social work practice—that between general and specialist practice—as a specific illustration of the quest to define social work. We have rooted this central tension in its historical context; an understanding of the recurring nature of these themes will help you to understand the present state of social work and better anticipate its future.

This debate and struggle are still prevalent today. At one of the author's own schools of social work, where there is both an undergraduate and graduate program (BSW and MSW program), since the inception of the master's program several years ago, there has been considerable debate about what distinguishes the MSW program from the BSW program. At the university in question, the undergraduate program is described as a Generalist Social Work Program, while the MSW program is referred to as an Advanced Generalist Community Social Work Program.

What Is a Specialty?

Going back almost half a century ago, Hollis and Taylor (CSWE, 1951) pointed to the "lack of adequate criteria for determining what is *basic* and what is *specialized* in social work" and considered this to be the main reason for the inability to develop a satisfactory social work curriculum. Bartlett

(1970, p. 94) noted that the concept of specialization is only valid "when there is a concept of a whole that can be divided into parts" and that social work's peculiar origins as "a profession growing *through* its parts" led to premature concepts of specialization. An aggregation can just as soon become desegregation. She declared that "practitioners not long in practice cannot be regarded as specialists because specialization rests on extended study and experience from which true expertise develops" (Bartlett, 1970, p. 195). Bartlett would, therefore, have considered the idea of developing a specialist area of practice as a social work *student* as very premature.

Bartlett (1970) argued for greater discrimination in the use of the terms *generic* and *specific,* as well as *basic* and *specialized.* Papell (1996) reminds us that the term *generic* first appeared in North American social work in the report of the Milford Conference in 1929, although only a single method (casework) was then involved. "The recommendation was that education presented in the university was to be generic while the specialized knowledge needed in settings wherever casework was practiced—such as psychiatric, medical, child welfare—was to be taught in the field" (Papell, 1996, p. 16).

The division between specialist and generalist remains far from clear. The distinctions can be drawn along many different lines, depending on time and place. Forty years ago, Bartlett (1970) noted that social workers were accustomed to think of their practice in terms of agencies, fields, and methods. She mused why it was proving so difficult for "social workers to take the necessary steps toward a perception of their practice as no longer fragmented" (Bartlett, 1970, p. 130).

In other words, there is an expectation at the advanced generalist level that the student will engage in more difficult practice tasks and, therefore, operate from an expanded knowledge base about individuals, groups, organizations, and communities. The advanced generalist must also develop increased skills to intervene in direct service provision with individuals, families, and groups at one end of the multiple-level practice spectrum and, at the other end, address more complex indirect practice situations such as supervision, administration, and policy and program evaluation.

Forms of Specialist Practice

Specialist social work practice can be characterized by the application of selected knowledge and skills to a narrowed area of practice based on practice setting, population served, social problems addressed, and/or practice intervention model used. The Curriculum Policy Statement of the Council on Social Work Education identifies the following categories of specializations that schools might offer (CSWE, 1992, p. 10):

1. Fields of practice: for example, services to families, children, and youth; services to the elderly; health; mental health; developmental disabilities; education

2. Problem area: for example, crime and delinquency, substance abuse, developmental disabilities, family violence mental illness

3. Populations at risk: for example, children and youth, the aged, women, single parents, migrants, gay and lesbian persons

4. Intervention models or roles: for example, specific practice approaches with individuals, families, and groups; community organization; administration social policy formulation

5. Practice contexts and perspectives: for example, school, hospitals, rural or urban area

Notwithstanding the conceptual difficulty in defining specialist and generalist social work, observation reveals that, in the real world, specialist practice comes in many shapes and sizes. Horwath and Shardlow (2003a, 2003b) have suggested that there are at least several different "territories"[2] of specialist practice:

1. *Service user group:* The social worker works mainly or exclusively with one type or group of service user: This has become the dominant paradigm of professional practice in the United States at the time of writing, to the extent that the term *specialist practice* has become synonymous with this type of specialism. Certainly, within the United States, there is an apparently ever-widening gap, in terms of practice skills and knowledge between those who work with children and families and those who work with adults. This has become the primary division in professional practice.

2. *Expertise:* Some social workers are recognized by others to have a particularly detailed knowledge or skill in some aspect of social work and become known as experts. Frequently, they are awarded that status informally by colleagues who will seek out such experts to consult. Some social workers also occupy specialist (senior practitioner) posts. However, in North America, the concept of specialist practice (sometimes called *concentration* in the curriculum) is concerned more with depth, so that one can have a generalist knowledge or a specialist knowledge of the same "territory," the difference being the depth of knowledge, not the

---

[2]In this view of specialism, social work is a land of many territories (defined by age, service user group, nature of problem, setting, etc.), and specialist workers become knowledgeable about their territory in more detail, rather like consultants carve up the territory of the human body—foot; heart; ear, nose, and throat; and so on.

"territory" itself. This is more akin to the notion of specialism in medical practice, where the consultant is the expert.

3. *Method:* Practitioners themselves often show skepticism toward the idea of models and methods, as suspect and restrictive. The nearest approach to a methodological specialism is group work. However, group work is as much a context for practice as it is a single method of practice (there are, for instance, as many methods of group work practice as there are individual practice). Adopting a self-definition as a group worker does allow practitioners to have an affinity with practitioners from other professional backgrounds.

4. *Mode:* Some 30 years ago, it was usual for social workers to define their orientation to their practice according to which "mode" of practice they were engaged with: individuals, families, groups, and communities. While some social workers may have defined themselves as being generalists and working across several different modalities, others would have specialized in one. As already noted earlier in the chapter, historically many agencies have been identified with a particular practice setting: elderly, children, health care, or mental health. On the basis of this, many social workers, especially those who are MSWs or licensed social workers, have viewed themselves as experts with a particular population or drawn to a particular practice setting. This area of preference is further encouraged by agencies for financial reimbursement reasons.

5. *Organizational form or structure:* Determining who works with a particular service user according to organizational form and structure has been a popular approach to specialization at various times; "intake" or "reception" teams consisted of social workers who dealt with the initial service user contact, with complementary "long-term teams" of social workers who took over responsibility after a certain period of time. These are specialisms by time, as is the work of the emergency duty team, which deals with service user need outside of normal office hours.

6. *Setting:* The setting in which the practitioner is based can also be seen as a specialism: hospital social work, school social work, child welfare, gerontology. Historically, setting has been an important definer of salary and status, but the trend has been for settings to be merged in the education of social workers.

In addition to these several different territories, the authors would propose that there are several further "territories" for consideration.

Education

There is continuing debate in the profession about the differences between undergraduate and graduate education. According to the CSWE (2008), there is an expectation that in the master's program, there is greater depth, breadth, and specificity of the advanced curriculum. Indeed, there are two ways in which students can enter into an MSW program. First, there is the traditional 2-year program known as the foundation year and concentration year. This venue is open to students who have an undergraduate degree in another discipline. The intent of this 2-year program is that in the first year, the student will take courses in the curriculum content areas. Again, the CSWE stipulates what content areas must be covered. In their second year, the student is expected to undertake more in-depth study in specified content areas (see above) and in addition can take several elective courses.

The other means by which students go on to take their MSW degree is through a program called Advanced Standing. This option is open to students who have obtained their BSW degree from an accredited school of social work. The student is exempt from the foundation year and goes straight into the concentration year. In addition to having this traditional program, schools of social work also offer this program on a 4-year and 2-year part-time basis.

The intent of this concentration year is to provide the student with the opportunity to address issues in more depth. Using Bloom's Taxonomy of Educational Objectives (Anderson et al., 2001), this would suggest that students are increasingly able to design, combine, justify, evaluate, and critique existing knowledge, as well as propose and create new knowledge.

So, the expectation from the CSWE is that social workers, on completion of their MSW, will have a more in-depth and extensive education. However, the CSWE also states that graduates will practice in "an area of concentration"—in other words, that they will "specialize." Not only have social work agencies and programs been pursuing the need for their employees to be MSWs but students themselves have realized the need to obtain an MSW degree and then to be licensed. There is a great deal of variance in the pay scale between those with a BSW and those with a MSW; by having an MSW degree, social workers have a great deal more autonomy, and they regard themselves as being more specialized.

Private Practice/Mental Health

The growth in private practice coincides with the development of mental health as the primary professional base of social work; there are over 200,000 social workers working in the area of mental health (Comer, 2002). In addition, there are 35,000 physicians currently in psychiatric practice, 70,000 psychologists, and 50,000 marriage and family therapists.

According to the U.S. Bureau of Labor Statistics, projected employment of social workers in mental health and private practice is expected to grow rapidly. In addition, studies indicate that between one fifth and one third of incoming MSW students ultimately plan to have full-time private careers. In addition, although social work in general is not a highly paid profession, according to the NASW, social workers at the BSW level who work in mental health earned about $20,000 to $30,000 a year, and those with MSWs earned a salary of approximately $41,000 to $46,000 (Linsley, 2003).

Field

In addition to setting, "field" has also been used to demarcate areas of social work practice: hospital, school, court, and so on. In these circumstances, social work is a *secondary activity* to the principal profession—medicine, education, the law, and so forth. Social work practice in a secondary setting is itself a form of specialism, and it seems likely to become ever more common as new organizational arrangements, particularly those that integrated health and social care, are developed for the delivery of welfare.

New forms of specialist practice are emerging: for example, in the United States, rapid-response teams providing immediate intervention in cases of financial abuse against elders—so-called financial abuse specialist teams (FAST). Interestingly, some areas of specialist practice are seldom considered specialisms. Is social work management a specialism?

The notion of specialization, although fashionable at present, is far from clear-cut. The terms of debate have been all but closed off by the assumption that the meaning of specialist work is defined by current forms of practice.

Generalist and Specialist—The Future

It is evident in the early years of the 21st century that the confusion between generalist and specialist practice is unlikely to go away. On one hand, the complexity of human problems requires a "generalist" approach, yet MSWs—the most highly qualified social workers—are considered "specialist" as they work in a particular field or work with a specific population. However, when working in these specialist fields, given their complexity, is it not necessary to be able to look at the problems from a generalist perspective?

Perhaps the most scathing criticism of this contradiction comes from Specht and Courtney (1995). In *Unfaithful Angels*, they asserted that the social work profession had abandoned its mission, that it had been more concerned with itself as a profession than with the populations it claimed to serve, and noted that social work had become more focused on private practice, licensure, and third-party payments:

CSWE's standards for accreditation stipulate that schools must have required classroom courses in the content of social policy and programs, methods of practice, human growth and development in the social environment, and research. In addition there is a requirement for a practicum. There are no requirements for any content about the poor, and deprived or dependent children, or the mentally ill, or the frail or the aged. Nor is there any requirement that students complete courses on the family, the publicly supported social services, community work, and work with groups, or the law. Thus CSWE leaves rather large gaps in the education of professional social workers. (Specht & Courtney, 1995, p. 149)

ASSESSING YOUR LEARNING

This question of generalist and specialist practice is fraught with contradictions, many of which the profession itself has perpetuated. As already noted in this chapter, social workers are expected to look at the person in the environment. On the other hand, many of the settings in which social workers work, and where you have your placement, see their mission as working with a specific population and require a focus on a specific type of problem, target population, or objective. The field instructor's role is not to teach you to become a specialist worker in their agency but to become a social worker with transferable skills so that you can bring your "social workness" to any situation. The assessment of your practice needs to reflect your ability to recognize and practice social work at large, not just the specific technical skills of any particular job role.

FURTHER READING

Anderson, L. W., Krathohl, D. R., Airasian, P. W., Cruikshank, K. A., Mayer, R. E., Pintirch, P. R., Raths, J., & Wittrock, M. C. (2001). *Taxonomy for learning, teaching, and assessing: A revision of Bloom's taxonomy of educational objectives.* Boston, MA: Allyn & Bacon.

Horwath, J., & Shardlow, S. M. (Eds.). (2003). *Making links across specialisms: Understanding modern social work practice.* Lyme Regis, UK: Russell House.

Specht, H., & Courtney, M. E. (1995). *Unfaithful angels: How social work has abandoned its mission.* New York, NY: Free Press.

CHAPTER 16

Comparative Social Work

ABOUT ACTIVITY 16: *VIEW FROM ANOTHER PLACE...ANOTHER TIME*

Being able to look at the world from the point of view of others is an essential aspect of social work—whether the others are service users, providers, or social workers from other places, at other times. Taking two approaches to comparing different views, those of people in other countries or changes in your view over time, *View From Another Place . . . Another Time* provides an opportunity to think about the key characteristics of social work in the student's own country and to consider how those characteristics could be presented to give an impression of social work to those from elsewhere or to compare practice learning experience from an earlier period of learning. Ideally, the activity is best undertaken with a group of two or three students—even better if they are from different countries or practice contexts.

NOTES FOR INSTRUCTORS[1]

PURPOSE

If we do not understand the context within which we practice social work, our practice will be circumscribed by the moment and by the demands of the agency in which we work. To have a broad vision of how social work is practiced

---

[1]See the Introduction to the book for suggestions about how instructors and students can, separately and together, use the activities in this book.

elsewhere provides grounding upon which to develop a critical and creative approach to social work practice.

METHOD

Students should have a copy of the activity *View From Another Place . . . Another Time* for about a week before their fieldwork seminar or supervision session. They should follow the guide notes for the activity and produce a written assignment before the session.

NOTES FOR STUDENTS AND INSTRUCTORS

VARIATIONS

This activity can be used singly or with several students as part of a practice tutorial. The content of the activity can be modified to take account of other forms of comparison and by selecting different "prompt" material for students. It may be difficult to develop the idea of comparative practice in relation to social work overseas, less so with respect to earlier practice learning. However, many other forms of comparison, many of which are frequently neglected, can be used to develop an appreciation of "comparative practice." For example, a comparison with a different region, between an urban and a rural area, or another historical comparison could be engendered by identifying suitable materials. Employing these other forms of comparison is of particular importance to generate a rounded notion of what is entailed by a comparative perspective.

It can also be used as an internet-based activity if you have contacts with students based in other countries—discussion and comment can be structured through e-mail discussion or, if the resources allow, through instructional technology and some type of virtual learning environment (VLE).

USE BY OTHER PROFESSIONS

View From Another Place . . . Another Time lends itself for use by other professions. It can be modified to suit the needs of any profession by, for example, using a definition taken from an international body about the particular profession. Importantly, the exercise can be used to promote interprofessional learning (see p. 267). A group of students from different professional backgrounds can be asked to prepare and present to each other their own views about their own and other professions—promoting a comparative dialogue about comparative professional practice. This could be through a comparison of different approaches to the same issue, such as how to interpret standards for professional practice (Shardlow et al., 2004).

EDUCATIONAL POLICY ACCREDITATION STANDARDS

The topics in this chapter relate to the following *Educational Policy and Accreditation Standards (EPAS)* 2008 Primary Core Competencies (Council on Social Work Education [CSWE], 2008):

1. Identify as a professional social worker and conduct oneself accordingly.

2. Apply social work ethical principles to guide professional practice.

3. Apply critical thinking to inform and communicate professional judgments.

4. Engage diversity and difference in practice.

5. Advance human rights and social and economic justice.

6. Engage in policy practice to advance social and economic well-being and to deliver effective social work services.

7. Respond to contexts that shape practice.

FOR STUDENTS AND INSTRUCTORS

ACTIVITY 16: *VIEW FROM ANOTHER PLACE . . . ANOTHER TIME*

There are two parts to this activity corresponding to the two different views, in place and time. You may choose to focus on one or the other or—if you have time—to consider both.

Part 1: View From Another Place . . . International Comparisons

Social work is an international activity; it takes place around the world in many different forms. Consider the definition of social work below, from the International Federation of Social Workers (IFSW, 2003).

International Federation of Social Workers Definition of Social Work[2]

Definition[a]

The social work profession promotes social change, problem solving in human relationships and the empowerment and liberation of people to enhance well-being. Utilizing theories of human behavior and social systems, social work intervenes at the points where people interact with their environments. Principles of human rights and social justice are fundamental to social work.

Commentary

Social work in its various forms addresses the multiple, complex transactions between people and their environments. Its mission is to enable all people to develop their full potential, enrich their lives, and prevent dysfunction. Professional social work is focused on problem solving and change. As such, social workers are change agents in society and in the lives of the individuals, families and communities they serve. Social work is an interrelated system of values, theory and practice.

Values

Social work grew out of humanitarian and democratic ideals, and its values are based on respect for the equality, worth, and dignity of all people. Since its beginnings over a century ago, social work practice has focused on meeting human needs and developing human potential. Human rights and social justice serve as the motivation and justification for social work action. In solidarity with those who are disadvantaged, the profession strives to alleviate poverty and to liberate vulnerable and oppressed people in order to promote social inclusion. Social work values are embodied in the profession's national and international codes of ethics.

Theory

Social work bases its methodology on a systematic body of evidence-based knowledge derived from research and practice evaluation, including local and indigenous knowledge specific to its context. It recognizes the complexity of interactions between human beings and their environment, and the capacity of people both to be affected by and to alter the multiple influences upon them including bio-psychosocial factors. The social work profession draws on theories of human development and behavior and social systems to analyze complex situations and to facilitate individual, organizational, social and cultural changes.

---

[2]This is correct at the time of writing, but further revision is anticipated in June 2010 at the World Conference in Hong Kong.

> *Practice*
>
> Social work addresses the barriers, inequities and injustices that exist in society. It responds to crises and emergencies as well as to everyday personal and social problems. Social work utilizes a variety of skills, techniques, and activities consistent with its holistic focus on persons and their environments. Social work interventions range from primarily person-focused psychosocial processes to involvement in social policy, planning and development. These include counseling, clinical social work, group work, social pedagogical work, and family treatment and therapy as well as efforts to help people obtain services and resources in the community. Interventions also include agency administration, community organization and engaging in social and political action to impact social policy and economic development. The holistic focus of social work is universal, but the priorities of social work practice will vary from country to country and from time to time depending on cultural, historical, and socio-economic conditions.
>
> ---
>
> [a]This international definition of the social work profession replaces the IFSW definition adopted in 1982. It is understood that social work in the 21st century is dynamic and evolving, and therefore no definition should be regarded as exhaustive.
>
> Adopted by the IFSW General Meeting in Montréal, Canada, July 2000.[3]

Does this definition highlight the key aspects of social work in your country—from your point of view? If not, how would you describe social work in your country to someone *from another place or another time?* Like most abstract questions, that is quite hard to do. To help with this task, think about one of the households of Derby Street (see Chapter 1, p. 29). Take one of the scenarios, about the residents, described in this book and consider how you would work with the individuals, family, or group. From this hypothesized practice example, try to draw out the key themes that define good practice. These might form the elements of social work that you would use to describe social work in your country.

- Discuss in the fieldwork seminar or in supervision.

- Find at least two articles in an academic journal (refereed) that discuss an area of practice that corresponds to your fieldwork but where the practice is located in another country. Then, reflect upon the similarities and differences from your own experience as compared with the view or practice in the articles.

- To complete the activity, draft an e-mail to send to a group of students in another country that describes social work in your country. This can be a simulation or, ideally, sent to initiate a dialogue.

---

[3]Found at www.ifsw.org/f38000138.html, the definition is also available in Danish, Finnish, German, French, Norwegian, Portuguese, Spanish, and Swedish.

Part 2: View From Another Time . . . Practice Learning Comparisons

Over the period of your practice learning, either during one practicum period or by comparing two separate practicum periods, your views will have developed and changed. Sometimes we find it difficult to be aware of such changes.

- Take one of the chapters from the book and review the activity—you may want to seek the advice of your field instructor about which one to select.

Part I.   Foundations of Practice
Context: Where does learning take place?
  1.   Learning about the service users
  2.   Learning about yourself
  3.   Learning about your role
  4.   Learning about value conflicts and ethical dilemmas

Part II: Direct Practice
Context: Interdisciplinary learning and practice
  5.   Preparation
  6.   Generating options
  7.   Making assessments in partnership
  8.   Working in and with groups

Part III: Agency Practice
Context: Creative practice and procedural requirements
  9.   Making priorities
  10.   Managing resources
  11.   Accountability
  12.   Challenging situations and resolving conflicts

Part IV: Themes of Practice
Context: Social worker as researcher: Evaluating practice
  13.   Multicultural practice
  14.   Law-informed practice
  15.   Generalist and specialist practice
  16.   Comparative social work

- Consider your response when you first completed the activity. If you have kept the notes, review these and recall your response to that activity. Try to identify the key principles of professional practice that informed your view at that time.

- Complete the activity again, using either the same or different material.

- Compare your earlier response with your current response.

- Discuss in the fieldwork seminar or in supervision the reasons for any differences, both between changes in your views and changes in the views of others. What is emphasized by one person may not be emphasized by another. Explore the scope and extent of the similarities of these different visions through discussion.

NOTES FOR INSTRUCTORS

TEACHING ABOUT COMPARATIVE SOCIAL WORK

In learning about how to do social work, we can draw a parallel with learning how to drive a car. In the early stages of driving, many students find that there are too many actions to perform in a very short time period, and there can be a similar feeling of being overwhelmed when learning social work. In such situations, a student may tend to focus on the minutiae of task performance rather than broader considerations about the meanings and significance of actions. The novice car driver may be unconcerned with asking questions about the mechanics of the car, the social symbolism of car ownership, or the impact of the car on urban life. Likewise, the beginner social worker may be unconcerned with questions about the need for social work as an activity in society, the impact of social work on individuals and the state, or whether social work takes different forms in different countries, regions, or societies and so on. Even so, students should be encouraged to ask these broader questions, from an early stage in their professional development. To explore social work comparatively is one way to promote this breadth of thinking.

OPPORTUNITIES FOR COMPARATIVE SOCIAL WORK

Traditionally, the term *comparative practice* has been used to denote social work as it is practiced in other countries. Here, we have used the term in a much broader context, although we have remained within the bounds of convention within the activity *View From Another Place . . . Another Time*. Comparative social work can and, we believe, should be used to denote any form of comparison, such as those that are international, historical, interprofessional, and those based on the perspectives of different stakeholders. There are many opportunities to help students explore comparative approaches (see below)—if we adopt this broad conceptualization of the notion of "comparative social work."

NOTES FOR STUDENTS

LEARNING ABOUT COMPARATIVE SOCIAL WORK

Comparison may be motivated by the desire to find out more about the *other*, who may be perceived as exotic or strange. Increasing familiarity with the other is likely to reduce this sense of "otherness" and lead instead to a greater understanding not just of the other but also—surprisingly—of the self and your own circumstances. Through comparison, the reasons and justifications for our own actions made within our own professional context are subject to challenge. We may be more inclined to ask questions such as, "Why do we do it this way?" Hence, focusing on the practice and policy of others may promote a greater sense of the possibilities of your own practice, a desire for and knowledge of other ways of working, than those that we see on a day-to-day basis. The boundaries of our imagination can be extended through comparison.

Dimensions of Comparison

As we have noted, there are several different dimensions of comparison.

International Comparison. Across the world, the social work profession is working to ameliorate the devastating effects of poverty, hunger, illness, homelessness, inequality, injustice, and violence. In recent years, the processes of globalization, such as rapid urbanization, increasing industrialization, and greater global financial interdependence have affected the lives of individuals and families worldwide. Previously, social workers may have seen themselves as dealing solely with the concerns of local communities, but now those very concerns are influenced by the effects of globalization. Sarri (1997) has urged the infusion of international content in social work education for exposure to comparative options and innovations for addressing economic and social issues.

As the world has become more interconnected, the social work profession must constantly reexamine its forms of professional practice to meet these challenges. Historically, the nations of the global North have dominated free market economies through technology. Social work knowledge and forms of practice from these same nations have similarly promulgated a conceptualization of social work that has flowed from North to South (van Wormer, 2006, p. 121). However, this interconnectivity provides an opportunity for reciprocal learning, and the profession should look to learn more from other countries and cultures. There is much talk about cultural competence, multicultural practice, and respecting diversity (Educational Policy 2.1.4 states, "Engage diversity and difference into practice"), and these imperatives apply to the international level as much as the federal or state levels.

To enhance this exchange of information and knowledge and to help students acquire an international perspective on their own work, international exchanges have been developed by some departments and schools of social work. Typically, in such exchanges, students and faculty take or teach courses on foreign campuses. In addition, a number of social work programs are now offering internet and instructional technology (IT) courses that provide an opportunity for students to enroll in courses at universities in another part of the country and also in another part of the world.

Comparative social work may be regarded, erroneously, as being synonymous with international social work. It is certainly the case that much of what is taken to be international social work has a comparative dimension. Midgely (2001, pp. 24–25), in a review of current developments in international social work, described three different types of international social work as follows:

1. Specialist social work conducted by international agencies such as the International Red Cross

2. Contacts and exchanges between social workers from different countries

3. A global awareness enabling social workers to transcend a concern for the local and particular

Of these types of social work, the first two are self-explanatory, and the meaning of the third is less immediately obvious. The ability of social workers to "transcend the local" implies an ability to appreciate, for example, the impact of global economic change on local communities and therefore to be able to frame realistic and achievable responses. Social work is practiced in many different ways around the globe (Tan, 2004; Tan & Dodds, 2002; Tan & Envall, 2000). An awareness of some of these differences and similarities will help you to understand this wider context of social work and reflect critically on your own social work practice.

Comparison Across Locality and Region. Is "good" social work the same everywhere? One challenge that confronts social workers in the United States is the diversity of the country with respect to time, climate, terrain, population density, dialects, religions, foods, pace of life, and so on. For instance, living in one of the five boroughs of New York City is a very different experience from living in Buffalo, upstate New York. Similar differences are replicated across and within each of the states.

Pavel Kowalski, a BSW student, who previously served in the military and who now attends university, noted,

> After living in Mississippi for a few years and eating their fried and spicy foods every day, then moving to the State of Maine, everything tasted plain for a while. From the clothes they wear to the food they eat, the houses, the flats, the mountains, and the weather. All these differences not only make the environment different, but the people as well.

Is the same true of social work? Does it have a different "taste" across state lines as well as across national borders?

Rural Social Work

Social workers practice in rural, urban, and suburban settings; each setting presents its own challenges. There is a substantial literature concerned with the nature of rural social work, although seeking to identify the core characteristics of a rural community is not an easy task. Davenport and Davenport (1995) noted that rural communities have three major facets: (1) having a low population density (i.e., number of residents per square mile), (2) being located a significant distance from large urban hubs, and (3) concentration of economic activities in a specialized area, such as lumbering, farming, ranching, or mining.

Carlton-LeNey, Edwards, and Reid (1999) took a numerical view and defined a rural community as one in which there are fewer than 2,500 inhabitants. Looking at the issues rural communities face, they identified these problems facing "rural" communities:

> Poverty, lack of transportation, inadequate child care, unemployment substandard housing, and insufficient health care. Problems of access and adequacy remain critical issues that must be addressed in rural social work practice. (p. 7)

To understand the nature of rurality, social workers must first be true generalists, prepared to work with individuals, families, groups, local organizations, and the wider community, using a wide range of skills to meet diverse needs (Daley & Avant, 2004). In a rural setting, a social worker would be expected to be able to address and deal with a broad range of issues such as substance abuse, protective services for elders, and people with cognitive disabilities, domestic violence issues, and sexual abuse issues. Rural social workers must be flexible and able to engage with people across a varied assortment of issues.

Second, in rural social work, it is particularly critical that there is a great deal of interagency cooperation (Carlton-LeNey et al., 1999, p. 10). As there are fewer and more general services, agencies and staffs must work even more closely together than in urban centers.

Third, there is the importance of understanding the community, knowing its values, and developing relationships with rural residents (Daley & Avant, 2004). Because there are fewer people in rural communities than in urban communities, social interaction and relationships tend to be much more informal. Rural social workers may attend the same church or shop at the same store as their service users.

Fourth, it is imperative that social workers emphasize the strengths inherent in rural communities. Because of the informal nature of relationships, rural clients are often integrally involved with informal support systems or social networks of other people willing to help out—sometimes referred to as natural helping networks (Tracy, 2002; Watkins, 2004). Such networks can include family members, neighbors, co-workers, church members, and others not providing formal agency services but who offer volunteer assistance.

Urban Social Work

Urban social work is practiced within the context of large cities, usually with a vast array of social problems, exceptional diversity, and potential range of resources. Urban areas are characterized by a number of conditions (Marsella, 1998).

First, a population that is dense often contains diverse population subgroups. Second, urban economic conditions involve a range of industries, businesses, and services; varying rent levels; and transportation availability and costs. Third, paradoxically, the urban environment is often more anonymous than rural ones, even though it entails more intensive interaction and contact with many people. Fourth, the environment may call into question issues of public health, such as air quality.

Phillips and Straussner (2002, p. 25) identified at least five clusters of problems that tend to characterize urban areas. First, although poverty, discrimination, overcrowded housing, crime and violence, homelessness, high rates of school dropouts, substance abuse, and HIV/AIDS exist in communities of all sizes, they occur with greater frequency and are more visible in the cities. Second, discriminatory behavior occurs because of the wide variety of ethnic, racial, religious, and cultural groups living in cities. Third, with forced migration and refugee status, many people are unprepared for the pressures and demands of urban living. "Some who migrate to urban areas whether from other parts of the US or from other countries, are faced with unemployment, underemployment, discrimination, poor housing, and language barriers" (Phillips & Straussner, 2002, p. 27).

Fourth, there are frequently inadequate resources to address the scale of the social problems. For example, some cities do not have the financial resources to provide services, while others choose not to provide them. The consequence is that there may be a lack of affordable housing, inadequate schooling, and recreational facilities. All of these problems can combine to exacerbate the social problems.

Finally, there are likely to be numerous psychological stressors such as noise, dirty streets, and abandoned buildings. Overcrowded housing, lack of geographic mobility, and substance abuse can impose psychological pressures and increase anxieties (Phillips & Straussner, 2002, p. 29). Social workers practicing in the cities are required to deal with numerous and very challenging situations.

Historical Comparisons

In your social work program, you are likely to complete two social welfare classes, one examining the social and political history of the problems and the second course looking at contemporary social welfare issues that confront the profession. Indeed, CSWE Educational Policy 2.1.8 requires that "social workers know the history and current structures of social policies and services."

To explore the history of social welfare, refer to these books: Albert and Skolnik (2006), DiNitto (2005), Jansson (2005), Gilbert and Terrell (2005), Kirst-Ashman (2007), Marx (2004), Popple and Leighninger (2005), Segal and Brzuzy (1998), Trattner (1999), and van Wormer (2006).

Let us consider child welfare policy and the development of foster care by way of example.

Child Welfare Policy

During the 1800s, public opinion was dominated by the view that children from poor homes might be better served in institutions. Hence, institutions such as the New York House of Refuge were established for neglected and abandoned and delinquent youth (DiNitto, 2005, p. 337). By the mid-1880s, some organizations such as the Children's Aid Society, founded by Charles Loring Brace in 1853, decided that children would be best served in rural areas, and they sent thousands of children to live and work with families on farms in the Midwest. In effect, Brace's scheme was to relieve the city of its youthful pauperism. Through his approach, we see an underlying philosophy of rescuing children.

This philosophy prevailed for over one hundred years, until the 1980 Adoption Assistance and Child Welfare Act. The 1980 law was a reaction to scathing indictments of the child welfare system and the fact that numerous children were spending their entire lives in the foster care system. Hence, rather than foster care becoming a temporary measure, it had become a permanent feature in the lives of many children within the welfare system. By 1984, the number of children in foster care declined to 275,000 as a result of vigorous permanency planning and family preservation (Downs, Moore, McFadden, Michaud, & Costin, 2004, p. 328).

By 1991, however, the number of children in care once again climbed, despite permanency planning, family preservation, and adoption reforms. The onset of the crack cocaine epidemic, the spread of HIV/AIDS to women and children, and economic stressors were contributing factors that fragmented families. Nonetheless, the prevailing philosophy was to keep children with their biological family. Hence, the focus shifted to the possibilities of placing children with relatives. Thus, in the mid-1990s, the emergence of kinship care emerged as a serious alternative to institutional care that provided a continuity of family relationships for the child and also helped alleviate the foster home shortage crisis (Allen, Larkin, McFadden, & Wasserman, 1992; McFadden & Downs, 1995).

This example reinforces the need to look at issues from a historical perspective and to have a good understanding of the issues and policies that have affected so many of the populations we encounter as social workers.

Interprofessional Comparison

Social workers work in a variety of settings, which necessitates that they are able to work with numerous other professionals and disciplines. In a school setting, social workers will interact with principals, teachers, nurses, psychologists, speech therapists, and guidance counselors (Allen-Meares, 2004).

In a medical setting, the professions will include doctors, nurses, psychiatrists, occupational therapists, physical therapists, and dieticians. In the legal/court system, the professions will include lawyers, judges, court officers, police officers, prison officers, and probation officers (Downs et al., 2004, pp. 182–220). Like social work, all of these several disciplines undertake their own formal education and training and take state licensing examinations, but they are likely to have their own perspectives when working with an individual, family, or group. For example, why was the nurse more concerned about the patient taking his or her medication than where the patient was going to go when he or she was discharged from the hospital? Why did the teacher complain at the Individual Education Program (IEP) meeting that the child is extremely disruptive in class, is not doing well academically, and should be held back? Why did the judge seem more concerned with the rights of the biological parents than how the children were progressing in the foster home? The challenge for you is to learn how to work effectively with all these different disciplines and to understand your own perspective as a social worker and to explain your own social work role.

ASSESSING YOUR LEARNING

When you seek to evidence your understanding of comparative social work, the primary concern should not be the details of your knowledge of social work practice in another country, location, time, place, and so on. What is important is to understand the significance of "comparison" as a technique to further our understanding about ourselves and others.

Social work practice can be based on quite fundamentally different premises. For example, Sacco (1996) describes an African paradigm as a foundation for spirituality in social work practice, which is in strong contrast to the Western materialist basis of social work. Through this understanding of difference, using comparison as a mechanism, it is possible to better understand ourselves. Demonstrating an appreciation of the importance of comparison throughout any placement and consistently across any assessment tasks is essential. It is not necessary always to seek out complexity or the more exotic comparisons. Drawing upon comparisons, for example, between yourself and your fieldwork supervisor, faculty liaison, other students, or the earlier and later parts of your practice learning experience can all be a highly constructive mechanism to promote a deeper understanding both of yourself and of "the other."

FURTHER READING

Albert, R., & Skolnik, L. (2006). *Social welfare programs: Narratives from hard times.* Belmont, CA: Brooks/Cole/Thompson.

Phillips, N. K., & Straussner, S. L. (2002). *Urban social work: An introduction to policy and practice in cities.* Boston: Allyn & Bacon.

Scales, T. L., & Streeter, C. L. (Eds.). (2004). *Rural social work: Building and sustaining community assets.* Belmont, CA: Brooks/Cole/Thompson.

van Wormer, K. (2006). *Introduction to social welfare and social work: The U.S. in global perspective.* Belmont, CA: Brooks/Cole/ Thompson.

References

Adams, J. (1995). *Risk*. London: UCL Press.

Adams, R., Dominelli, L., & Payne, M. (2009). *Social work: Themes, issues and critical debates* (3rd ed.). Houndmills, Basingstoke, UK: Palgrave.

Albert, R., & Skolnik, L. (2006). *Social welfare programs: Narratives from hard times*. Belmont, CA: Brooks/Cole/Thompson.

Alexander, L. B., & Solomon, P. (Eds.). (2006). *The research process in the human services behind the scenes*. Belmont, CA: Brooks/Cole/ Thompson.

Allen, M., Larkin, D., McFadden, E. J., & Wasserman, K. (1992). *Family continuity: Practice competencies*. Ypsilanti, MI: National Foster Care Resource Center.

Allen-Meares, P. (2004). *Social work services in schools* (4th ed.). Boston, MA: Allyn & Bacon.

Alsop, A., & Vigars, C. (1998). Shared learning, joint training or dual qualification in OT and SW: A feasibility study. *British Journal of Occupational Therapy, 61*(4), 146–152.

Anderson, L. W., Krathohl, D. R., Airasian, P. W., Cruikshank, K. A., Mayer, R. E., Pintirch, P. R., & Wittrock, M. C. (2001). *Taxonomy for learning, teaching, and assessing: A revision of Bloom's taxonomy of educational objectives*. Boston: Allyn & Bacon.

Asch, S. E. (1952). *Social psychology*. Englewood Cliffs, NJ: Prentice Hall.

Association of Baccalaureate Social Work Program and Directors. (2009). Retrieved 1 August, 2009, from www.bpdonline.org

Astor, R. W., Behre, W. J., Wallace, J. M., & Fravil, K. A. (1998). School social workers and school violence: Personal safety, training, and violence programs. *Social Work, 43*(3), 223–232.

Attlee, C. (1920). *The social worker*. London: Bell.

Ball, C., Harris, R., Roberts, G., & Vernon, S. (1988). *The law report: Teaching and assessment of law in social work education* (Paper 4.1). London: Central Council for Education and Training in Social Work.

Baltimore, M., Hickson, J., George, J., & Crutchfield, L. (1996). Portfolio assessment: A model for counselor education. *Counselor Education and Supervision, 36*(2), 113–121.

Bamford, T. (1982). *Managing social work*. London: Tavistock.

Banks, S. (2006). *Ethics and values in social work* (3rd ed.). New York, NY: Palgrave Macmillan.

Barker, R. L. (2003). *The social work dictionary* (5th ed.). Washington, DC: NASW.

Barr, H. (2002). *Interprofessional education today, yesterday and tomorrow.* London: LTSN for Health Sciences and Practice.

Barsky, A. E. (2006). *Successful social work education: A student's guide.* Belmont, CA: Thomson Wadsworth.

Bartlett, H. (1970). *The common base of social work practice.* Washington, DC: National Association of Social Workers.

Beaver, H. W. (1999). Client violence against professional social workers: Frequency, worker characteristics, and impact on worker job satisfaction, burnout and health. *Dissertation Abstracts International Section A: Humanities and Social Sciences, 60*(6A), 2227.

Beck, U. (1990). *Risk society: Towards a new modernity.* Thousand Oaks, CA: Sage.

Becker, H. S. (1986). *Doing things together: Selected papers.* Evanston, IL: Northwestern University Press.

Bergmark, A. (1996). Need, allocation and justice: On priorities in the social services. *Scandinavian Journal of Social Welfare, 5*(1), 45–56.

Billington, J., & Roberts, S. (2002). Creative practice learning: Exploring opportunities to fulfil students' requirements. *Practice, 14*(4), 29–41.

Birkenmaier, J., & Berg-Weger, M. (2007). *The practicum: Companion for social work integrating class and field work.* Needham Heights, MA: Allyn & Bacon.

Birnbaum, M., & Auerbach, C. (1994). Group work in graduate social work education: The price of neglect. *Journal of Social Work Education, 30*(3), 325–335.

Birnbaum, M., & Wayne, J. (2000). Group work content in foundation generalist education: The necessity for change. *Journal of Social Work Education, 36*(2), 347–356.

Blenkner, M. (1950). Obstacles to evaluative research casework: Part II. *Social Casework, 31,* 97–105.

Bloom, M., Fischer, J., & Orme, J. G. (2006). *Evaluating practice: Guidelines for the accountable professional* (5th ed.). Boston: Allyn & Bacon.

Bodenheimer, T. S., & Grumbach, K. (2002). *Understanding health policy: A clinical approach* (3rd ed.). New York, NY: McGraw-Hill.

Bogo, M., & Vayda, E. (1998). *The practice of field instruction in social work: Theory and process* (2nd ed.). Toronto: University of Toronto Press.

Braye, S., Lebacq, M., Mann, F., & Midwinter, E. (2003). Learning social work law: An enquiry-based approach to developing knowledge and skills. *Social Work Education, 22,* 479–492.

Braye, S., & Preston-Shoot, M. (1990). On teaching and applying the law in social work: It is not that simple. *British Journal of Social Work, 20*(4), 333–353.

Braye, S., & Preston-Shoot, M. (1992). Honourable intentions: Partnership and written agreements in welfare legislation. *Journal of Social Welfare and Family Law, 6,* 511–528.

Braye, S., & Preston-Shoot, M. (1995). *Empowering practice in social care.* Buckingham, UK: Open University Press.

Braye, S., & Preston-Shoot, M. (1997). *Practising social work law* (2nd ed.). New York, NY: Macmillan.

Braye, S., & Preston-Shoot, M. (2002). Social work and the law. In R. Adams, L. Dominelli, & M. Payne (Eds.), *Social work: Themes, issues and critical debates* (2nd ed.). London: Macmillan.

Briar, S. (1974). *Social casework: Generic and specific* (A Report of the Milford Conference, 1929). New York, NY: American Association of Social Workers.

Briar, S. (1980). Toward the integration of practice and research. In D. Fanschel (Ed.), *Future of social work research*. Washington, DC: NASW.

Broadbent, G., & White, R. (2003). Identifying underlying principles in social work law: A teaching and learning approach to the legal framework of decision making. *Social Work Education, 22*, 445–459.

Brodie, I. (1993). Teaching practice in social work education: A study of the content of supervision. *Social Work Education, 13*(2), 71–91.

Brown, A., & Bourne, I. (1996). *The social work supervisor*. Buckingham, UK: Open University Press.

Burr, V. (2003). *Social constructionism* (2nd ed.). New York, NY: Routledge.

Butler, A. (2004, July). *START (students and refugees together): Towards a model of practice learning as service provision*. Paper presented at the Joint Social Work Education Conference, Glasgow, UK.

Butrym, Z. (1976). *The nature of social work*. New York, NY: Macmillan.

Cabot, R. C. (1931). Treatment in social casework and the need for tests of its success and failure. In *Proceedings of the National Conference of Social Work (Fifty-Eighth Annual Session) Minneapolis MN* (pp. 3–24). Chicago: University of Chicago Press.

Carlton-LeNey, B., Edwards, R. L., & Reid, P. N. (1999). Small towns and rural communities: From romantic notions to harsh realities. In I. B. Carlton-LeNey, R. L. Edwards, & P. N. Reid (Eds.), *Preserving and strengthening small towns and rural communities* (pp. 5–12). Washington, DC: NASW Press.

Caspi, J., & Reid, W. J. (2002). *Educational supervision in social work: A task-centred model for field instruction and staff development*. New York, NY: Columbia University Press.

Central Council for Education and Training in Social Work (CCETSW). (2000). *Working in multi-disciplinary settings in Northern Ireland*. Belfast, Ireland: Author.

Chand, A., Doel, M., & Yee, J. (1999). Tracking social work students' understanding and application of anti-discriminatory practice. *Issues in Social Work Education, 19*(1), 55–74.

Chaskin, R. J. (2003). Fostering neighborhood democracy: Legitimacy and accountability within loosely coupled systems. *Nonprofit and Voluntary Sector Quarterly, 32*(2), 161–189.

Chiaferi, R., & Griffin, M. (1997). *Developing fieldwork skills*. Pacific Grove, CA: Brooks/Cole/Thompson.

Christie, A., & Weeks, S. (1998). Life experience: A neglected form of knowledge in social work education and practice. *Practice, 10*(1), 55–68.

Clark, C. L. (2000). *Social work ethics, politics principles and practice*. Houndmills, Basingstoke, UK: Palgrave.

Clarke, C. L., Gibb, C. E., & Ramprogus, V. (2003). Clinical learning environments: An evaluation of an innovative role to support preregistration nursing placements. *Journal of Learning in Health and Social Care, 2*(2), 105–115.

Clough, R. (Ed.). (1996). *Abuse in residential institutions.* London: Whiting and Birch.

Cohen, C. S. (1995). Making it happen: Building successful support group programs. *Social Work With Groups, 18*(1), 67–80.

Comer, R. J. (2002). Foreword. In D. W. Sifton (Ed.), *PDR: Drug guide for mental health professionals* (pp. V–VI). Montvale, NJ: Thompson Medical Economics.

Corby, B. (1996). Risk assessment in child protection work. In H. Kemshall & J. Pritchard (Eds.), *Good practice in risk assessment and risk management* (pp. 13–30). Philadelphia, PA: Jessica Kingsley.

Corcoran, K., & Gingerich, W. J. (1994). Practice evaluation in the context of managed care: Case recording methods for quality assurance reviews. *Research on Social Work Practice, 4*(3), 326–337.

Coulshed, V., & Orme, J. (2006). *Social work practice: An introduction* (4th ed.). New York, NY: Macmillan.

Coulshed, V., & Mullender, A. (2006). *Management in social work* (3rd ed.). Houndmills, Basingstoke, UK: Palgrave.

Council on Social Work Education (CSWE). (1992). *Curriculum policy statement for master's degree programs in social work education.* Alexandria, VA: Author.

Council on Social Work Education (CSWE). (2008). *Educational policy and accreditation standards.* Alexandria, VA: Author.

Courtney, M. E., Piliavin, I., Grogan-Kaylor, A., & Nesmith, A. (2001). Foster youth transitions to adulthood: A longitudinal view of youth leaving care. *Child Welfare, 80,* 685–717.

Cree, V. E. (1996). Why do men care? In K. Cavanagh & V. E. Cree (Eds.), *Working with men* (pp. 65–86). New York, NY: Routledge.

Cree, V. E., & Macaulay, C. (2000). *Transfer of learning in professional and vocational education.* New York, NY: Routledge.

Daley, M. R., & Avant, F. L. (2004). Rural social work: Reconceptualizing the framework for practice. In T. L. Scales & C. L. Streeter (Eds.), *Rural social work: Building and sustaining community assets* (pp. 34–41). Belmont, CA: Brooks/Cole/Thompson.

Danowski, W. A. (2005). *In the field: A real-life survival guide for the social work internship.* Needham Heights, MA: Allyn & Bacon.

Davenport, J. A., & Davenport, J., III. (1995). Rural social work overview. In R. L. Edwards (Ed.), *Encyclopedia of social work* (19th ed., vol. 3, pp. 2076–2085). Washington, DC: NASW Press.

Davies, M. (1994). *The essential social worker: An introduction to professional practice in the 1990s* (3rd ed.). Aldershot, UK: Arena.

de Bono, E. (2000). *Six hat thinking.* New York, NY: Penguin.

Degenhardt, D. (2003). Teacher or supporter? The social work tutor's role in students' professional development. *Journal of Practice Teaching in Health and Social Care, 4*(3), 54–67.

Dent, T., & Tourville, A. (2002). University-community partnerships: Practicum learning for community revitalization. In S. M. Shardlow & M. Doel (Eds.), *Learning to practise social work: International approaches* (pp. 25–42). Philadelphia, PA: Jessica Kingsley.

Devore, W., & Schlesinger, E.G. (1999). *Ethnic-sensitive social work practice* (5th ed.). Boston: Allyn & Bacon.

Dewees, M. (2006). *Contemporary social work practice*. New York, NY: McGraw-Hill.

Diller, J. V. (2004). *Cultural diversity: A primer for the human services*. Belmont, CA: Brooks/Cole Wadsworth.

DiNitto, D. M. (2005). *Social welfare: Politics and public policy* (6th ed.). Boston, MA: Allyn & Bacon.

Do you need treatment? (1989, November). *New Internationalist,* p. 10.

Doel, M. (1988). A practice curriculum to promote accelerated learning. In J. Phillipson, M. Richards, & D. Sawdon (Eds.), *Towards a practice led curriculum* (pp. 45–60). London: National Institute for Social Work.

Doel, M. (2002a). Interprofessional working: Berlin walls and garden fences. *Learning in Health and Social Care, 1*(3), 170–171.

Doel, M. (2002b). Creativity and practice teaching: Editorial. *Practice Teaching in Health and Social Work, 4*(1), 3–7.

Doel, M. (2006). *Using groupwork*. New York: Routledge.

Doel, M. (2010). *Social work placements: A traveller's guide*. New York, NY: Routledge.

Doel, M., Allmark, P., Conway, P., Cowburn, M., Flynn, M., Nelson, P., & Tod, A. (2010). Professional boundaries: Crossing a line or entering the shadows? *British Journal of Social Work*. doi:10.1093/bjsw/bcp106

Doel, M., & Best, L. (2008). *Experiencing social work: Learning from service users*. London: Sage.

Doel, M., & Cooner, T. S. (2002). *The virtual placement* [Interactive Web-based program]. www.routledge.com/textbooks/9780415499125/ch03.asp

Doel, M., & Lawson, B. (1986). Open records: The client's right to partnership. *British Journal of Social Work, 16*(4), 407–430.

Doel, M., & Marsh, P. (1992). *Task-centred social work*. Aldershot, UK: Ashgate.

Doel, M., & Sawdon, C. (1999). *The essential groupworker: Teaching and learning creative groupwork*. Philadelphia, PA: Jessica Kingsley.

Doel, M., Sawdon, C., & Morrison, D. (2002). *Learning, practice and assessment: Signposting the portfolio*. Philadelphia, PA: Jessica Kingsley.

Doel, M., & Shardlow, S. M. (1995). *Preparing post qualifying portfolios: A practical guide for candidates*. London: Central Council for Education and Training in Social Work.

Doel, M., & Shardlow, S. M. (1996). Simulated and live practice teaching: The practice teacher's craft. *Social Work Education, 15*(4), 16-33.

Doel, M., & Shardlow, S. M. (1998). *The new social work practice*. Aldershot, UK: Arena.

Doel, M., & Shardlow, S. M. (2005). *Modern social work practice: Teaching and learning in practice settings*. Surrey, UK: Ashgate.

Doel, M., & Shardlow, S. M. (Eds.). (2009). *Educating professionals: Practice learning in health and social care*. Aldershot, UK: Ashgate.

Douglas, T. (1993). *A theory of groupwork practice*. New York, NY: Macmillan.

Downs, S. W., Moore, E., McFadden, E. J., Michaud, S. M., & Costin, L. B. (2004). *Child welfare and family services: Policies and practice* (7th ed.). Boston, MA: Allyn & Bacon.

DuBois, B., & Miley, K. K. (2005). *Social work: An empowering profession* (5th ed.). Boston, MA: Allyn & Bacon.

Duncan, T., Piper, C., & Warren-Adamson, C. (2003). Running rings round law? An ecological approach to teaching law for child-centered practice. *Social Work Education, 22*(5), 493–503.

Dyche, L., & Zayas, L. H. (1995). The value of curiosity and naivety for the cross cultural psychotherapist. *Family Process, 34*(4), 389–399.

Ebenstein, H. (1999). Single session groups: Issues for social workers. *Social Work With Groups, 21*(1/2), 49–60.

Encarta. (1999). *Dictionary.* London: Bloomsbury.

Epstein, L. (1987). Pedagogy of the perturbed: Teaching research to the reluctant. *Journal of Teaching in Social Work, 1*(1), 71–89.

Evans, G. (1997). The rationing debate: Rationing healthcare by age; the case against. *British Medical Journal, 314,* 822–825.

Fischer, J. (1973). Is social casework effective? A review. *Social Work, 18*(1), 5–20.

Fong, R. (2004). *Culturally competent practice with immigrant and refugee children and families.* New York, NY: Guilford.

Fong, R., & Furito, S. (2001). *Culturally competent practice: Skills, interventions, and valuations.* Boston, MA: Allyn & Bacon.

Fook, J. (2002). *Social work: Critical theory and practice.* London: Sage.

Fortune, A. E., & Abramson, J. S. (1993). Predictors of satisfaction with field practicum among social work students. *The Clinical Supervisor, 11*(1), 95–110.

Fortune, A. E., Miller, J., Rosenblum, A. F., Sanchez, B. M., Smith, C., & Reid, W. J. (1995). Further explorations of the liaison role: A view from the field. In G. Rogers (Ed.), *Social work field education: Views and visions* (pp. 273–293). Dubuque, IA: Kendall/Hunt.

Gambrill, E. (2000). Evidence-based practice: An alternative to authority-based practice. *Families in Society, 80*(4), 341–350.

Gambrill, E. (2006). Evidence-based practice and policy: Choices ahead. *Research on Social Work Practice, 16*(3), 338–357.

Gardiner, D. (1989). *The anatomy of supervision.* Milton Keynes, UK: SRHE and Open University Press.

Garthwait, C. L. (2008). *The social work practicum: A guide and workbook for students* (4th ed.). Needham Heights, MA: Allyn & Bacon.

Gelman, S. R., & Wardell, P. J. (1988). Who's responsible? The field liability dilemma. *Journal of Social Work Education, 24*(1), 70–77.

Gelman, S. R., Pollack, D., & Auerbach, C. (1996). Liability issues in social work education. *Journal of Social Work Education, 351*(3), 351–361.

Gibbs, L., & Gambrill, E. (2002). Evidence-based practice: Counter arguments to objections. *Research on Social Work Practice, 12*(3), 452–476.

Gil, D. G. (1994). Confronting social injustice and oppression. In F. G. Reamer (Ed.), *Foundations of social work knowledge* (pp. 231–263). New York, NY: Columbia University Press.

Gilbert, N., & Terrell, P. (2005). *Dimensions of social welfare policy* (6th ed.). Boston, MA: Allyn & Bacon.

Ginsberg, L. H. (2001). *Careers in social work* (2nd ed.). Boston, MA: Allyn & Bacon.

Gitterman, A., & Salmon, R. (Eds.). (2008). *Encyclopedia of social work with groups.* New York, NY: Haworth.

Glendinning, C., Coleman, A., & Rummery, K. (2002). Partnerships, performance and primary care: Developing integrated services for older people in England. *Ageing and Society, 22*(2), 185–208.

Goldberg, M. (2000). Conflicting principles in multicultural social work. *Families in Society, 81*(1), 12–21.

Goleman, D. (1996). *Emotional intelligence.* London: Bloomsbury.

Gordon, W. E. (1950). The research project: Its educational value and its contribution of social work knowledge. *Social Work Journal, 31*(3), 110–116.

Gray, J. A. M. (2001). Evidence-based medicine for professionals. In A. Edwards & G. Elwyn (Eds.), *Evidence-based patient choice: Inevitable of impossible* (pp. 19–33). Oxford, UK: Oxford University Press.

Graybeal, C. (2001). Strengths-based social work assessment: Transforming the dominant paradigm. *Families in Society, 82*(3), 233–242.

Green, J. W. (1999). *Cultural awareness in the human services.* Boston, MA: Allyn & Bacon.

Gutierrez, L. M. (2001). Working with women of color: An empowerment perspective. In J. Rothman, J. L. Erlich, & J. E. Tropman (Eds.), *Strategies of community intervention* (6th ed., pp. 209–217). Itasca, IL: Peacock.

Guttman, D. (2006). *Ethics in social work: A context of caring.* Binghamton, NY: Haworth.

Haber, M., & Toro, P. A. (2004). Homelessness among families, children and adolescents: An ecological-developmental perspective. *Clinical Child and Family Psychology Review, 7*(3), 123–164.

Harries, P. A., & Harries, C. (2001). Studying clinical reasoning: Part 2. Applying social judgement theory. *British Journal of Occupational Therapy, 64*(6), 285–292.

Hawkins, P., & Shohet, R. (2006). *Supervision in the helping professions* (3rd ed.). Maidenhead, UK: Open University Press.

Hepworth, D. H., Rooney, R. H., Dewberry Rooney, G., & Larsen, J. (2006). *Direct social work practice, theory and skills.* Belmont, CA: Brooks/Cole/ Thompson.

Herod, J., & Lymbery, M. (2002). The social work role in multi-disciplinary teams. *Practice, 14*(4), 17–28.

Hewison, A., & Sim, J. (1998). Managing interprofessional working: Using codes of ethics as a foundation. *Journal of Interprofessional Care, 12*(3), 309–321.

Hollis, E. V., & Taylor, A. L. (1951). *Social work education in the United States.* New York: Columbia University Press.

Holme, A., & Maizels, J. (1978). *Social workers and volunteers.* London: Allen & Unwin.

Horwath, J. (2009). *The child's world: The comprehensive guide to assessing children in need* (2nd ed.). Philadelphia, PA: Jessica Kingsley.

Horwath, J., & Shardlow, S. M. (Eds.). (2003a). *Making links across specialisms.* London: Russell House Publishing.

Horwath, J., & Shardlow, S. M. (2003b). Specialism: A force for change. In J. Horwath & S. M. Shardlow (Eds.), *Making links across specialisms: Understanding modern social work practice* (pp. 1–21). Lyme Regis: Russell House.

Houston-Vega, M. K., Neuhring, E. M., & Daguio, E. R. (1996). *Prudent practice.* Annapolis, MD: NASW Press.

Howard, M. O., McMillen, C. J., & Pollio, D. E. (2003). Teaching evidence-based practice: Toward a new paradigm for social work education. *Research on Social Work Practice, 13*(2), 234–259.

Howe, D. (1996). *Social workers and their practice in welfare bureaucracies.* Aldershot, UK: Gower.

Howe, D. (2003). *An introduction to social work theory.* Aldershot, UK: Ashgate.

Hugman, R. (1991). *Power in caring professions.* New York, NY: Macmillan.

Humphries, B. (2003). What *else* counts as evidence in evidence-based practice? *Social Work Education, 22*(1), 83.

Institute of Medicine. (2001). *Crossing the quality chasm: A new health system for the 21st century.* Washington, DC: National Academy Press.

International Federation of Social Workers (IFSW). (2003). *The ethics of social work: Principles and standards.* http://www.ifsw.org/Publications/4.4.pub.html

Jansson, B. S. (2005). *The reluctant welfare state: American social welfare policies: Past, present, and future* (5th ed.). Belmont, CA: Brooks/Cole/Thompson.

Jayaratne, S., Croxton, T., & Mattison, D. (1997). Social work professional standards: An exploratory study. *Social Work, 42*(2), 187–198.

Jayaratne, S., & Levy, L. (1979). *Empirical clinical practice.* New York, NY: Columbia University Press.

Jayaratne, S., Vinkur-Kaplan, D., Nagda, B. A., & Chess, W. A. (1996). A national study on violence and harassment of social workers by clients. *Journal of Applied Social Sciences, 20*(1), 1–14.

Johns, R. (2003). *Using the law in social work.* Exeter, UK: Learning Matters.

Johnson, P. (2004, January 7). Unhealthy states. *Community Care,* p. 41.

Johnson, P. G., Beckerman A., & Auerbach, C. (2002). Researching our own practice: Single system design for groupwork. *Groupwork, 13*(1), 57–72.

Jones, C. (2001). Voices from the front line: State social workers and New Labour. *British Journal of Social Work, 31*(4), 547–562.

Jordan, B. (2003). Tough love: Social work practice in UK society. In P. Stepney & D. Ford (Eds.), *Social work models, methods and theories.* London: Russell House Publishing.

Joseph, M. V. (1989). Social work ethics: Historical and contemporary perspectives. *Social Thought, 15*(3/4), 4–17.

Ka Tat Tsang, A., & George, U. (1998). Towards an integrated framework for cross-cultural social work practice. *Canadian Social Work Review, 15*(1), 71–93.

Kadushin, A. E. (1992). *Supervision in social work.* New York, NY: Columbia University Press.

Kant, I. (1785). Groundwork of the metaphysic of morals. In H. J. Paton (Ed.), *The moral law* (pp. 53–123). New York: Routledge.

Katz, J. (1978). *White awareness: Handbook for anti-racist training.* Norman, OK: University of Oklahoma Press.

Kemshall, H. (1996). Offender risk and probation practice. In H. Kemshall & J. Pritchard (Eds.), *Good practice in risk assessment and risk management* (pp. 133–145). Philadelphia, PA: Jessica Kingsley.

Kemshall, H., & Pritchard, J. (Eds.). (1996). *Good practice in risk assessment and risk management.* Philadelphia, PA: Jessica Kingsley.

King, A. W., Fowler, S. W., & Zeithaml, C. P. (2001). Managing organizational competencies for competitive advantage: The middle management edge. *Supervision, 15*(2), 95–106.

Kirk, S. (1991). Scholarship and the professional school. *Social Work Research Abstracts, 27*(1), 3–6.

Kirst-Ashman, K. (2007). *Introduction to social work and social welfare: Critical thinking perspective* (2nd ed.). Pacific Grove, CA: Brooks/Cole/Thompson.

Kirst-Ashman, K. K., & Hull, G. H., Jr. (2001). *Generalist practice with organizations and communities* (2nd ed.). Pacific Grove, CA: Brooks/Cole/Thompson.

Kitwood, T., & Bredin, K. (1992). *Person to person.* Essex, UK: Gale Centre.

Klassen, D., & O'Connor, W. A. (1994). Demographic and case history variables in risk assessment. In J. Monahan & H. J. Steadman (Eds.), *Violence and mental disorder: Developments in risk assessment* (pp. 229–257). Chicago: University of Chicago Press.

Knight, C. (1997). A study of MSW and BSW students' involvement with group work in the field practicum. *Social Work with Groups, 20*(2), 31–49.

Kronenberg, F., Algado, S. S., & Pollard, N. (2004). *Occupational therapy without borders.* Oxford, UK: Elsevier.

Kupperman, J. J. (1999). *Value . . . and what follows.* New York, NY: Oxford University Press.

Kurland, R., & Salmon, R. (1998). *Teaching a methods course in social work with groups.* Alexandra, VA: Council on Social Work Education.

Langan, M., & Day, L. (1992). *Women, oppression and social work.* New York, NY: Routledge.

Lefevre, M. (1998). Recognising and addressing imbalances of power in the practice teacher/student dialectic: An anti-discriminatory approach. In H. Lawson (Ed.), *Practice teaching changing social work.* Philadelphia, PA: Jessica Kingsley.

Levitt, L., Beckerman, H., & Johnson, P. (1999). Defending social and health services under threat: Questions and strategies. *Journal of Social Work Practice, 13*(1), 59–67.

Levy, C. S. (1973). The value base of social work. *Journal of Education in Social, 9,* 34–42.

Levy, C. S. (1976). *Social work ethics.* New York, NY: Human Sciences Press.

Linsley, J. (2003). Social work salaries: Keeping with the times? *The New Social Worker, 10*(1), 1–5.

Lishman, J. (2002). Personal and professional development. In R. Adams, L. Dominelli, & M. Payne (Eds.), *Social work: Themes, issues and critical debates* (pp. 95–108). Basingstoke, UK: Palgrave.

Lishman, J. (2009). *Communication in social work* (2nd ed.). Houndmills, Basingstoke, UK: Palgrave Macmillan.

Loewenberg, F. M., & Dolgoff, R. (2000). *Ethical decisions for social work practice* (6th ed.). Itasca, IL: Peacock.

Lum, D. (1999). *Culturally competent practice: A framework for growth and action.* Pacific Grove, CA: Brooks/Cole/Thompson.

Lum, D. (Ed.). (2003). *Culturally competent practice: A framework for understanding diverse groups and justice issues* (2nd ed.). Pacific Grove, CA: Brooks/Cole/Thompson.

Lum, D. (2004). *Social work practice with people of color: A process-stage approach.* Pacific Grove, CA: Brooks/Cole/Thompson.

Lymbery, M. (2000). The retreat from professionalism: From social worker to care manager. In N. Malin (Ed.), *Professionalism, boundaries and the workplace* (pp. 123–138). New York, NY: Routledge.

Lyter, S. C., & Martin, M. (2000, February). *Playing it safe: A survey addressing dangers in the field.* Paper presented at the annual program meeting of the Council on Social Work Education, New York, NY.

Mace, P. (1989). The effect of attitude and belief on social workers judgments concerning potentially dangerous clients. *Dissertation Abstracts International, 50*(2A), 544.

Manthorpe, J. (2000). Risk assessment. In M. Davies (Ed.), *The Blackwell encyclopaedia of social work* (pp. 298–299). Oxford, UK: Blackwell.

Mark, R. (1996). *Research made simple: A handbook for social workers.* Thousand Oaks, CA: Sage.

Marsella, A. J. (1998). Urbanization, mental health, and social deviancy. *American Psychologist, 53*(6), 624–634.

Marsh, J. C., D'Aunno, T. A., & Smith, B. A. (2000). Increasing access and providing social services to improve drug abuse treatment for women with children. *Addictions, 95*(8), 1237–1247.

Marsh, P., & Doel, M. (2005). *The task-centred book.* New York: Routledge.

Marx, J. D. (2004). *Social welfare: The American partnership.* Boston, MA: Allyn & Bacon.

Maslow, A. H. (1962). *The farther reaches of human nature.* New York, NY: Penguin.

McDonald, A. (1999). *Understanding community care: A guide for social workers.* New York, NY: Macmillan.

McFadden, E. J., & Downs, S. W. (1995). Family continuity: The new paradigm in permanency planning. *Community Alternatives: The International Journal of Family Care, 7*(1), 44.

McPhatter, A. R. (1997). Cultural competence in child welfare: What is it? How do we achieve it? What happens without it? *Child Welfare, 76*(1), 255–278.

Menscher, S. (1959). *Research methods in social work education.* New York, NY: Council on Social Work Education.

Meyer, D. R. (1995). Supplemental security income. In R. L. Edwards (Ed.), *Encyclopedia of social work* (19th ed., Vol. 3, pp. 2379–2385). Washington, DC: NASW Press.

Middleton, L. (1997). *The art of assessment.* Birmingham, UK: Venture Press.

Midgley, J. (2001). Issues in international social work. *Journal of Social Work, 1*(1), 21–35.

Miller, C., Ross, N., & Freeman, M. (1999). *Shared learning and clinical teamwork: New directions in education for multiprofessional practice*. London: English National Board for Nursing, Midwifery and Health Visiting.

Milner, J. (1986). *The Child Abuse Potential Inventory: Manual* (2nd ed.). Webster, NC: Psytec.

Milner, J., & O'Byrne, P. (2002). *Assessment in social work* (2nd ed.). New York, NY: Macmillan.

Minuchin, S., & Fishman, C. (1981). *Family therapy techniques*. Cambridge, MA: Harvard University Press.

Mullen, E. J., & Dumpson, J. R. (Eds.). (1972). *Evaluation of social intervention*. San Francisco: Jossey-Bass.

Mullen, E. J., & Magnabosco, J. L. (1997). *Outcomes measurement in the human services: Cross cutting issues and methods*. Washington, DC: NASW Press.

Mullender, A., & Ward, D. (1991). *Self-directed groupwork: Users take action for empowerment*. London: Whiting and Birch.

Muzumdar, K., & Atthar, R. (2002). Social work placements in police stations: A force for change. In S. M. Shardlow & M. Doel (Eds.), *Learning to practise social work: International approaches* (pp. 43–58). Philadelphia, PA: Jessica Kingsley.

National Association of Social Workers (NASW). (1982). *Standards for the classification of social work practice*. Washington, DC: Author.

National Association of Social Workers (NASW). (1988). *Council on Social Work Education (1988) curriculum policy statement* (Section, 6.13). Washington, DC: Council on Social Work Education.

National Association of Social Workers (NASW). (1996). *Code of ethics*. Washington, DC: Author.

National Association of Social Workers (NASW). (1999). *NASW code of ethics* (amended). Washington, DC: Author.

National Association of Social Workers (NASW). (2001). *Standards for cultural competence in social work practice*. Washington, DC: Author.

National Organisation for Practice Teaching (NOPT). (2000). *Code of practice*. www.nopt.org

Newhill, C. E. (1995). Client violence toward social workers: A practice and policy concern. *Social Work, 40*(5), 631–636.

Newhill, C. E. (2003). *Client violence in social work practice: Prevention, intervention, and research*. New York, NY: Guilford.

Newhill, C. E., & Wexler, S. (1997). Children and youth services social workers experiences with client violence. *Children and Youth Services Review, 19*(3), 195–212.

O'Hagan, K. (2001). *Cultural competence in the caring profession*. Philadelphia, PA: Jessica Kingsley.

O'Melia, M., & Miley, K. K. (2002). *Pathways to power: Readings in contextual social work practice*. Boston, MA: Allyn & Bacon.

Orme, J. (2002). Feminist social work. In R. Adams, L. Dominelli, & M. Payne (Eds.), *Social work: Themes, issues and critical debates* (pp. 218–226). Basingstoke, UK: Palgrave.

O'Sullivan, T. (1999). *Decision making in social work.* New York, NY: Macmillan.

Øvretveit, J., Mathias, P., & Thompson, T. (Eds.). (1997). *Interprofessional working for health and social care.* New York, NY: Macmillan.

Papell, C. (1996). Reflection on issues in social work education. In N. Gould & I. Taylor (Eds.), *Reflective learning for social work.* Aldershot, UK: Arena.

Parker, J., & Bradley, J. (2003). *Assessment, planning, intervention, and review.* Exeter, UK: Learning Matters Ltd.

Parker, J., & Merrylees, S. (2002). Why become a professional? Experiences of caregiving and the decision to enter social work or nursing education. *Learning in Health and Social Care, 1*(2), 105–114.

Parton, N. (2000). Some thoughts on the relationship between theory and practice in and for social work. *British Journal of Social Work, 30*(4), 449–463.

Payne, M. (1996). *What is professional social work?* Birmingham, UK: Venture Press.

Pelosi, A., & Birchwood, M. (2003). Is early intervention for psychosis a waste of valuable resources? *British Journal of Psychiatry, 182*(3), 196–198.

Phillips, N. K., & Straussner, S. L. (2002). *Urban social work: An introduction to policy and practice in cities.* Boston: Allyn & Bacon.

Phillipson, J. (2002). Creativity and practice teaching. *Practice Teaching in Health and Social Work, 4*(1), 8–26.

Pincus, A., & Minahan, A. (1975). *Social work practice: Model and method.* Itasca, IL: F. E. Peacock.

Pithouse, A. (1998). *Social work: The social organisation of an invisible trade* (2nd ed.). Aldershot, UK: Ashgate.

Popple, P. R., & Leighninger, L. (2005). *Social work, social welfare and American society* (6th ed.). Boston, MA: Allyn & Bacon.

Preston-Shoot, M. (1993). Whither social work law? Future questions on the teaching and assessment of law to social workers. *Social Work Education, 12*(Suppl. 1), 65–78.

Preston-Shoot, M. (2001). A triumph of hope over experience? On modernizing accountability in social services—the case of complaints procedures in community care. *Social Policy and Administration, 35*(6), 701–715.

Protocky-Tripodi, M. (2002). *Best social work practice with immigrants and refugees.* New York, NY: Columbia University Press.

Quinny, A. (2004, July). *Supporting practice learning: The placements on-line project.* Paper presented at the Joint Social Work Education Conference, Glasgow, UK.

Reamer, F. G. (1994). *Social work practice and liability.* New York, NY: Columbia University Press.

Reamer, F. G. (1999). *Social work values and ethics* (2nd ed.). New York, NY: Columbia University Press.

Redl, F. (1957). Research needs in the delinquency field. *Children, 4*(1), 15–19.

Reed, M. (2002, April). The practitioner's perspective: Practice focus. *Professional Social Work,* pp. 16–17.

Reid, W. J. (1992). *Task strategies: An empirical approach to clinical social work.* New York, NY: Columbia University Press.

Rey, L. (1996). What social workers need to know about client violence. *Families in Society, 77*(1), 33–39.

Richmond, M. (1917). *Social diagnosis.* New York, NY: Russell Sage.

Roberts, A. L., & Yeager, K. R. (2006). *Foundations of evidence-based social work practice.* New York, NY: Oxford University Press.

Roberts, H., Smith, S. J., & Bryce, C. (1995). *Children at risk.* Buckingham, UK: Open University Press.

Rose, S. M. (1992). *Case management and social work practice.* New York, NY: Longman.

Rosenthal, R. N. (2006). Overview of evidence based practice. In A. R. Roberts & K. R. Yeager (Eds.), *Foundations of evidence based social work practice* (pp. 67–80). New York, NY: Oxford University Press.

Rothman, J. (2000). *Stepping out into the field: A field work manual for social work students.* Boston, MA: Allyn & Bacon.

Royse, D., Dhooper, S., & Rompf, E. (2007). *Field instruction: A guide for social work students* (5th ed.). Needham Heights, MA: Allyn & Bacon.

Rubin, A., & Babbie, E. (2008). *Research methods for social work* (6th ed.). Belmont, CA: Brooks/Cole/Thompson.

Rush, B. L. (2009). U.S. health care: A matter of answering the right question. *Chicago Defender, 104*(2), 1.

Sacco, T. (1996). Spirituality and social work students in their first year of study at a South African university. *Journal of Social Development in Africa, 11*(2), 43–56.

Sackett, D. L., Richardson, W., Rosenberg, W., & Haynes, R. B. (1997). *Evidence-based medicine: How to practice and teach evidence-based medicine.* New York, NY: Churchill Livingstone.

Sackett, D. L., Straus, S. E., Richardson, W. S., Rosenberg, W., & Haynes, R. B. (2000). *Evidence based medicine: How to practice and teach EBM* (2nd ed.). London: Churchill Livingstone.

Saleebey, D. (1992). *The strengths perspective in social work.* New York, NY: Longman.

Sarri, R. (1997). International social work at the millennium. In M. Reisch & E. Gambrill (Eds.), *Social work in the 21st century.* Thousand Oaks, CA: Pine Forge Press.

Schön, D. A. (1987). *Educating the reflective practitioner: Toward a new design for teaching and learning in the professions.* San Francisco: Jossey-Bass.

Schubert, L. (2006, July). *Is social work art, or is art social work?* Paper presented at the Humanities Conference University of Carthage, Tunis, Tunisia.

Segal, E., & Brzuzy, S. (1998). *Social welfare, policy, programs, and practice.* Itasca, IL: Peacock.

Senge, P. (1990). *The fifth discipline: The art and practice of the learning organization.* New York, NY: Currency Doubleday.

Shardlow, S. M. (1988). The economics of student help. *Insight, 3*(23), 24–25.

Shardlow, S. M. (2000). Legal responsibility and liability in fieldwork. In L. Cooper & L. Briggs (Eds.), *Field in the human services* (pp. 117–130). Sydney, Australia: Allen & Unwin.

Shardlow, S. M., Davis, C., Johnson, M., Murphy, M., Long, T., & Race, D. (2004). *Standards and inter-professional education in child protection.* Salford, UK: Salford Centre for Social Work Research.

Shardlow, S. M., & Doel, M. (1996). *Practice learning and teaching.* New York, NY: Macmillan.

Shardlow, S. M., Nixon, S., & Rogers, J. (2002). The motivation of practice teachers: Decisions relating to involvement in practice learning provision. *Learning in Health and Social Care, 1*(2), 67–74.

Sheafor, B., & Horejsi, C. (2008). *Techniques and guidelines for social work practice* (8th ed.). Needham Heights, MA: Allyn & Bacon.

Sheppard, M. (2006). *Social work and social exclusion.* Aldershot, UK: Ashgate.

Shields, G., & Kiser, J. (2003). Violence and aggression directed toward human service workers: An exploratory study. *Families in Society, 84*(1), 13–20.

Shulman, L. (2006). *The skills of helping individuals, families, groups and communities* (5th ed.). Belmont, CA: Brooks/Cole/Thompson.

Singleton, W. T., & Holden, J. (Eds.). (1994). *Risk and decisions.* London: John Wiley.

Siporin, M. (1975). *Introduction to social work practice.* New York, NY: Macmillan.

Skolnick-Acker, E., Atkinson, J., Frost, A. K., Kaplan, B., & Pelavin, A. (1993). *Violence against social workers.* Unpublished manuscript.

Smith, B. D. (2003). How parental drug use and drug treatment compliance relate to family reunification. *Child Welfare, 82*(3), 335–365.

Specht, H., & Courtney, M. E. (1995). *Unfaithful angels: How social work has abandoned its mission.* New York, NY: Free Press.

Spencer, P. C., & Munich, S. (2003). Client violence toward social workers: The role of management in community mental health programs. *Social Work, 48*(4), 532–544.

St. Thomas, B., & Johnson, P. G. (2003). In their own voices: Play activities and art with traumatized children. *Groupwork, 13*(2), 34–48.

St. Thomas, B., & Johnson, P. G. (2004). Play the lantern of hope. *Journal of Poetry Therapy, 17*(2), 81–90.

St. Thomas, B., & Johnson, P. G. (2007). *Empowering children through art and expression: Culturally sensitive ways of healing trauma and grief.* Philadelphia, PA: Jessica Kingsley.

Stalker, K. (2003). Managing risk and uncertainty in social work. *Journal of Social Work, 3*(3), 211–233.

Stanley, T. L. (2002). Architects of change: A new role for managers. *Supervision, 63*(10), 10–14.

Stein, T. J. (2004). *The role of law in social work practice and administration.* New York, NY: Columbia University Press.

Stevenson, O. (1988). Law and social work education: A commentary on The Law Report. *Issues in Social Work Education, 8*(1), 37–45.

Stevenson, O., & Parsloe, P. (1993). *Community care and empowerment.* York, UK: Rowntree Foundation with Community Care.

Sullivan, H. (2003). New forms of local accountability: Coming to terms with "many hands"? *Policy and Politics, 31*(3), 353–369.

Swigonski, M., Ward, K., Robin, S., Mama, R. S., Rodgers, J., & Belicose, R. (2006). An agenda for the future: Student portfolios in social work education social work. *Education, 25*(8), 812–823.

Tajfel, H. (1981). *Human groups and social categories.* Cambridge, UK: Cambridge University Press.

Tan, N.-T. (Ed.). (2004). *Social work around the world III.* Berne, Switzerland: International Federation of Social Workers.

Tan, N.-T., & Dodds, I. (Eds.). (2002). *Social work around the world II.* Berne, Switzerland: International Federation of Social Workers.

Tan, N.-T., & Envall, E. (Eds.). (2000). *Social work around the world.* Berne, Switzerland: International Federation of Social Workers.

Thomlison, B., & Collins, D. (1995). Use of structured consultation for learning issues in field education. In G. Rogers (Ed.), *Social work field education: Views and visions* (pp. 223–228). Dubuque, IA: Kendall/Hunt.

Thompson, N. (2000a). *Tackling bullying and harassment in the workplace.* Birmingham, UK: Pepar Publications.

Thompson, N. (2000b). *Understanding social work: Preparing for practice.* New York, NY: Macmillan.

Thompson, N. (2002). Developing anti-discriminatory practice. In D. Tomlinson & W. Threw (Eds.), *Equalising opportunities, minimising oppression.* New York, NY: Routledge.

Thompson, N. (2003). *Promoting equality.* New York, NY: Palgrave Macmillan.

Tracy, E. M. (2002). Working with and strengthening social networks. In A. R. Roberts & G. J. Greene (Eds.), *Social workers desk reference* (pp. 402–405). New York, NY: Oxford University Press.

Trattner, W. I. (1999). *From poor law to welfare state: A history of social welfare in America* (6th ed.). New York, NY: Free Press.

Trevithick, P. (2005). *Social work skills: A practice handbook.* Maidenhead, UK: Open University Press.

Trotter, C. (1999). *Working with involuntary clients: A guide to practice.* Thousand Oaks, CA: Sage.

Tully, C. T. (2000). *Lesbians, gays, and the empowerment perspective.* New York, NY: Columbia University Press.

Underhill, D. (with Betteridge, C., Harvey, B., & Patient, K.). (2002). Learning opportunities and placements with asylum seekers. In S. M. Shardlow & M. Doel (Eds.), *Learning to practise social work: International approaches* (pp. 77–90). Philadelphia, PA: Jessica Kingsley.

University of Southern Maine. (2009). *School of Social Work BSW field work manual academic year 2009–2010.* Portland, ME: Author.

U.S. Department of Labor Statistics. (2009). *Occupational outlook handbook, 2008–09 edition: Social workers.* Retrieved October 4, 2009, from http://www.bls.gov/oco/ocos060.htm

Vallianatos, C. (2001, May). Profession extolled on Hill. *NASW News, 46*(5), 1.

van Wormer, K. (2006). *Introduction to social welfare and social work: The U.S. in global perspective.* Belmont, CA: Brooks/Cole/Thompson.

Ward, D. (2000). Totem not token: Groupwork as a vehicle for user participation. In H. Kemshall & R. Littlechild (Eds.), *User involvement and participation in social care.* Philadelphia, PA: Jessica Kingsley.

Watkins, T. R. (2004). Natural helping networks: Assets for rural communities. In T. L. Scales & C. L. Streeter (Eds.), *Rural social work: Building and sustaining community assets*. Belmont, CA: Brooks/Cole/Thompson.

Wayne, J., & Cohen, C. (2001). *Group work education in the field*. Alexandra, VA: Council on Social Work Education.

Webster's new world dictionary of American English (3rd college ed.). (1990). New York, NY: Simon & Schuster.

Weedon, C. (1987). *Feminist practice and poststructuralist theory*. Oxford, UK: Basil Blackwell.

Weinstein, J. (1997). The development of shared learning: Conspiracy or constructive development? In J. Øvretveit, P. Mathias, & T. Thompson (Eds.), *Interprofessional working for health and social care*. New York, NY: Macmillan.

Weinstein, J., Whittington, C., & Leiba, T. (2003). *Collaboration in social work practice*. Philadelphia, PA: Jessica Kingsley.

West, J., & Watson, D. (2002). Preparing for practice: The use of personal learning audits in social work education. *Practice, 14*(4), 43–52.

Whitaker, D., & Archer, J. L. (1989). *Research by social workers: Capitalizing on experience*. London: Central Council for Education and Training in Social Work.

Whittington, C. (2003). *Learning for collaborative practice*. London: Department of Health.

Williams, A. (1997). The rationing debate: Rationing health care by age. The case for. *British Medical Journal, 314*, 820–822.

Williams, R. M., Jr. (1967). Individual and group values. *Annals, 371*, 20–37.

Wolins, M. (1960). Measuring the effects of social work intervention. In N. Polansky (Ed.), *Social work research*. Chicago, IL: University of Chicago Press.

Woolhandler, S., & Himmelstein, D. (1998). *For our patients, not for profits: A call for action*. Cambridge, MA: The Center for National Program Studies, Harvard Medical School.

Yee Lee, M. (2003). A solution-focused approach to cross-cultural clinical social work practice: Utilizing cultural strengths. *Families in Society, 84*, 385–395.

Zastrow, C. (2008). *Introduction to social work and social welfare* (9th ed.). Belmont, CA: Brooks/Cole/Thompson.

Index

Accountability, 150, 175
assessing student's learning, 185–186
client outcomes
    assessment, 177
forms of, 181
Held to Account activity, 175
horizontal and vertical, 182
learning about, 181
legal, 185, 244–245
managed care and, 176–177
monitoring, 169
opportunities for learning about, 180
personal, 181–182
priorities and, 178
private sector agencies and, 141
professional, 184–185
program evaluation, 24, 176, 182–183
public, 182–183
record keeping, 180
research and, 214
single-case evaluation
    designs, 177
teaching about, 180
to employer, 182
to other agencies, 182
to service users and providers,
    183–184
Accreditation standards, 2, 263
legal education, 240
See also Educational Policy and
    Accreditation Standards

Action techniques for generating options,
    110–111
Active listening, 113
Activities, 5–6
A-Z of the Law: Spirit and Letter
    (Activity 14), 233–237
Boundaries (Activity 3), 53–58
Dial "D" for Danger (Activity 12),
    187–193
The Drawbridge (Activity 13),
    217–223, 226
Essence of Social Work (Activity 15),
    247–254
Held to Account (Activity 11),
    175–179
Hold the Front Page (Activity 7),
    113–116, 119–120
Home Truths (Activity 9), 145–150
No One Is an Island (Activity 8),
    125–128
Open Ends (Activity 6), 101–106
Permission to Learn (Activity 1),
    27–32
Points of View (Activity 2), 39–45
Starting Out (Activity 5), 89–92
The Myth of Sisyphus (Activity 4),
    67–73
Travel Agent (Activity 10), 159–167
*View from Another Place . . . Another
    Time* (Activity 16), 265–271
virtual learning environments, 266

Activity-based learning, 7
Actuarial risk assessment, 195
Ad hoc contacts, 97
Adoption law, 242
Advanced social work practice, 14,
    255–256
  defining, 256
  See also Specialist or advanced practice
Advocacy, 169
African paradigm, 278
Age and health care rationing, 155–156
Agency mission, 93
Agency practice, 137
  accountability, 182
  creative practice issues, 137, 141–143
  importance of procedures, 137–138
  interdisciplinary practice, 82–83
  priorities, 152
  private sector agencies and, 140–141
  problems with procedures, 138–140
  public and private settings, 16
  retreat from professionalism, 140–141
  student induction, 94
  successful organization
      characteristics, 169–170
  See also Interprofessional practice
Albert, R., 276
Appeal mechanisms, 183
Appointment management, 172–173
Appointments with
    yourself, 173
Art of social work, 142
Asch, S. E., 134
Asperger syndrome, 198
Assessing student
    performance, 18
  accountability, 185–186
  assessment in partnership, 123
  communication and generating
      options, 111
  comparative social work, 278
  contrast errors, 18
  defining professional
      boundaries, 65–66

generalist and specialist practice, 263
group work practice, 134–135
law-informed practice, 246
learning agreement and, 22
learning-practice escalator, 23
making priorities, 158
multicultural practice, 231
resource management, 174
self-knowledge, 50
understanding service users, 37
Assessing students' learning, 6
Assessment:
  active listening, 113
  assessing student's
      learning, 123
  defining, 117
  documenting, 118
  government guidance, 120–121
  Hold the Front Page activity,
      113–116, 119–120
  holistic, 122
  intervention and, 118–119, 122–123
  judgment, 119, 121
  of needs, 120, 168–169
  opportunities for making in
      partnership, 117
  risk, 203
  task-centered practice, 123
  teaching and learning about, 117–118
  wide range of, 120
  working in partnership, 121–122
Attlee, Clement, 2
Audio-video feedback, 98
Austin, David, 205
Autonomy and risk, 198
Awareness. *See* Self-awareness
A-Z of the Law: Spirit and Letter
    (Activity 14), 233–237

Babbie, E., 43
Baccalaureate social work (BSW)
    education, 14–15, 254–255, 257,
    260–262
Bamford, T., 181

Barker, R. L., 167–168

Bartlett, H., 257–258

Benefits of supervising students, 19–21

Bergmark, A., 157

Best practice, 137

Bilateral working, 83. *See also* Interprofessional practice

Blaming, 227

Blenkner, Margaret, 206

Bloom's Taxonomy of Educational Objectives, 261

Boundaries (Activity 3), 53–58, 60–61

Bourne, I., 130–131

Brace, Charles Loring, 277

Braye, S., 238, 240, 241

Briar, S., 205–206

Broadbent, G., 241

Brown, A., 130–131

Brzuzy, S., 276

Burnout, 142

Butrym, Zofia, 257

Cabot, R. C., 207

Careers in social work, 3

Carlton-LeNey, B., 274–275

Case management, 159, 167–169
  change approach, 170–171
  components of, 168–169
  time management, 171–173
  See also Resource management

Categorical imperative, 181

Certification, 184

Challenging situations, 187
  assessing student's learning, 203
  Dial "D" for Danger activity, 187–193
  harm-benefit analysis, 199–200
  opportunities for learning about, 194
  risk assessment, 194–196
  teaching about, 193–194
  See also Risk

Change approach, 170–171

Change attitudes, 96

Child Abuse Prevention and Treatment Act (CAPTA), 242

Child care centers, 140

Child protection:
  history of child welfare, 276–277
  legal requirements, 242, 244
  risk assessment, 195

Children, enquiry with, 102, 110

Child Study Center, 251–252

City subway maps, 8–10

Clark, C. L., 18, 181

Class paradigm, 221

"Clients," 7, 33–34. *See also* Service users

Clinical risk assessment, 195

Codes of ethics, 17, 60, 63, 68, 74–75, 184–185, 239, 244, 255

Cognitive-behavioral approaches, 42, 127

Coleman, A., 158

Collaboration cooperation, 83
  accountability issues, 181
  assessment in partnership, 121–122
  See also Interprofessional practice

College-filed liaison, 24–25

Collins, D., 25

Common law, 239

Communication cooperation, 83

Communication patterns, 106–108

Communication skills:
  assessing student's learning, 111
  enquiry with children, 102, 110
  nonverbal, 110
  positive reframing, 109–110
  recognizing and interrupting patterns, 106–108
  recording, 111
  spirit of enquiry, 108–109
  symbolic, 110
  taboo topics, 96–97

Comparative social work, 265
  assessing student's learning, 278
  historical comparisons, 276–277

international comparisons,
    267–269, 272–273
interprofessional comparison, 277–278
learning about, 272
local/regional comparison, 274
opportunities, 271–272
rural practice, 274–275
teaching about, 271
urban practice, 275–276
*View from Another Place . . . Another
    Time* activity, 265–271
Competencies, 13–14
    accountability and, 181
    activities and, 6
    cultural, 223–225
    successful organization
        characteristics, 170–171
    synthesizing competence and
        context, 14
    See also Educational Policy and
        Accreditation Standards
Complaint procedures, 183
Confrontational responses, 108
Constitutional law, 238–239
Constructionist approach, 48, 106
Consultation cooperation, 83
Contemporary field social work, 1–4
Context and competence, 14
Continuing education, 24, 82
Contrast errors, 18
Control:
    occupational, 63–64
    risk management, 198
    service user and provider, 36
    See also Power issues
Corby, B., 195
Council on Social Work Education
    (CSWE), 180, 184
    accreditation standards
        limitations, 263
    BSW and MSW differences,
        15, 260–261
    no law studies requirements, 239–240
    purpose of social work profession, 205
    signature pedagogy, 14

specialist/advanced practice
    definition, 256
specialization categories, 258–260
values and ethics policies, 74
See also Educational Policy and
    Accreditation Standards
Courtney, M. E., 156, 262–263
Creative practice, 137, 141–143
Critical empathy, 206
Cultural competence, 223. *See also*
    Multicultural practice
Culturally responsive practice. *See*
    Multicultural practice
Cultural relativism paradigm, 221

Davenport, J., III, 274
Davenport, J. A., 274
de Bono, E., 109–110, 197
Decision making about resources. *See*
    Resource management
Decision making priorities. *See*
    Prioritization
Democracy and groups, 134
Depression support group, 127–128
Descriptive research, 213
Dial "D" for Danger (Activity 12),
    187–193
DiNitto, D. M., 276
Disabled persons' rights, 167–168
Discretionary procedures, 139–140
Diversity, 223, 230–231
    international comparisons of social
        work, 273
    social work profession and, 46
    student-supervisor relationship, 18
    See also Multicultural practice
Documenting placement learning and
    experiences, 98–99, 118, 180
Doel, Mark, 25
Domestic violence, 242–243
The Drawbridge (Activity 13),
    217–223, 226
DuBois, B., 181
Dumpson, J. R., 208
Duncan, T., 241

Educational Policy and Accreditation Standards (EPAS), 12, 13
  accountability, 177
  BSW and MSW differences, 254–255
  comparative social work, 267
  Core Competencies, 13–14
  generalist and specialist practice, 248
  generating options, 103
  group work practice, 126
  law-informed practice, 234
  learning about service users, 29
  making assessments in partnership, 114–115
  making priorities, 147
  managing resources, 161
  multicultural practice, 218–219
  preparation for practice, 90
  professional relationships, 55
  risk, 189
  self-learning, 41
  signature pedagogy, 4–5
  values ethical dilemmas, 69
Education of social workers.
  See Social work education
Edwards, R. L., 274–275
Elderly people, 46, 227–228
  abuse, 243
  health care rationing, 155–156
Emotional risk, 197
Empirical practice, 43
Employment of social workers, 3
Empowerment, 36, 168, 198
Enquiry, 108–109
  discerning appropriate and inappropriate responses, 107–108
  Open Ends activity, 101–106
  self-awareness, 107
  with children, 102, 110
  See also Communication skills
Essence of Social Work (Activity 15), 247–254
E-support systems, 24–25

Ethical dilemmas, 67, 78–79
  assessing student's learning, 79–80
  Boundaries activity (professional relationships), 53–58
  conflicting values, 75–76
  how to address, 76
  learning about, 76–79
  other professions and, 68
  teaching about, 74–76
Ethical principles, CSWE policy statement, 74
Ethical review, 212
Ethics codes, 17, 60, 63, 68, 74–75, 184–185, 239, 244, 255
Evaluation research. *See* Program evaluation
Evans, G., 156
Evidence-based practice, 43, 208–210
Executive branch of government, 239
Expectations, role, 59–60, 62
Explanatory research, 213
Exploratory research, 212–213

Faculty liaison role, 24–25
Families and the law, 242
Family Violence Prevention and Services Act, 243
Federal and state constitutional law, 238–239
Feedback, 97–98
Feminism, 44, 221–222
Field education:
  core values, 17
  learning agreement, 21–22
  learning-practice escalator, 23
  placement as learning experience, 25
  signature pedagogy, 4–5, 14
  support for practice learning, 24–25
  See also Social work education; Supervision
Field instructor, 7, 27. *See also* Supervision
Fields of social work practice, 262
Financial abuse specialist teams (FAST), 262

First contact with service
   users, 95–96
First impressions, 94–95
Fischer, Joel, 208
Flipcharts, 111, 114, 141
Fook, J., 51
Friendships, 53
Fundamentalist paradigm, 222
Funding issues, 15, 82, 129

Gambrill, E., 157
Gay aging, 228
Generalist practice, 14, 254–256
   assessing student's
      learning, 263
   Essence of Social Work
      activity, 247–254
   future and critique of, 262–263
   learning about, 257
   opportunities, 256
Generic, 258
Gibb, C. E., 18
Gibbs, L., 157
Gilbert, N., 276
Glendinning, C., 158
Globalization, 272
Good practice, 63–64
Gordon, William, 215
Grant writing, 24
Group activities, 28
Group supervision, 130–131
Group work, 125
   assessing student's learning,
      134–135
   balancing needs, 129
   fears about, 130
   learning from, 134
   meetings and sessions,
      133–134
   No One Is an Island
      activity, 125–128
   opportunities for learning
      about, 128–131
   power issues, 130
   social action model, 132

specialist practice, 260
teamwork, 131–133
visibility, 134
Guilt, 227

Harm-benefit analysis, 199–200
Health care financial risk, 189
Health care legal issues, 243
Health care priorities, 153–155
   rationing, 155–158
   triage, 156–157
Health insurance, 153–154
Held to Account (Activity 11), 175–179
Herod, J., 87–88
Historical social work comparisons,
   276–277
HIV/AIDS status, 227
Hold the Front Page (Activity 7),
   113–116, 119–120
Holistic assessment, 122
Home Truths (Activity 9), 145–150
Homosexual (LGB) people, 228–229
Horizontal accountability, 182
Hospice social work manager, job
   description, 250
Howe, D., 64
Human services organizations, 140
Humphries, B., 51

Imprint effect, 173
Individualism paradigm, 221
Individuality, 34
Induction, 94
Insider-outsider tensions, 227–228
Institutional Review
   Board (IRB), 212
Institutional support, 24
Interdisciplinary learning and practice.
   See Interprofessional practice
International Federation of Social
   Workers (IFSW), 180, 184, 267–268
International social work, 273
International social work comparisons,
   267–269, 272–273
Internet-based activity, 266, 273

Internet-related legal issues, 244
Interprofessional learning, 85–86
Interprofessional practice,
    68, 81–82, 83, 88
  comparative social work, 277–278
  existing networks, 93–94
  group work activity, 126
  harmful collusion, 85–86
  interprofessional practice
    issues, 68, 83–85
  issues concerning, 84–85
  modes of interaction, 83
  multidisciplinary teams,
    16, 81, 83, 87–88
  networking, 84
  power and status differentials, 85
  Starting Out activity, 89–92
  working with multiple
    agencies, 82–83
Intervention and assessment,
    118–119, 122–123
Intervention and risk, 195
  assessing student's learning, 203
  Dial "D" for Danger
    activity, 187–193
  risk assessment, 194–196
  risk management, 197–198
  See also Risk
Intervention prioritization. *See*
    Prioritization
Interview lines of enquiry, *Open Ends*
    activity, 101–106
Introduction methods, 95–96
"It depends" type answers, 61

Jansson, B. S., 276
Jayaratne, S., 208
Jewish stereotyping, 230–231
Job descriptions, 249–254
Job satisfaction, 142
Joint working, 83
Journal writing, 118
  time management, 172–173
Judgment and assessment, 119, 121
Judicial review, 239

Kant, I., 181
Katz, Judith, 217
Kemshall, H., 195
Kinship care, 277
Kirst-Ashman, K., 168, 276
Kowalski, Pavel, 274

Language and multicultural practice, 226
Law-informed practice, 233, 237
  accountability issues, 185
  approval-disapproval continuum, 245
  assessing student's learning, 246
  assessment considerations, 120–121
  A-Z of the Law: Spirit and Letter
    activity, 233–237
  consequences of professional actions,
    244–245
  legal sources, 238–239
  linking social work and law, 238–240
  opportunities, 240–243
  seeking legal expertise, 241
  social work educational requirements,
    239–240
Learning about yourself. *See* Self-
    knowledge
Learning agreement, 21–22, 98
Learning by doing, 7
Learning by simulated practice, 7–10
Learning-practice escalator, 23
Legal accountability, 185. *See also* Law-
    informed practice
Legal authority and assessment, 120–121
Legal context. *See* Law-informed practice
Legal paradigm, 221
Leighninger, L., 276
Lesbian, gay, and bisexual
    (LGB) people, 228–229
Levy, L., 208
Liability insurance, 185
Liaison, college-field, 24–25
Licensing, 184
Life experiences and social
    work practice, 45–47
Lifestyle and health care rationing, 156
Linking or referring, 169

Listening skills, 113
Location of social work, 15–17
Lymbery, M., 36, 50, 87–88

Managed care, 140–141, 176–177
Management by objectives (MBO), 183
Management role, 77–78
Managing resources. *See* Resource
    management
Manthorpe, J., 194
Maps, 8–10
Marx, J. D., 276
Master's social work (MSW) education,
    14–15, 255, 257, 260–262
McDonald, A., 120
Meetings, 133–134
Menscher, S., 207
Mental health and the law, 243
Mental Health Block Grant, 243
Mental health-related practice
    specialties, 261–262
Mental health teams, 133
Mental maps, 8
Messiness of practice, 42
Metaphors for social work role, 64
Midgely, J., 273
Miley, K. K., 181, 229
Mission of social work, 2
Modern Social Work Practice
    (Doel & Shardlow), 5
Monitoring, 169
Motivations for social work
    careers, 39, 46–47
Mullen, E. J., 208
Multicultural practice, 217
    assessing student's learning, 231
    competence, 223–225
    diversity and difference, 230–231
    The Drawbridge activity,
        217–223, 226
    insider-outsider tensions, 227–228
    international comparisons, 273
    language, 226
    opportunities, 222–223, 225
    political correctness, 226

power and empowerment, 229–230
practitioner attitude, 223–224
practitioner knowledge, 224
practitioner skills, 224–225
responsibility, 227
teaching about, 220–222, 225–226
See also Diversity
Multidisciplinary teams, 16, 81, 83,
    87–88, 133
    paradigms, 220–222
The Myth of Sisyphus (Activity 4), 67–73

National Association of Social Workers
    (NASW), 17, 180, 198, 207
    Code of Ethics, 60, 63, 74–75, 184,
        239, 255
    goals of social work practice, 168
    liability insurance resources, 185
National Organisation for Practice Teaching
    (NOPT), 17
Needs assessment, 120, 168–169
Needs focus, 36
Networks, 84, 93–94
The New Social Work Practice
    (Doel & Shardlow), 25
Newhill, C. E., 194, 197
Nixon, S., 19–21
Nonverbal communication, 110

Observer feedback, 97–98
Occupational control, 63–64
O'Melia, M., 229
Open Ends (Activity 6), 101–106
Opportunities for practice
    learning, 18, 25
Options for service users, 101
    action techniques, 110–111
    assessing student's learning, 111
    learning about generating, 108–111
    lines of enquiry, *Open Ends* activity,
        101–106
    opportunities for generating, 105–106
    recognizing and interrupting patterns,
        106–108
Organizational change, 170–171

Organizational specialisms, 260
O'Sullivan, T., 196
Outcome preference values, 77–78
Outcomes evaluation, 177
   evidence-based practice, 208–210
   need for, 210–211
   See also Program
      evaluation; Research
Out-groups, 227–228

Papell, C., 258–260
Paradigms, 220–222
Parenting skills group, 127
Parsloe, P., 197
Participative learning, 7
Partnership, assessment in, 121–122
Pathologizing the person, 35
Payne, Malcolm, 257
Performance assessment. *See* Assessing
   student performance
Permission to Learn
   (Activity 1), 27–32
   Held to Account activity, 177
   Hold the Front Page activity, 115
   Home Truths activity, 145, 147
   No One Is an Island
      activity, 125, 126
   Open Ends activity, 102–103
   Starting Out activity, 89–91
Phillips, N. K., 276
Physical risk, 197
Piper, C., 241
Placement as learning experience, 25
Placement first impressions, 94–95
Play, 102, 110
Points of View (Activity 2),
   39–45, 50–51
Political correctness, 226
Political support for social work, 3
Popple, P. R., 276
Populations at risk, 46
Portfolio, 98–99, 174
Positive reframing, 109–110
Positivist evaluation methods, 42
Postmodern, 48

Power issues, 42–43, 51
   group leadership, 130
   interprofessional practice, 85
   multicultural practice,
      225–226, 229–230
   occupational control
      and status, 63–64
   procedures, 139
   professional relationships, 60
   supervisory context, 23
   See also Empowerment
Power paradigm, 222
Practice learning, support for, 24–25
Practice teacher, 7
Practicum as a culture, 11
Preferred conceptions values, 77
Preferred instrumentalities
   values, 77
Preferred outcomes values, 77–78
Preparation for practice, 89
   ad hoc contacts, 97
   attitude, 96
   direct feedback, 97–98
   documenting, 98
   documenting experiences, 98–99
   expectations, 93
   first contacts and introduction
      methods, 95–96
   first impressions, 94–95
   induction, 94
   opportunities for learning
      about, 92–93
   service user existing networks, 93–94
   Starting Out activity, 89–92
   taboo topics, 96–97
Prescriptive responses, 108
Preston-Shoot, M., 184, 238, 240
Prioritization, 145
   accountability issues, 178
   agency priorities, 152
   assessing student's
      learning, 158
   health care issues, 153–155
   Home Truths activity, 145–150
   learning about, 152–154

mental health care, 153
opportunities for learning about, 152
public choice, 152
ranking criteria, 150–151
rationing, 155–158
teaching about, 150
Pritchard, J., 195
Private organizational settings, 16, 140–141, 261–262
Procedures, 137–138
creative practice issues, 137, 143
defining, 143
problems with, 138–140
Professional accountability, 184–185
Professionalism:
managed care versus, 140–141
occupational control and status, 63–64
process and outcome, 63
situations for different professions, 62–63
Professional relationships:
assessing student's learning, 65–66
Boundaries activity, 53–58, 60–61
different expectations, 59–60
friendships and workships, 53
style development, 61–62
See also Social worker-service user relationship; Social work role
Professional social work values, 74–75
Professional standards, 60, 180
Program evaluation, 24, 176, 182–183, 213–214
single-case evaluation designs, 177, 209
See also Research
Psychological paradigm, 221
Public accountability, 182–183
Public choice in setting priorities, 152
Public housing scenario, *Permission to Learn* activity, 29–31
Public organizational settings, 16

Qualities of a good social worker, 47
Quasi-legal statements, 239

Ramprogus, V., 18
Rationing, 155–158
Record keeping, 180, 209
Redl, Fritz, 207
Reflection, 10–11
Reflective practitioner, 14, 48, 89
Reframing, 109–110
Regulations, 239. *See also* Law-informed practice
Reid, W. J., 51, 274–275
Relationships, professional. *See* Social worker-service user relationship
Religious paradigms, 222
Reminiscence therapy, 211
Research:
accountability issues, 214
challenges for teaching, 206
empirical practice, 43
essential elements, 215
ethical and governance review, 212
evidence-based practice, 208–210
historical context, 206–210
methodologies or designs, 212–214
need for outcomes evaluation, 210–211
research and practice connection, 211–212
researcher versus practitioner qualities, 206
single-subject design, 214
See also Program evaluation
Resource management, 159
assessing student's learning, 174
case management, 159, 167–169
teaching about, 161
time management, 171–173
Travel Agent activity, 159–167
See also Case management
Responsibility and multicultural practice, 227
Retirement communities, 140
Richmond, Mary, 207

Risk:
  ascertaining levels of, 193
  assessing student's learning, 203
  avoidance, 201–202
  Dial "D" for Danger activity, 187–193
  empowerment and autonomy, 198
  health care issues, 189
  opportunities, 194
  propensity to intervene, 189–191
  strengths/hazards matrix, 196
  teaching about challenging
      situations, 193–194
  third party warning
      requirements, 244
  typology of, 197
  violence against social workers, 202
Risk assessment, 194–196
  harm-benefit analysis, 199–200
Risk management, 197–198
Rogers, J., 19–21
Role of social worker.
    See Social work role
Role of student, 64–65
Rose, S. M., 168
Rubin, A., 43
Rummery, K., 158
Rural social work, 274–275

Sacco, T., 278
Sarri, R., 272
Schön, D. A., 11
School refusal group, 127
Segal, E., 276
Self-awareness, 47–48, 107, 150
  cultural, 223–224
  See also Self-knowledge
Self-knowledge:
  assessing learning, 50
  learning about yourself, 39, 45–47
  opportunities, 43–45
  Points of View activity, 39–45
  use of self, 47–48
  worldviews, 48–49
Service or treatment planning, 169
Service user and provider control, 36

Service user options. *See* Options for
    service users
Service users, 7
  accountability to, 183–184
  assessing student's learning, 37
  attitudes toward change, 96
  direct feedback from, 97
  first contacts, 95–96
  individuality of, 34
  needs focus, 36
  Permission to Learn activity, 29–32
  social worker relationship, 35–36, 42
  strengths perspective, 34–35
  teaching about, 32–33
  "Who is the 'client'?," 33–34
  worldviews, 50
Service user-social worker relationship.
    See Professional relationships; Social
    worker-service user relationship
Sessions, 133–134
Shardlow, S. M., 19–21, 25
Signature pedagogy, 4–5, 14
Simulation and learning, 7–10
Single-case evaluation designs, 177, 209
Single-subject research design, 214
Skilled incompetence, 10
Skolnik, L., 276
Social action model of group work, 132
Social constructionism, 48, 106
Social justice and social work mission, 2
Social risk, 197
Social service organization,
    characteristics for success, 169–170
Social services resource management. *See*
    Resource management
Social welfare history, 276–277
Social welfare law, 238
Social work, defining, 257, 267–269
Social work "clients," 7, 33–34. *See also*
    Service users
Social work education:
  BSW and MSW differences, 14–15,
      254–255, 257, 260–262
  classroom and field importance, 4
  core competencies, 13–14

core values, 17
curriculum, 1–2
interdisciplinary learning and
      practice, 81–82
limitations of CSWE standards, 263
no law studies requirements,
      239–240
signature pedagogy, 4–5, 14
See also Educational Policy and
      Accreditation Standards; Field
      education
Social work employment
   and careers, 3
   Essence of Social Work activity,
      247–254
   job descriptions, 249–254
   job satisfaction, 142
   motivations for, 39, 46–47
Social worker qualities, 47
Social workers' constructions of
      power, 42–43
Social worker-service user relationship,
      34–35, 42
   Boundaries activity, 53–58
   introduction methods, 96–97
   taboo topics, 96–97
   See also Professional relationships
Social worker's purpose, 42
Socialworkland, 11
Social work law, 238. *See also* Law-
      informed practice
Social work manager, job
      description, 251
Social work mission, 2
Social work practice:
   contemporary field social
      work, 1–4
   creative practice issues, 137, 141–143
   Essence of Social Work activity,
      247–254
   evidence-based practice, 208–210
   fields, 262
   goals of, 168
   messiness of, 42

practitioner life experiences
      and, 45–47
   researcher versus practitioner
      qualities, 206
   use of self in, 47–48
Social work practice, comparative. *See*
      Comparative social work
Social work practice settings, 15–17,
      140–141, 261–262
Social work practice supervision. *See*
      Supervision
Social work practitioner-researcher,
      210–211
   history, 206–210
   researcher versus practitioner
      qualities, 206
   See also Research
Social work profession
   occupational control and
      status, 63–64
   purpose of, 205
Social work research. *See* Research
Social work role, 53
   Boundaries activity (professional
      relationships), 53–58
   expectations, 59–60, 62
   learning about, 62–63
   management role versus, 77–78
   metaphors for, 64
   occupational control and
      status, 63–64
   opportunities for learning about,
      58–59
   role as student, 64–65
   style, 61–62, 65–66
   supervision-therapy boundary, 64–65
   See also Professional relationships
Social work supervisor, job descriptions
      and qualifications, 249, 252–253
Specht, H., 156, 262–263
Specialist or advanced practice,
      14, 255–256
   assessing student's learning, 263
   defining, 256

Essence of Social Work activity, 247–254
 fields, 262
 forms of, 258–260
 future and critique of, 262–263
 learning about, 257
 opportunities for learning about, 256
 private practice/mental health, 261–262
 specialization concept, 257–258
Speculative thinking, 110
Starting Out (Activity 5), 89–92
State sovereign immunity, 244
Statutory law, 239
Stein, T. J., 237
Stereotypes, 46, 50, 85–86, 230–231
Stevenson, O., 197, 241
Straussner, S. L., 276
Strengths/hazards matrix, 196
Strengths perspective, 34–35, 168, 255
Stress an burnout, 142
Student performance assessment. *See* Assessing student performance
Student role, 64–65
Students as a resource, 19–21
Student self-learning. *See* Self-knowledge
Student supervision. *See* Supervision
Student-supervisor fit, 18
Style, 61–62, 65–66
Subjectivity, 224
Subway maps, 8–10
Successful social work agencies, 169–170
Sullivan, H., 182
Supervision, 17–18
 benefits of supervising students, 19–21
 boundary with therapy, 64–65
 context of, 23
 faculty liaison role, 24–25
 group, 130–131
 relevant codes of ethics, 17
 role expectations, 62
 student performance assessment, 18
 student-supervisor fit, 18, 28
 tides in progress of, 25

Support for practice learning, 24–25
Supportive responses, 108
Symbolic communication, 110

Taboo topics, 96–97
Task-centered practice, 123, 143
Teachable moment, 6
Teams:
 groups and, 132–133
 learning from, 134
 meetings and sessions, 133–134
 multidisciplinary, 16, 81, 133
Teamwork, 131–133
Terminology, 7, 33
Terrell, P., 276
Theory, 43
Therapy-supervision boundary, 64–65
Thomlison, B., 25
Tides in supervision progress, 25
Time management, 171–173
Transferability of knowledge, 11, 23
Trattner, W. I., 276
Travel Agent (Activity 10), 159–167
Triage, 156–157

United Nations (UN) Declaration of Rights for Disabled People, 167–168
Unlearning, 10
Urban social work, 275–276
U.S. Department of Labor Statistics, 3
Use of self, 47–48
Utilitarianism, 182

Values, 67
 assessing student's learning, 79–80
 CSWE policy statement, 74
 defining, 76–77
 ethical dilemmas, 75–76
 learning about, 76–78
 other professions and, 68
 preferred conceptions, 77
 preferred instrumentalities, 77

preferred outcomes, 77–78
professional social work, 74–75
teaching about, 74–76
The Myth of Sisyphus
    activity, 67–73
van Wormer, K., 276
Vertical accountability, 182
Victim Compensation and Assistance
    Fund, 243
*View from Another Place . . . Another
    Time* (Activity 16), 265–271
Violence:
    domestic, 242–243
    risks, 202
Violence Against Women Act
    (VAWA), 243
Virtual learning environment
    (VLE), 266
Virtual Placement, 47

Volunteering, 46
Volunteers group, 127

Warren-Adamson, C., 241
White, R., 241
*White Awareness: Handbook for Anti-
    Racist Training* (Katz), 217
Williams, A., 155
Workships, 53
Worldviews, 48–50
    Points of View activity,
        39–45
    service users, providers, and other
        professionals, 50
    teaching about, 43–45
Written appointments of
    introduction, 95–96

Younghusband, Eileen, 2

About the Authors

Professor Mark Doel, Ph.D., M.A. (Oxon), CQSW, is Research Professor of Social Work in the Centre for Health and Social Care Research at Sheffield Hallam University, England. He is a registered social worker and was in practice for almost 20 years, including two separate years living and working in the United States. His research focuses on groupwork, social work practice, service evaluation, professional boundaries and practice education, and he has an international reputation in these fields.

Professor Doel is widely published. His fifteenth book, *Social Work Placements: A Traveller's Guide* (Routledge), introduces readers to *Socialworkland*, a travel guide approach to practice learning. Other recent books include *Educating Professionals: Practice Learning in Health and Social Care* (Ashgate, with Shardlow), which explores how students learn their practice in nine different professions, using a virtual local community to bring the professions together; *Experiencing Social Work: Learning From Service Users* (Sage, with Best), which tells the stories of service users who have had positive experiences of social work and reflects on what we can learn from this; *Using Groupwork* (Routledge); and *The Task-Centred Book* (Routledge, with Marsh). He is coeditor of the journal *Groupwork* and founding coeditor of the journal *Social Policy and Social Work in Transition*.

Professor Doel directs a 3-year, EU-funded project to develop social work education and research in the republic of Georgia and the Ukraine, and he is a consultant with UNICEF and EveryChild. He has had visiting professorial appointments in the United States, Russia, and Georgia. He regularly leads training workshops in social work agencies in practice education and groupwork.

Dr Paul G. Johnson, DSW, LCSW, is an Associate Professor of Social Work at the University of Southern Maine. He is a licensed social worker in the state of Maine. Prior to coming to USM, Dr. Johnson worked at Lehman College, CUNY, where he was the fieldwork coordinator for the BSW program. For several years, Dr. Johnson was affiliated with Jewish Child Care Association

(JCCA) in New York City. His responsibilities included the agency-owned Group and Boarding Home Programs. Prior to joining JCCA, Professor Johnson worked for United Cerebral Palsy Association of NYS, where he was a social worker for 42 dual-diagnosed clients in a residential setting. Before coming to the United States in 1986, he did residential social work in England.

At USM, Professor Johnson teaches primarily BSW courses, including Introduction to Social Work, Introduction to Social Welfare, the Fieldwork Seminar, and both sections of the undergraduate research sequence. In 2007, he coauthored (with Bruce St. Thomas) *Empowering Children through Art and Expression: Culturally Sensitive Ways of Healing Trauma and Grief.* Over the past several years, he has published 15 referred articles and 6 nonrefereed articles in *Community Care.* For the past 12 years, he has been a member of the Association for the Advancement of Social Work with Groups. Since 2006, he has been a member of the Caring Across Communities Steering Committee for the Portland Public Schools Multilingual & Multicultural Center. In March 2007, this organization was awarded a Robert Wood Johnson Foundation Grant for Mental Health Services for $300,000.

Professor Steven M. Shardlow MA (Oxon), MSc (Oxon), PhD, Doc. Soc. Sci.(h.c.), CQSW, AASW, RSW was educated at that University of Oxford and is Foundation holder of the Chair of Social Work at the University of Salford, England, where until recently he was Director of the Institute for Health and Social Care Research. He has held visiting professorial appointments in Norway, Italy, and Hong Kong—currently at City University Hong Kong. Previously, he was Director of a UK social work masters professional qualification programme. He is founding Editor-in-Chief of the *Journal of Social Work.* Previously chairperson of The Association of Teachers of Social Work Education (ATSWE-UK) and UK representative on the Executive Committee of the European Association of Schools of Social Work (EASSW): he has worked as a social work practitioner and manager. He is a registered social worker in England and has worked extensively in international social work, through research, consultancy and development work. His current research is focused upon: *program evaluation* that enhances evidence-based policy and practice— underpinned by social capital theory, particularly in respect of social work with children and families and older people to promote research utilization by practitioners and policy makers; *applied professional ethics; professional knowledge and education for the human services workforce* with a focus on field education. Much of his work is conducted using comparative research methodologies. He has published widely in these fields, including fifteen books, and his work has been translated into several languages.

Supporting researchers for more than 40 years

Research methods have always been at the core of SAGE's publishing program. Founder Sara Miller McCune published SAGE's first methods book, *Public Policy Evaluation*, in 1970. Soon after, she launched the *Quantitative Applications in the Social Sciences* series—affectionately known as the "little green books."

Always at the forefront of developing and supporting new approaches in methods, SAGE published early groundbreaking texts and journals in the fields of qualitative methods and evaluation.

Today, more than 40 years and two million little green books later, SAGE continues to push the boundaries with a growing list of more than 1,200 research methods books, journals, and reference works across the social, behavioral, and health sciences. Its imprints—Pine Forge Press, home of innovative textbooks in sociology, and Corwin, publisher of PreK–12 resources for teachers and administrators—broaden SAGE's range of offerings in methods. SAGE further extended its impact in 2008 when it acquired CQ Press and its best-selling and highly respected political science research methods list.

From qualitative, quantitative, and mixed methods to evaluation, SAGE is the essential resource for academics and practitioners looking for the latest methods by leading scholars.

For more information, visit **www.sagepub.com**.